A Deadly Suggestion

Cyn Lawrence

Francinepearl Publishing

A Deadly Suggestion is a work of fiction. The story, all names, characters, and incide
contained within are fictitious.

info@francinepearl.com

Contents

Even the darkest night will end

and the sun will rise...

Victor Hugo

Chapter One

SECRETS

Saturday, December 3, 2022. 7:30PM – 10:30PM
During: the discovery

*A*ngela is dead.

    I am swathed in blackness, and the stench of decaying flesh rushes through my nostrils, threatening to overturn my stomach and sense of duty. The flashlight almost slips from my shaking hand ... as I force my right index finger to click the tiny switch that will illuminate the reality that we've found her much too late. Every fiber of my being rejects that fact but five years on the force speaks its truth. A chill works its way down my spine.

"Yeah, it's cold as hell in here." Officer Doherty's voice brings me back to my senses. "Smells bad too." Our shoulders bump as I pass through the narrow bedroom doorway ahead of him. Service weapons in one hand and flashlights in the other, wavering, we cannot help but pick up on each other's body language.

I want to tell him it isn't the cold room that makes me shiver. This is a home—a bedroom—I've been in many times, and I can smell death. But I swallow my remorse. Those details will get me kicked off this case. Or make me a suspect.

"Right," I say.

The crossing beams of our flashlights sweep the room, revealing pristine pink and white pinstripe walls that show no evidence of weapon or blood spatter. The oak floors, which I have always admired, are clear. "No sign of a struggle." I say, an instant before my eyes land on her.

She is laying supine on the bed, tucked within the embrace of a fluffy pink comforter covered in cabbage roses that resemble leering demonic faces in our hazy beams.

"Damn, looks like she's sleeping, don't it?"

His mangled grammar grates on my already frayed nerves. His voice feels too loud—too cheerful—too everything to fit the situation. "Pretty sure she's not," I say, not bothering to hide the sarcasm from my voice.

I can feel the weight of his eyes on me. My terse reply caught his attention.

I stare hard at her for a long minute. Blonde hair splayed atop a white eyelet pillow, the four- inch batten lace creased and folding onto her neck. He is right. From this angle, she does look like she is sleeping. I am being tough on him for no good reason.

"Come on," I say, consciously making my voice more affable. Simultaneously, we move with stealth further into the room.

"I got no obvious weapons. You see any?" He asks.

'Have' no obvious weapons, I think automatically. Where did this guy go to school? I wonder if this is his first murder scene. His excitement disgusts me. But he is also right. I can see no weapons. I also can't see any evidence of violence on the body: no knife wound, no gunshot wound, no apparent evidence of assault. But her head is tilted to one side. *What are we missing?*

"Keep the beam steady while I check the other side," I say as I circle the bed, bending down for a close inspection. Sunken milky eyes, eerily reflecting the beam of light, connect with mine accusingly. An involuntary gasp escapes my lungs, sounding loud and obscene in the eerie quiet of the space.

"You okay Neely?" Doherty is alarmed. Now I'm almost certain this is his first crime scene.

"Yeah. Her eyes are open. Took me by surprise."

Shame and regret twist my insides into a painful knot. Grateful for the dark, I squeeze my eyelids against the liquid gathering there. Inhaling, I square my shoulders. This is no time to think of myself. As the detective on the scene, I must confront her accusing stare and examine every inch of her decaying body. It is my duty as an officer of the law . . . and as someone who loves her.

"Hey, that you?" Doherty's abrupt question jolts me out of my thoughts.

The beam of his flashlight illuminates a picture on the bedside stand. It is a photo from a couple of months ago. Two smiling women, sitting by the waterfront, a firepit blazing in front of us, boats tethered but ready to set sail against an azure sky. We had taken the ferry over to Hingham for a celebratory dinner at Alma Nove. Her beautiful face smiled up from the picture, the glow of the blaze reflected in her sparkling blue eyes. Eyes that will never glow again.

"Yes." The challenge in my voice tells him not to question me further.

Doherty stares at me for a long minute as he weighs the situation. "Looks like another one of them suicides."

I have to fight down my disgust. I know he is a brand-new officer, but there are two things I hate: people with poor grammar and officers who make instant conclusions. Now he has committed both sins. A crime scene is to be *investigated*, not summarized. Nonetheless, he was throwing me a bone. I had to show some appreciation.

And the crime scene does look like the others—the ones that have been keeping me up at night for well over a month. It is all here: the empty glass with dried milk residue, the empty prescription bottle that I am sure we will later identify as the anti-anxiety drug Zanacan, the peaceful way she appears to have lain down and gone to sleep. I can understand his eagerness to solve the case. It would look good for a new cop. The local media has made it so easy for him, eagerly jumping on board, labeling them the Virgin Suicides. It is their golden opportunity to steal the spotlight from Christmas bargains and holiday good will.

"No matter how 'this' looks," I gesture to the side table and around the room, "this is not a suicide. This is a crime scene. I guarantee it."

The silence tells me Doherty is struggling to decide. At last, he says, "I'm assuming you will want to notify the family? We've got a lot of guys on vacation this week, so we can handle this scene alone, don't you think?"

Smart guy. I am going to owe him. Big time.

"Makes sense. I'll notify her mother after we've processed the crime scene. Do you have your kit?"

He nods.

Again, grateful for the shelter of the darkness, I exhale a sigh of relief. I wish Doherty knew that my upbringing taught me to respect rules. I am only bending them now because the person lying dead in front of me changed my life. Without her, I would have remained a shell of a human. But a vulnerability like that is not something to share—especially not with a man. I've learned the hard way I can't trust them.

"And Doherty? Can you please keep a lid on it and not mention the picture? I'll owe you."

Despite his deficiencies, Doherty understands the value of a detective owing him. He smiles slowly, with certainty, nods again and dials Jake, the medical examiner. My anger flares—a sudden urge to slap the smile off his face consumes me, but I swallow it down.

When Doherty goes outside to get his crime kit and lantern, I move about the room quickly, snapping pictures. I silently thank the guy who'd recently pressured me into my upgraded phone with the remarkable night photo capability. When I angle it to the nightstand, rapidly squeezing the raised side button, I notice something I have not seen before. I lean in closer. I can hardly believe my eyes: fresh evidence not found at the other crime scenes.

Excitement causes my heart to pound loudly in my ears. Can this be the missing link I have been searching for? The superstitious wish I made earlier in the evening? I examined and re-examined the other four crime scene photos enough times to know that this is an unknown element: a simple sheaf of papers lying beneath the glass and pill bottle. A contract? An electric jolt courses through my veins, the desire to pick it up so intense I clench my hand, inadvertently clicking off several photos of my palm. If I can just examine it . . . But I know I cannot disturb the crime scene. Bending the rules is one thing, but I cannot break the law.

"Jake won't be long." I jump at the sound of Doherty's voice. I hope he didn't see me taking pictures. But he is already keeping secrets for me. What is one more?

"Let's get to it then."

I open up a small square of plastic and set the lantern atop it so as to not contaminate the crime scene in any way. Light. I almost dread what it will show me.

We get to work photographing, measuring, and taking detailed notes. Our communications are brief and clipped. Doherty seems to understand I cannot banter. Although he knows nothing about the bile my throat works convulsively to hold down, he does notice the furtive glances I continue to throw at the body. Every brief look brings a fresh wave of guilt, scorching my chest like a branding iron searing into my flesh.

I finally speak. "I'll meet Jake at the morgue."

If there is one thing I know with absolute certainty, it is that I cannot allow Doherty to be there when Jake opens her up. She has worked too long and too hard to become the beautiful woman that lay before us. She deserves to be remembered this way. I must protect her the way she has always protected me.

"Yeah. Sure." He keeps working doggedly, whether it is to avoid awkward conversation with me or to get out of this ice box, I'm not certain. Either way, I'm grateful.

How the heck has she tolerated the cold? When she told me her bedroom was cold, I had no idea it was downright frigid. Someone should sue her landlord—or at least make them spend the night in the room. I know my churning mind is creating mindless drivel to anesthetize my aching heart. I allow it.

Doherty does not ask me her name. Instead, he leans over the bedside stand and copies her information from the ID left sitting out, just as I hoped. Had it been me, I would question the strange coincidence that the deceased had the foresight to leave her identification handy. But this once, his inexperience helps me. That single act has just bought me time to continue to work on Angela's case. I can't bear losing a place on this case. I'll deal with the chief soon enough when he discovers my deception. Hopefully I can hold him off until I...*I have to find Angela's killer.*

Chapter Two

THE CALL

Saturday, December 3, 2022. 5:55 PM
Before: mystical thinking

The call came in at precisely 5:55 pm. I had just made a wish, a foolish leftover superstition from childhood, but one of those silly little habits I just couldn't seem to give up. Maybe because it was one of the only pieces of information about my birth that had ever been shared with me. I was born at 5:55 pm on May 5. I clung to this tiny bit of information like a rare jewel. It had become my personal "bewitching" moment, and it certainly came along more often than falling stars.

In this instance, a wish couldn't hurt. I was losing sleep over the nagging certainty that I was missing a key piece of evidence in the series of teenage deaths I was investigating. I'd pored over the information endlessly; each page was a piece of a puzzle I couldn't seem to quite fit together. No matter how many times I reviewed them, the gnawing feeling that I was overlooking something critical—something 'telling'—had taken root. I knew the answer was there, lurking in the recesses of my mind if only I could grab hold of it. So, I was willing to take any tidbit of help I could get, even if it was magical thinking.

"Neely, you praying over there?"

Murphy was Boston born and bred. They all were, which was part of their pride and what made them such great cops, but it drove me crazy that 'r' simply did not exist in their vocabulary. I involuntarily recoiled then tried to hide my reaction by acting as if I dropped my pen. How the heck did these guys get through school without speech therapy? I was a classic introvert and something as simple as bad grammar could cause sensory overload pretty quick. It was a strange quirk that used to make me feel like a freak, but I'd learned it was very real and not my fault at all—another perk of an isolated childhood.

My raised eyes revealed four sets trained on me expectantly. "You know it. Thought it might help."

I forced a smile. I hadn't realized my eyes were closed. Some of the things I did without thinking, automatically made "fitting in" impossible. I didn't need any more strikes against me. It was hard enough being the only female detective; I was 25 and the youngest detective to ever be shielded in the city. My peers had yet to agree that my father's bank account hadn't bought my position. I'd also received some offbeat questions about my parentage that made me take a second look at the color of my skin and hair. Political correctness had not yet infiltrated the BPD, certainly not when it came to me.

The sudden burst of raucous laughter was loud. I blushed, then realized they had moved on. Their joviality had nothing to do with me. The precinct had been low in calls but high in spirit all day, and when I say high, I mean soaring. Violent crime always took a dive close to Christmas— proof that even criminals loved their families. I knew I would love mine too if I had one. The guys were chatting it up like it was Christmas already. Me, I always kept my head low and my nose to the grindstone. My partner was always telling me to lighten up. *If they're teasing you, they like you* was his theory. But 25 years is enough time to understand that pointed looks and backhanded comments were meant to exclude me—make me feel unbalanced and unsure. Did I feel some type of way about it? Sure, and my methods worked for me. Protected me. Kept me out of the spotlight.

Fortunately, my desk sat at a right angle to theirs, which were lined up like school desks, creating a somewhat private space for me while still allowing me to observe the heartbeat of what was going on. A detective's job is like that: included but still separate. I was still trying to figure it out. There were a couple of private offices, but those were taken by the senior detectives and my chief. My partner, O'Malley, occupied one of those offices, although if he'd been here, he would've been shooting the bull with the rest of the guys tonight, talking about who was able to get what "impossible to find" toy for their kid for Christmas. I didn't have a kid or a husband or a family.

Heck, I didn't even have a boyfriend, and I only had one friend. So that knocked me out of any conversation they might have. These were family guys, good guys. And with my partner out on medical leave, leaving me alone for another three weeks still, I was the odd man out, so to speak.

I sure could've used both his help and one of those private offices today. It would've made it a lot easier to work while they goofed around. Don't get me wrong. These guys deserved the break. The things they dealt with most days could bring the toughest man to their knees. I was just feeling left out and surly. Maybe because I had been beating my head against the wall for the past month working on a case that had mysteriously grown into a series of dead-end cases, and Christmas or not, they were consuming every waking moment.

I looked up to see Harry Sullivan, the middle-aged duty cop moving in my general direction.

"Hey Sullivan, got a minute?" He sidestepped my desk on his way to the bathroom and peered over my shoulder.

"What you need, Neely?" He asked. I was glad that nobody called me Daniela here. Funny how desperate I once was to be known by that name, when the mean kids in school tormented me for my tomboyish appearance. Before Angela made me realize my name wasn't the problem. How I viewed myself was the problem. But at work, I was just Neely, and that worked fine for me.

"I have to get this last vic's info in the system and I keep getting this 'error' screen when I put in her address. I'm trying to populate all fields to see if I can find any crossovers."

He grunts, not bothering to answer. I can feel his hot breath in and out more than I can actually hear it. I'm generally good with computers but have not found this new system—the Lifestream 911—to be user friendly. It was supposed to save us so much time that we were going to be able to double our caseloads. So far, the only thing it has done is double our training time, although as I watched Sullivan change the zip code, press enter and the screen advance to the next prompt, I knew this time the user error was mine.

"Sorry," I mumble.

I've been on the job long enough to know what the zip code is for Weymouth. I can tell by the look on his face as he continues on his way to the bathroom that he shares that thought. My self- loathing has nearly reached a tipping point after I finish entering the newest case data: only the same key evidence is shared and no new substantiating factors. *What the hell is going on here?*

It first started about a month and a half ago with eighteen-year-old Kayleigh O'Brien. Her brokenhearted mother knew her way around the social media circuit and utilized all of them to share her loss. She started out on Caring Bridge and Facebook and then moved on to Instagram and TikTok. Who could fault her? She openly shared her daughter's story, its ending a profound tragedy.

"My daughter was body shamed most of her life. She tried every diet on the market, but nothing worked because she had thyroid and hormonal issues. But after taking part in a miraculous clinical trial, she was finally able to achieve a healthy weight." Her grief-stricken mother was never focused on Kayleigh becoming thin but rather she just wanted her daughter to become healthier and satisfied with herself. "With every pound she lost, she became happier. She began to believe in herself more. No more doctors acting like she was stuffing her face with junk food secretly. No more mean teenagers calling her fatso or Teletubby. She dreamed of dating and her first kiss, and it was all about to come true for her."

The "first kiss" statement is the one that made the media go wild, immortalizing Kayleigh as The Virgin Suicide. Something had driven her to dissolve an entire bottle of Zanacan, the new designer drug that relieves anxiety, into her evening milk and fall asleep forever just as she had finally achieved her lifelong goal. A goal that both she and her family had believed would make her happy had instead made her take her life.

So, when three more suicides followed in rapid succession—each girl the same age, using the same method—the media very quickly got on board with the notion of a virgin suicide pact. The headlines, insensitive as they were, took off like a wildfire in the dry California mountains.

But the truth was that they were not a pact, and the similarities ended with the method and circumstance of death. These girls did not know each other and not all of them appeared to be virgins either. How could four completely unrelated teenagers commit suicide in exactly the same way within 36 days? This was the conundrum I had been trying to figure out for the past month. Why? What was the connection between the girls? The only obvious connection was that they all participated in a weight loss clinical trial, but those documents were medical records and protected since I had no evidence of foul play.

But according to their family members, each girl was prescribed Zanacan early in the trial "just in case" it was needed for anxiety. And all the girls had held on to it for the duration of the trial without touching it. Then one day, each just woke up and decided to take an entire bottle. Why would a group of young women work so hard toward a new life and then end it? They didn't leave angry or sorrowful suicide notes.

If anything, my best evidence was the lack of evidence. These young women should have been plastering their successes all over social media, yet there was not one Facebook post, one text, one Instagram, one Tik Tok, nor one email for months prior to their deaths. I scoured each of their social media accounts. Each had no social media presence at all, which was incredibly odd considering what they had accomplished.

I had tried, unsuccessfully, to sell this theory to the rest of the team.

"Not everybody lives on social media, Neely. Some people got a real life, you know?" Sass had been on the BPD for 27 years. Trying to convince him was like watching generational gaps play out in real time.

But the facts were the facts, and these facts didn't add up. Unfortunately, I was the only one doing modern addition at this time.

I leaned back in my chair staring at the screen, gently twisting side to side, contemplating the possibilities. Could there be a mastermind behind the deaths? Could it be a serial killer? Who would have known all of them? Had they all attended the same gym?

In the background, I could hear Murphy and Duffy in a lighthearted battle over who was next in line for unit chief. "You ain't got the guts," I hear Murphy say, then Duffy says, "You ain't got the balls." Laughing, they slap each other on the back, still friends. I twist away from them. *Is that funny?* Men are hard to understand.

When the Johnson Street address in Mattapan scrolled over the Lifestream screen, it instantly caught my eye. It was one I often visited. Alarmed, I stood so quickly I sent my chair spinning into Sullivan's knee as he was returning from the bathroom.

"I'll take this one," I said. Without waiting for permission or approval, I grabbed my overcoat and demanded, "What are the details?" knowing nobody would bother to answer my rhetorical question. The details were going to a centralized printer. That was the new system. We all knew that and hated it.

A couple of guys gave each other the side eye. Sullivan's yelp of pain had caught their attention. I wasn't sure if they were wondering why I was so jumpy or if I knew detectives didn't take cases like this. I caught one subtle shoulder lift and more than one smirk before they returned to their bantering. Reactions like that made my guts twist. Did they think I was stupid or that I didn't notice?

Regardless, nobody else was eager to jump up to take a case on a quiet night like tonight. They were just counting their lucky stars I was doing it. I knew once I walked out the door, the comments would fly and they'd all have a good laugh at my eagerness—or was it ignorance? *Let them laugh*. I knew who lived at this address.

I paced in front of the duty desk, counting steps to avoid considering the situation, waiting impatiently for the detailed report. My practical black rubber soled Clarks squeaked methodically on the over polished wood floors. I found myself mesmerized by the dazzling sheen. I couldn't imagine how many coats of varnish lay beneath my foot, and I often wondered, as my chair rolled back and forth on the glossy surface, just how many toxins I might be releasing into my unsuspecting lungs.

My patience snapped. I could no longer hide my exasperation.

"Sullivan! Where's the damn report?"

The new system only sends a summary to the detectives. The duty desk gets the details. How's that for a timesaver? Me having to wait to get the details from someone else. *Ridiculous.* I stopped myself before I rolled my eyes. That would not win me any cred with the guys. Eye rolls were not something a detective would do. Sometimes my age caught up with me. Even though "detective" was a promotion, it was only going to remain a word until I earned the respect that goes behind the title with these guys.

"Here. Don't get your panties in a wad." He handed me the report in what felt like slow motion. "Some whacky old guy says his neighbor is missing. Says she's been acting crazy lately—running around outside naked."

Sullivan gives me a nod and look that says, "like you, just now," expecting me to say something—maybe apologize for slamming his leg with my chair and change my mind about taking the case. But my anxiety overrode my decorum, and anyhow, it wasn't my fault he was hovering behind my chair in the first place.

I stopped pacing abruptly and asked, "So . . . Is she missing or running around outside naked?"

Without O'Malley here, getting information was like pulling teeth. Maybe this really was a crank call, and I had overreacted because I haven't seen much of Angela recently. When had I last spoken to her? A week? Two? I couldn't discount the call no matter how crazy it sounded.

Angela's tiny one bedroom apartment wasn't exactly in the high-rent district.

"This guy says he puts a flower in a flowerpot by her front door every morning—they have an 'understanding.'"

He raises his thick, manicured eyebrows twice and I wince inwardly, thinking that if he knew Angela's history, he probably wouldn't joke like that. Most people wouldn't, and as macho as he is—I hate to think what he would have to say about Angela. We have a long way to go as a society towards understanding and acceptance.

"Anyhoo, he hasn't seen her, and she didn't take her flower for the past couple of days."

That explanation got my attention, and my stomach sank. I knew exactly what he was talking about.

"Got it." I said.

"You need me to send you the address?" Sullivan asks, already losing interest as he eavesdropped on a conversation about whether Tom Brady will ever become a coach for the Patriots now that he's retired and Belichick is struggling without him.

Unlike some precincts, the duty cop at our local was a pretty important guy—not someone banned to desk duty—and Sullivan had the perfect arrogant look to go with it. Not only did he sport the high, flat New England forehead and thick mane of hair, but he also had a strong aristocratic nose and luminous olive skin that women pay a lot of money to get. I'd be willing to bet his mother was of Italian or Greek descent. He exuded authority with his appearance alone. Even though technically I outranked him, I looked insignificant in comparison. I did my best to pull off a serious detective look, keeping my thick dark hair in a low ponytail, wearing a minimum of makeup, and ensuring any curves of my five-foot two-inch frame were well hidden behind custom tailored suits. But standing my ground would have been a lot easier if I had a sturdier build—say, something more along the lines of Venus Williams, my dream body.

I saved my words and headed out, wondering if he forgot that the address was the only thing the stupid system did give me or if Tom was still the most important thing happening in New England. This call was no joke to me. Someone had reported my best friend missing.

Chapter Three

FOREBODING

Saturday,December 3, 2022. 7:10 PM
20 minutes before

I made it to Angela's apartment in record time, feeling my hysteria grow each time Siri received no answer to the six calls I had placed. New England traffic can be a bear, especially during the holidays, but thankfully, they respect their law enforcement and scatter like cockroaches in the light when they see men in blue coming through.

When I arrived at Angela's building, I skipped the elevator and took the stairs two at a time. Walking briskly down the hall, I inhaled and exhaled deeply, trying to regain my composure. The wild beating of my heart had nothing to do with the stairs. They'd had no effect on me. It wasn't the first time I was grateful for my many childhood years of elite gymnastics training. I guess my father did something right. Even during the worst of times, I was searching for positive attributes in him. Pathetic.

Further along the hallway, I spied the shelf outside Angela's door, remembering when we built it. Since she had a second-floor apartment in a neighborhood fighting to overcome its crime statistics, that little shelf was as close to a garden as she could get, her own private flowerbox. As I drew closer, I saw three different sprigs of flowers floating in the vase we had found at the arts festival in Chelsea the summer before last. Ang was always trying to make her living environment happier—more feminine. Mine was pretty much just a place to sleep.

I rapped three times on the stark white door, irritated now that I hadn't helped her fight harder for the paint she'd wanted to put on the door. This shocking white must have been an assault on her senses every time she came home. I made a mental note to help her scour her lease agreement for caveats; maybe we *could* paint the door after all.

Her key hung on the ring in my front jacket pocket. I didn't know what I would find inside, so protocol had to be followed to the T. Two things I knew I *would* find inside were my picture and my fingerprints. For an instant, I wondered if answering the call was a wise decision, but my love for Angela wiped away reason.

"Angela!" I yelled, loudly enough for the neighbors to hear me, especially Mr. Smithers, who had called in the missing person report.

Of course, this was most likely a misunderstanding. Angela couldn't be missing. There was a chance she was at her mother's house. Instead of panicking, I should have called there. This thought made my body suddenly limp with relief.

Then it hit me: Mrs. Monn had gone to Rhode Island with a friend just last week, and she probably wasn't back yet. She'd been waiting for years to see Christmas at the Newport Mansions and had Nutcracker tickets. The chances of Ang staying at her mom's place were slim, unless there was a big issue with her apartment, and she was there temporarily. It was possible, but unlikely.

I yelled once more, louder this time, then tried calling her again, but there was no answer. I did not hear the cellphone ringing, which comforted me. If she was here, I would have heard her cell, right? Then I remembered she had a landline and tried that number twice. I could hear the landline ringing through the door.

The key felt like it was burning a hole through my pocket into my chest. I wanted desperately to just walk in, but I knew I should not have taken the case and didn't want to jeopardize anything by improper procedure. Before I entered, I decided to try to contact her mother.

With shaking fingers, I called.

"Mrs. Monn. Hi. This is Dan. Have you talked to Angela today?" I knew I should have asked about her trip and made small talk, but concern took control, and the words flew out of my mouth before I could stop them.

Mrs. Monn didn't seem put off by my direct questions. "Well, hello Dan! How are you doing?

How's the job going?"

I could tell from her voice that she was delighted to hear from me. Guilt flooded my body. What was wrong with me that I ignore the two people who cared for me when nobody else did? When I had nobody—a dead mother, a father who ignored me, and an emotionally devoid nanny— Mrs. Monn was there to show me what a loving parent looked like. She was the one who helped me through the traumas I faced as a youth. I scanned my brain for the last time I had spoken to her and came up with Thanksgiving.

"Fine, thank you."

Even I could hear the guilt in my words, but no matter how hard I tried to be different, my father raised me to be a nose to the grindstone person, and that shaped my work ethic. I eagerly took on any available cases. I didn't mind working day and night, but sometimes I forgot about the people I cared about—since caring about people and being cared about had not been part of my life for so long.

"I'm so sorry to be short with you," I continued. "But would you mind telling me if you've spoken to Angela today—or yesterday perhaps? It's important."

She tsk-tsked under her breath. "Oh no worries sweetheart, I understand you young people have so much going on. But now that you mention it, Dan, I haven't spoken to Angela since Monday." I can almost hear her thinking about it over the phone line. The pause increases my anxiety over the situation a hundredfold. "You know I've been in Newport—having a wonderful time, I might add— and it's not all that uncommon for us to not talk much this time of year. There are so many people who count on her for holiday pies and cakes. It's her busy time, you know."

Pride was evident in her words. Angela had worked long and hard to build the bakery up to what it had become. Angela was a child to be proud of. The knot in my shoulders eased a bit.

"I hope you've ordered your holiday pies, Dan. I know how your dad loves her apple strudel." Standing there with my head leaning against Angela's door, I thought about how my dad loved

Angela's apple strudel. He always made an appearance at her house on Thanksgiving, no excuses. It sometimes made me wonder if he liked her better than me—maybe because she began her existence as a male? But that was my own ugly unresolved childhood insecurity and had no place in my mind right now. I needed to remain focused on the call, exactly as it had come in.

"Is there any chance Angela might be staying at your house for a few days?"

Mrs. Monn laughed. "Oh, I doubt that. She would never choose to fight the holiday traffic when she lives so close to the bakery. Are you having a hard time reaching her?"

"Mrs. Monn, could I have your permission to enter Angela's apartment?" I knew that I didn't technically need her permission, but now I was certain I had made the wrong decision in taking the call involving my best friend. I was crossing a line and doing as much damage control in advance as I possibly could.

"Dan, should I be worried?" Mrs. Monn asked, her voice now quiet and cautious. I had never asked for permission to enter either of their homes since that first day so many years ago.

"I'm sure it's nothing," I lied. "The neighbor and Angela have a daily flower thing going on between them, and apparently, she has not picked up her flower in a few days, so he reported her missing." I gave in to the roll of my eyes as I said this, thankful nobody could see my childish release. It sounded so silly as I said it. Why was I even here? Most likely, it was just my own guilt at not being a better friend, for not taking more time to call her myself, that had me at her door acting like a crazy person. If it was anyone else, we wouldn't even have taken a report for something so ambiguous.

"Oh Dan, she loves those flowers. She tells me about them all the time. He looks up different types of flowers and sends messages to her through their meanings." Her concern was evident now. "It is a little game they play. I don't think she would ignore him."

My forced casual demeanor disappeared. The crushing fear returned. "I've tried calling several times and have received no answer. This is why I'd like your permission to enter." I had the key in hand, ready to jam it into the lock.

"Yes. Please, Dan. Go ahead. You'll let me know she's okay, won't you?"

"Of course. Talk soon." I wasn't sure I got all the words out before I hung up the phone, but my focus had switched. Full detective mode kicked in as the door swung open.

Weapon drawn, I entered the apartment, my back flat to the wall. "Angela?" I was no longer shouting her name and didn't really expect a response. The lights were on in both the living room and kitchen, as if someone was home. Making a quick visual inspection of the small space, I continued, rounding each corner carefully. I searched each room, afraid of who or what I might encounter at any moment, grateful not to see any blood spatter or body.

Angela's apartment was easy to navigate—only about 900 square feet. Her tiny kitchen, lacking its perpetual stack of pots and pans in the strainer since she began the clinical trial, was immaculate. I always used to marvel that someone who baked for a living would come home and cook too, but it seemed that Ang never tired of cooking. You'd never find pots and pans, dirty or otherwise, at my house. Food was generally bought prepackaged and nuked as needed. I always tried to eat healthy, but cooking was definitely not part of that equation.

The two rooms were divided by a counter that served as the eating space with two stools pushed neatly beneath. Edging beyond, I threw open the coat closet, my gun pointed determinedly at a tidy row of hanging jackets, coats, and department store bags sitting on the floor. The next doorway I knew was the bathroom. The door was partially open, and I could see that the light had been left on in that room as well.

It was not unlike Angela to leave all of these lights on in the house. She had never been a fan of the dark.

I placed one foot inside the bathroom, trying to squeeze into the space without disturbing the door. *This is it* I thought. *I am going to find my best friend slaughtered in the bathroom*. Who would do this to her? Why? Heart hammering, I walked quietly to the bathtub, grabbed the edge of the shower curtain with one hand, making sure to keep my gun trained with the other and yanked as quickly as I could.

The bar clattered loudly on the stark white tiled floor. I screamed. But it wasn't my best friend lying slaughtered in the bathtub; just the Lily Pulitzer shower curtain I'd picked up for her last year at Pottery Barn lying in a heap. In my haste, I'd yanked down the shower curtain rod. I sat down on the toilet seat and put my head in my hands. I was losing it. I had to get a grip on myself. My imagination was running away with me. Now I understood why I should not have been the one to take this call. It is impossible to think rationally—to act rationally—when it involves someone you love.

Determined to finish up here and figure out where the heck Ang had gotten to, I completed my search of the bathroom. The sink was completely dry—not a droplet in sight. Good sign that Ang had not been here. Feeling a tiny bit reassured, I exited the bathroom and turned down the hallway toward the bedroom. I stumbled and put a shaking hand against the wall to catch myself. My breath shuddered as my last shred of hope dissolved.

The bedroom door, located at the end of the hallway, was closed. There was no beam of light coming from beneath the door. Angela did not close that door—ever. The HVAC system had somehow not been vented back there and the room had no climate control. This time of the year, that room would be freezing with the door closed. My car had registered 18 degrees on the drive over.

For several seconds, I stared at the door. I knew this was not something I should handle alone. *O'Malley, where are you when I need you?* Same place all men had always been when I needed them. Absent.

Lifting my collar, I whispered into the mike. "This is Detective Daniela Neely, current location 115 Johnson Street, Unit 2B, Mattapan. Requesting backup at a potential crime scene. Come in quiet."

My backup arrived seven minutes later in the form of shiny new Officer Brian Doherty. For every second of those seven minutes, I never gave up hope that Angela would walk out of the bedroom with her big bright smile and say, "Dan, what the heck are you doing?"

Officer Doherty looked scared as he fumbled his way down the hall. There was something about him that reminded me of a Saint Bernard puppy—all head, hands, and feet. I supposed that once he grew into them, he would become a strapping man, but for now, he was just too tall, awkward, and kind of clumsy. He nodded hello.

"What ya got?" he whispered.

I didn't answer. My muscles quivered in anticipation as I reached for the door handle, throwing the door open. Icy darkness blasted through the doorway and stole any remaining warmth left in my body. We stood, stunned, disoriented. And then the smell rose up to choke us.

Chapter Four

DEAD TO ME

Saturday, December 3, 2022. 11:00 PM
30 minutes after

The throbbing red and blue lights kept pace with the erratic pulse in my chest. Processing this crime scene was the worst three hours of my life. Although I had tried everything to avert my eyes from the form lying on the bed, a magnetic-like force pulled them there repeatedly. And each time I viewed her, the guilt seared me anew like I was being branded with a hot iron rod. If I hadn't been so caught up in my caseload, Angela would not be getting zipped into a bag for transportation to the city morgue. This was my fault, pure and simple, and I had to make it right. How ironic that the very cases that had taken me from her now brought me to her in this horrific manner.

And now, I had to do the unthinkable; tell a mother her daughter was dead. And not just any mother. A mother I knew and loved. It felt like I had killed her myself.

Despite the presence of the squad car and ambulance, the street remained empty around me—no crowd of looky-loos in this neighborhood. These were people who would peer out of their window and wonder but would rather google it or watch the evening news than get involved. This was a neighborhood where society's misfits felt comfortable with each other but still didn't trust the cruel and dangerous people of the world who had put them here. They instinctively knew their own and would discuss it amongst themselves when the outsiders had cleared. No matter how many times they had seen me visiting, the badge I carried made me an outsider.

I couldn't stop questioning myself. Why hadn't I worked harder to get Angela out of this neighborhood? Why hadn't I pushed past her protests? Was her killer watching me now? Wondering if the trail of evidence was copied perfectly enough to throw me off?

An ominous roll of thunder startled me out of my trancelike state. I glanced at the evening sky, looking for signs of the storm I hoped was not brewing there. A thundersnow event was not something to take lightly in New England. The flash of lightning was brief—partially hidden by the heavy, dark clouds—but its ghoulish stab through the night sky was a sharp reminder to me I needed to keep all my senses on high alert. This wasn't just another case. This was the most important case of my life. Someone had murdered my best friend.

Retrieving my phone, I pressed my most recent call. Mrs. Monn answered on the first ring.

"Dan! It's been so long. I was getting worried." I could hear the fear in her voice. The unspoken questions.

"Mrs. Monn, I need to talk to you. Could I meet you?" I didn't think I could deliver this news over the phone.

"Is she there Dan? Is she missing? Of course, you're always welcome, you know that, but is she there?" Even through her fear and anxiety, she was kind.

"She's not missing," I said.

"Dan." Her voice broke.

"Could we meet somewhere, Mrs. Monn?" I tried one more time.

"Tell me. Please tell me what has happened to my girl." She sounded so desperate; I knew she couldn't wait.

"Mrs. Monn, I found Angela in her room and she has passed."

"Passed? How? What happened to her?" Now she sounded frantic.

"We have no answers yet. But I promise you'll be the first to know," I said, and I meant every word.

"Oh my God," she wailed. "Was she murdered? How did she die? How long was she dead? I should've been there!"

Her sorrow was unbearable. *No, I should have been there.* It was my job to keep her safe. She always kept me safe. She was the one who saved me when the boys . . . No, I couldn't go there right now. This wasn't a time to think of me.

Feeling suddenly limp from hours of emotional upheaval, I leaned heavily against the first hard surface my body encountered: my trusty SUV. As always, I was grateful for its strong, dependable frame. I affectionately called it the "Beast." The Beast was the only constant in my life other than Angela—beautiful, effervescent Angela who would be ushered out the door on a gurney shrouded in black plastic any minute now.

Angela loved to tease me about the Beast. "Between me and that car, you'll never need a man, Dan."

I could see her leaning back in the seat, eyes closed as the luxury of the contoured leather enveloped her. In my mind's eye, I lingered on the smooth, milky planes of her face; her newly hollowed cheekbones; her straight nose with a little ball on the end that she constantly referred to as a "cherry ball" because it was often red; and her huge mouth that was always stretched in a smile.

She was right. It was a truly magnificent vehicle. I was glad she loved it too. I was also glad she didn't judge me for loving my vehicle the way I did. It was big; it was masculine—it worked for me. The memory now filled my eyes with tears. I blinked rapidly. Angela knew me better than anyone. She knew it wasn't that I didn't need a man, but rather that I just didn't trust them—which made it very hard to date. With an education in criminal justice and a lifelong distrust of men, I could have a pretty interrogatory first date—which is why there were never second dates—not to mention the fact that I had a terrible habit of introducing myself as Detective Dan Neely. Not exactly a "nice to meet you."

Thank God I had Angela in my life. But I didn't have her—not anymore. I would have to somehow face that cold, hard fact.

Right now, I had to face her mother. A mother who had loved me like her own just because her daughter had loved me. A mother who did not deserve this heartbreak.

"Mrs. Monn, she looked very peaceful. She did not look like she suffered," I offered. I knew it was evasive, but I didn't want to say the truth—what it really looked like.

"But how, Dan? How did she die?" Her voice had become high pitched in a way I'd never heard before. I wondered exactly where she was and hoped she was somewhere private, because I sensed she was about to lose control.

"Is your friend nearby? Do you have someone to be with you?" I asked.

"Dan, just tell me, sweetheart." She made a conscious effort to calm herself, probably because I'd drawn attention to her hysteria. I felt bad.

"It looked like she was sleeping. There was a glass with residue in it on the bedside stand and an empty prescription bottle." I paused. "We'll do an autopsy."

"Nooooo," she wailed. "Are you trying to say she's one of those virgin suicide cases? My girl would never kill herself!"

I cursed the media and their careless labels. "I know, I know." I tried to soothe her with my words. "I promise to get to the bottom of this. You know I love her too."

She was openly sobbing now. "I know. I must go. I'm sorry Dan." The line went dead.

I felt the first drops of precipitation as the front door to the apartment complex swung wide and was propped open. Showtime. I unclenched my phone, stretching out my white knuckles, zipped it into my department issue jacket, and jumped into the Beast just as icy shards of freezing rain hit my windshield so sharply. I was instantly reminded of the old metaphor "nails being driven into a coffin."

Coffin. My body convulsed involuntarily at that thought. I was determined not to cry. With my nearly clinical upbringing, I had never believed in old adages about a broken heart. I knew it was scientifically impossible, which made it pure nonsense in my world—until now. The ache in my chest was so intense there could be no other explanation. Science be damned.

Although the reflux boiling in my throat was a constant reminder that a quiet hysteria continued to brew, I refused to give in to it. If there was one thing my father had raised me to be, it was responsible. "Put aside all emotion and do your damn job." That I could do. Next stop, city morgue—a place I often visited, but not one where I often visited my best friend.

I cranked up both the heater and Pandora, already tuned in to Taylor Swift radio. Angela and I had fallen in love with Taylor Swift back in the early years when she sang songs about being bullied. We both knew how that felt, each of us in a different way. We loved her spunk and determination— her refusal to let critics or haters change who she was or how she made her music. I say we, but really Angela had taught me to admire people like that—like her. Life is hard, but some people just seem to understand how to make it better for both them and the people around them.

But even Taylor Swift couldn't stop the scenes that ran through my head on a loop. Was I too distracted at the crime scene? What did I miss? What was there that shouldn't have been? What wasn't there that should've been? I wished I had looked more deeply at her surroundings; at the pill bottle on the bedside stand, at the contract sitting beneath. But I was forced to act detached—like it was any other case. Angela took prescription medication? Not likely. She was too concerned about destroying the delicate balance of hormones her doctors worked so diligently to maintain. She was completely faithful to her medical regime. Where had it come from?

I scanned my brain for any memory of Angela mentioning anxiety medication. How could she have kept a secret like that from me? What else didn't I know?

When I spoke to Ang a few weeks ago, she was bubbling with excitement. She was eager to find her soulmate and had decided to spend some of her future "surrogate" money to buy a new wardrobe. You'd have to know Angela to understand the significance of that statement. Ang had a plan—Ang had always had a plan—from the time she was six years old. She was going to grow up and officially become a woman, get married to a man, and have three babies. She knew all of those babies would need to be carried by a surrogate, had researched the expense, and every spare penny had gone to that account after paying for her gender change operation. So, her decision to dip into her surrogate fund for a new wardrobe for the next step in her "happily ever after plan" told me with absolute certainty, this was not a female who would kill herself. This was a woman whose life had just begun. Someone else must have wanted her dead and either copycatted the other suicides or they were all forced suicides. I knew this from the bottom of my detective's gut.

I threw the Beast into park at the next stop sign, nearly jamming the zipper on my inside pocket in my hurry to get the phone out. I pulled up the photographs I'd snapped at the scene earlier, enlarging the pill bottle. The prescription had been filled a little over a week ago. Had I spoken to her since then? Why didn't she tell me? Was she anxious? Depressed? Even though I didn't believe for one minute that Angela had committed suicide, at the very least, I knew she had filled the prescription and had not told me. Was I that unavailable to her? Or was she hiding something from me, and if so, why?

A loud and extended honking told me it was time to move on. As hard as it would be, I knew I was lucky that I was getting to process her body at the morgue. It probably should've been Doherty. I had certainly given him every indication that the victim was someone important to me.

But I had not said it. I had not put him in a position where he had to lie for me. I would never do that to anyone. I believed in the truth. Which was why I had to go to the morgue instead of him. I had never thought about the truth as a slippery slope before, but now I wondered. Was avoiding the truth a lie? Or was it simply avoiding the truth? These new questions required answers I didn't have right now. I had no answers right now.

I chided myself. Thoughts like this would do nothing but distract me from what was really important: solving the case. Since this scene looked so much like the others I had been researching, I knew the higher-ups would want to close it up nice and neat with Christmas on the horizon. Nobody wants a murderer on the loose right before Christmas—especially not one who is killing women in their beds. Not to mention the fact that once my captain discovered my relationship with Angela, I would be removed from the case. The clock was ticking. It was time to put on my big girl panties and get my ass moving.

But there were things about this case that I knew and nobody else did. Important things—things that would affect the way the case was investigated . . . which was why I had to make sure her autopsy would be protected. I did not want Angela to be part of tomorrow's sensational headline, labeling her as anything other than who I knew her to be. She had worked too hard to become who she was.

She was not who the ID on her nightstand would say she was. She was not who the autopsy would say she was, either. She was so much more.

Chapter Five

CITY MORGUE

Sunday, December 4, 2022. 12:02 AM
92 minutes after

Only dead people lived here.

For the first time, the thought of going into the morgue alone overwhelmed me. Nobody *lived* in a morgue. A hysterical giggle bubbled in my throat. I always laugh when I'm nervous. That's definitely my worst trait. People just don't expect a woman to laugh when things get ugly. For the most part, we're still expected to be the softer sex, although I'm not sure I've ever been soft. I've heard the guys whisper that I'm heartless more than once, but really, I'm just uncomfortable with emotions, and my affect can be a bit flat too. There weren't any warm fuzzies floating around my barren upbringing, so I developed defense mechanisms. Or maybe I was just making excuses for myself. I don't really allow myself to get emotionally attached to most people. I've found people to be generally unreliable and uncaring.

Dread slowed my usually quick and nimble pace. Although I had no real passion for gymnastics as a young girl, the endless hours of training often came in handy when trailing a perp. But as I made my way to the underbelly of the old hospital, down the well-worn and familiar hallways to the morgue, with each step bringing me closer to an inevitability I did not want to face, my feet felt like they had lead in them.

I'd spent a fair amount of time here with Jake, between my freshman and sophomore years of college. I had little desire to go back home on breaks to a house that had never felt like home to me. And with all of

Boston's wonderful public transportation at my fingertips from the city, it was simple to navigate passage.

That summer, Jake allowed me to assist on several autopsies. He was surprised I had the stomach for it, but I found them fascinating. Autopsies felt honorable, like we were helping those people regain their dignity by finding their cause of death. I learned a lot from Jake that summer. I think what I learned made me a better detective. He and I have worked on numerous cases since I became a detective. He was someone whose ability and opinion I respected.

As I now approached his domain, I was glad this case landed on his table. If I was never again going to speak to my best friend, surely there was nobody better than Jake to help me give a voice to her final hours.

Right then, I made a promise to myself and to Angela that I would find the truth no matter the risk or cost to me professionally. She deserved that much. Angela was always a beacon of strength and resilience even in the face of all the challenges and obstacles that she had faced in life. She did not deserve to have "suicide" on her death certificate. It was like a slap in her face. She had saved me once. Now I would save her no matter what it took.

During the past two years, Angela completed a metamorphosis that had begun in childhood. When the gender change surgery that she desired for so many years was completed, the first thing Ang wanted to do was try out the "new equipment." I mean, who could blame her? She had waited such a long time to be fully female.

It had started with her decision to hire a gigolo named Joaquin from a company she found online called Romeo to the Rescue. Romeo to the Rescue was a male escort service, apparently designed to deflower virgins.

"Would you get a load of these guys?" she had said.

The ad was egotistical, promising a heavenly orgasm amongst other unmentionable things. We were enjoying a couple of glasses of wine, joking back and forth over the many possibilities. While she didn't agree with their moral compass, Angela knew exactly what she wanted, and it sounded like they would serve her purpose.

I frowned now, remembering the phone call I had received after her session.

"Well Dan, everything works as promised. Seriously. For 23 lovely minutes, I felt like a desirable woman for the first time in my life."

Even before she continued, I could hear the "but" coming. The usual joy was missing from her voice.

"But," she continued, "I got up to go pee afterward as instructed by Dr. Braun—no UTIs, thank you very much—and I could hear Joaquin talking."

She took a deep breath then. This was an uncharacteristic gesture for Angela—one that sounded like she was perhaps calming herself. It made me feel on high alert for what had happened next.

Had he somehow known she had just completed gender reassignment surgery? Had he ridiculed her as a woman? Rejected her? I would smash his face!

"I overheard him whispering that he had just spermed another whale and then he laughed," she said. "I was shocked. I've been so focused on becoming female, I guess I didn't realize that being overweight was that big of a deal."

I had been more relieved than shocked. At least it was only about weight—which still didn't make it right, but it was better than attacking her gender . . . maybe? Or maybe that was just a matter of opinion.

My experience with both men and women was that they were excruciatingly critical about women's bodies. I had often wondered why nobody nitpicks men's bodies the same. I would often see a super skinny guy with a gorgeous woman or a heavy guy with a gorgeous woman, but rarely did I see a gorgeous man with a super skinny or heavy woman. It seemed that women were expected to look one specific way—a way neither Angela nor I had ever looked.

"Geez, Ang. I'm so sorry. That must have crushed you." I felt so bad for her. To be so high one minute and brought so low the next must have been so painful. But Ang was having none of my sympathy.

"Don't feel bad for me. I'm only upset that I didn't think of it," she said, but the impatience in her voice told me a different story. For once,

Angela had been hurt. I wanted to punch that stupid Joaquin in the face. I wanted to tell him that someday he was going to probably be bald and have a dad bod and that I hoped someone would tell him he looked like shit when he did—but realistically, I knew that he would laugh in my face. After all, I'm not exactly someone he would look at either.

"Ang..." I began, but she cut me off.

"I'm just going to have to lose weight. It's that simple. If the media is telling men that they should desire a woman that looks like a Victoria Secret model and they crawl into bed with me, they are bound to be a little shocked." She was very matter of fact. "I've dealt with bigger obstacles. I just hate the message I'm sending to the women of the world—that now that I'm a woman, I need to be thin."

I could imagine how much she would hate the message. Angela was never unhappy with her size. She was always a healthy person.

"But I'm ready to move forward now with my HEAP, so if I need to lose weight to do it, I'm losing weight. End of story. I have to do what I need to do."

Her HEAP—her Happily Ever After Plan. She was completely committed to it. And true to her word, that was the last time we had that discussion. Right after that, she located the clinical trial online and it was completely free. The only small hiccup was that it was designed for 18-year-old co-eds. But true to Ang, she did not let that stop her. She had been told she looked like a teenager for years. She still had times when customers came into her bakery and asked to speak to her mother, assuming she was too young to be the owner. Feeling confident she could fool the administrators of the clinical trial; she went online and found a source for a very impressive fake ID—only $80. She never intended to cheat the trial—her only desire was to achieve her goals without further delay. It had never occurred to her that adult men would be so shallow as to first look at her size. She's made no plan for that blip.

Relying on both a nickname from childhood and the name she was born with, she combined them to create Angel Adams. The regulators of the trial barely looked twice at her ID other than verifying her age. She was officially part of the clinical trial. Right from the beginning, the results had been remarkable. The weight had come off quickly and painlessly.

I passed Jake as I rounded the last corner, briefly wondering how he had beat me here. Didn't he ride with the body? *God, did I really just call Angela "the body?"* What was wrong with me?

"Go ahead and go in, Dan. You know the drill. There's a warm one coming in. I'll be just a minute."

I did know the drill, but the morgue had never made me feel this way before. I pulled on the heavy door, the swoosh from its seal adding to my sense of foreboding. Jake's desk was on the left and I grabbed a few small containers of Vicks from the orange bowl.

"Why 'orange,'" I'd asked Jake, "when everything else is white?"

"To catch your eye so that, hopefully, everyone entering grabs one and uses it. Can't be too careful."

Now I opened one to dab a small amount under each nostril before adding all three to my left pocket. I had to have my wits about me and couldn't afford to be affected by things like the smell of decaying skin.

Jake always kept his lab in perfect order. The white sheets were examined meticulously before they were placed on the gurneys. Each morning, he walked the room to make certain every surface had been wiped clean. More than once, he had ordered a "re-clean" of the legs of the gurneys. Now, nobody forgot. Every surface was to be cleaned. He made sure the body bags were incinerated each evening and always carried a fresh one with him in case the paramedics were short. You could always be sure the crime scene evidence was intact.

He said the dead deserved respect. Also, when he first started, the lab had been a disaster.

Bodies had stacked up while he organized and cleaned. He didn't ever want that to happen again. He was a good guy—always thinking ahead.

I walked past the first body, which had been abandoned by Jake mid-processing earlier when he had left to meet us at Angela's crime scene. The next gurney had a large sealed black plastic bag sitting atop it. That would be Angela. It killed me to think of her inside that bag. She would've hated the dark space.

My legs wobbled as I slowly unzipped the bag, seeing her beautiful face now mottled in shades of deathly purple. My reaction felt disrespectful, but I couldn't control the swell of emotion.

Swallowing hard against the thickness in my throat, I slowly pealed back the plastic and gazed upon Angela's face, looking beyond the erosion of death—her blonde hair scattered in disarray around her head, clinging statically to the sides of the plastic bag in places; her long brown eyelashes naturally tipped in black lying deep in the sockets where her once beautiful blue eyes had begun to recede and discolor at the corners; her perfect bow shaped lips slightly plumped from the putrefactive gases— and seeing only her clear smooth skin. Even in death, she was a lovely woman.

"You did it Ang," I whispered. My voice sounded strangely small in the stark, fluoresced room. "You are finally everything you ever wanted to be." Except alive, of course. It was still impossible to believe my best friend—my only friend—lay dead before me.

Without warning, a sensation of creeping and crawling coursed through me, causing an involuntary shiver. The hairs on the back of my neck rose to attention. This wasn't about Angela. It was something more. I sensed a presence in the room. On high alert, I quickly scanned every corner of the room with law enforcement detail.

"Jake? That you? Didn't take long to roll that one in." But Jake didn't answer. And why would he? He was clearly allowing me some time alone with Angela. Doherty must have said something to him. I felt unhinged and confused in a way that I hadn't felt since my first visit to the morgue in high school. But then again, I'd never visited anyone I loved there before.

Unzipping the bag farther, I pulled open the plastic to her waist. I had little opportunity to really look at her body during the crime scene investigation. I had worked too hard at not looking at it— avoiding the vacant and cloudy stare of her once sparkling eyes, which I now ran my hands over to close once again. I caught sight of a tiny, incised wound on her left bicep. *Odd.* I leaned down quickly to examine it more closely just as a single "pop" shattered the silence. I felt a sharp sting near my left ear. I whirled around—but there was nobody there. God, my imagination was in serious overdrive. I actually thought I'd heard a gunshot.

Turning back to Angela, I touched the area behind my ear as I noticed blood on Angela's cheek.

Dead people don't bleed. Hysteria crept in as I discovered my hand was covered in blood—my own.

My vision blurred as the reality of the situation began to sink in. *I've been shot!* I grabbed the edge of the gurney with both hands, watching the blood drip steadily onto Angela's beautiful skin, the red and purples swirling together and puddling in her eye sockets like some garish work of art.

"Oh God!" My voice echoed against white tiled walls. I thought I heard the whoosh of the door, but whether it was opening or closing, I didn't know. *I will* not *pass out.* But as I tightened my grip on the gurney, I could feel it begin to give way and topple over onto me.

The sudden weight on my chest seemed to push out the hysterical giggle that I had fought so valiantly to suppress, and it echoed throughout the void. Angela. *Thank God she doesn't weigh 300 pounds anymore.* My laughter was enveloped by darkness.

ChapterSix

A PAST MONSTER

3:48 pm

Ten years ago

The backpack feels heavy laying atop me. What does she carry in it? Bricks? I start to sit up, but she holds up her hand.

"No, wait a minute," she says.

I stop moving. My heart is still jumping in my chest erratically. I try to slow it to match the barely audible beeping in the background.

She grabs the heavy glass doors to the school building, jiggling them to ensure they had firmly closed behind me. Then she peers outside, flattening her face on the glass to see as far as she can to the left and right.

"He's gone."

"It wasn't just him," I said quickly.

"All of them?" she asked.

I nodded.

"Nobody is out there now." She glances at my skinned knees and bloodied hands clutching at her backpack. "Give me a minute."

I look over to see Angela ripping down the "Welcome Back Students" banner along the wall. I sit up then. I'm naked from the waist down. I try to spread her backpack to cover myself, daring to look through the doors that mark the back entrance to the high school building, but she is right; nobody is outside trying to get in. Then I look down the hallways that fan out to the office and classrooms. They are empty. The whole school seems to be empty—except for Angela. Thank God.

"Thank you, Angela."

It is the first time I've ever spoken to her, even though we have been in school together most of our lives. It isn't that we don't like each other; we don't know each other. It is more of an unspoken rule that freaks don't befriend each other—we'd each been labeled freaks by the popular kids years ago—and magnify one another's torture. Angela is mocked because she is very overweight. Rumors circulate that she is intersexual—that she has both boy and girl parts. But who knows the truth. I have enough trouble dealing with my own freak status. I've been called a boy as long as I can remember. My name doesn't help: Daniela, better known as Dan the Man. But there is nothing but girl parts hiding beneath my clothes. I guess that rumor has just been put to rest.

Her voice startles me.

"Here. Stand up."

She wraps the paper banner twice around my skinny frame. As I meet her gaze, I see a confidence in her look that surprises me—and sympathy. Maybe I am the only freak avoiding people.

"Don't you want to know what happened?" I ask. I can't believe she hasn't asked. She just started helping me as if it was the most natural thing in the world.

"Did they...you know, hurt you?"

I knew what she was asking. "Not the way they wanted to."

"Good. There will be time for talking later," she said. "First, let's take care of you. How do you get home?"

"I walk." I say, although I know there isn't anything in this world that can convince me to walk today. I wonder what the beeping sound is in the hallways.

"Walking is not safe today. Walking might not ever be safe again. We need to tell someone."

She is handling the entire situation with such ease; it feels like she's an adult. I wonder what made her so mature.

I nod uneasily. This is not how I imagined my first day of high school ending; it is the worst day of my life. Where will I go from here?

Angela leads me to the guidance office. It is empty. The whole school appears to be empty.

The beeping grows louder as we walk down the hallway.

Finally, we spy Mr. Osteen, who is staying late to line up the microscopes for the next day.

"My God Daniela, what happened to you?"

Only then do I fully realize I am wearing a paper banner. And my face is scratched and bleeding. Am I in shock? Is that why I keep hearing the beeping?

"Jeremy Richards—the 6-Pack. The boys . . ." My voice quivers on the words. That's all I can say. He nods.

"Let's call your mother."

That simple phrase breaks me. Tears burn my face in rivulets where the gravel is still buried.

"I don't have a mother."

"Well I do," says Angela. "We will call my mom. She'll come and get us."

Us. Like I am her friend.

"Angela, thank you for saving me." I want to hug her, but I am not a hugger. I feel a strong urge to be a hugger, just this once. But I can't change who I am. Huggers have feelings and feelings make you hurt.

Ugh. The darn beeping is making my head hurt. Why won't the beeping stop?

Chapter Seven

TRAPPED

Sunday, December 4, 2022. 4:30 AM
6 hours after

I had to get to the source of the beeping. The pain in my head was excruciating. Every time I tried to open my eyes, glaring white lights penetrated my cracked lids and seared my pained skull. Reality came crashing back. Where was I? Was I still in the morgue? An involuntary shiver went through my body as I remembered the weight of Angela's body on me. Her dead body.

I was lying in a bed so maybe I'd been moved upstairs? Had I really been shot? Who shot me? Why? Was my shooter in the room with me? My mind darted over the possibilities until I had no option other than to force my eyes open.

Cautiously, I peeked through my lids. I was instantly transported back in time again. James Hawthorne. He was one of six people I had dreamed about moments earlier, and one I had hoped to never see again in my lifetime.

"What are you doing here?" I demanded, before he even realized I had become conscious.

I startled him. He quickly sat up, spilling coffee all over his ridiculously expensive suit. That made me smile inwardly, even if the sight of him made me want to vomit. Or that could have just been a result of the blow to the head, I guess.

"I've been assigned to the case," my nemesis sputtered. "I stopped by the morgue to examine the newest victim," he continued to explain.

The words "newest victim" did not escape my notice, nor did the fact that an FBI agent was sitting in a hospital room with me. *Why would they assign the FBI to a series of local suicides? Does he really expect me to believe that?* Maybe I was no longer the only one who believed there was foul play involved. I struggled to sit up, fighting against the IV line, the heart monitor, and the excruciating pounding in my head. Why did they hook people up to all of this stuff just for a gunshot?

Instinctively I reached to where I last felt blood and found a gauze patch on the left side of my skull, just above my ear. *Must have only been a flesh wound.*

"Please stop referring to Angela as 'the victim.' For once in your life, have the decency to call her by her real name." Spittle flew from my lips as the pent-up anger and hurt from high school pulsed through me like I was fifteen just yesterday, wiping out the ten years between in one clean swoop. *Damn it. Act like a professional!*

"How long have I been here?" I asked, trying to regain control over both me and the situation.

James Hawthorne, freshly minted FBI member and one of the "6-Pack," a group of mean boys from high school, had the decency to look puzzled. "I came here to see the newest virgin suicide victim—18-year-old; female; Angel Adams? And in the process, I found you, apparently shot in the head."

"She's not 18 and she's not Angel Adams! I just told you---it's Angela," I repeated with emphasis. Wasn't he listening to anything I said? "And I wasn't shot in the head, or we wouldn't be talking." My words were full of venom, making my heart monitor gain in momentum like a runaway horse. I swallowed back some of the choice words I wanted to hurl at him.

But I still wasn't done with him yet. "And since when does the FBI get involved in suicides? Why are you *really* here?" I shook my head in disgust and immediately regretted it when the knifelike pain sliced behind my right eye. "Am I supposed to believe it is coincidence that I get shot, then I wake up and 'ta da!' There you are! My hero this time?"

The look on his face told me I had gone too far. I do that some-times—maybe a lot of the time. Ang says it is a defense mecha-nism—that I want to hurt people before they hurt me—especially if they've hurt me before. And this guy was at the top of my hurt list.

"You mean Mon.....?"

Harshly, I cut him off before he could finish. "No! I mean *Angela*!" I couldn't believe he was still going to refer to Angela by her old high school nickname—Monstrosity. Could this man still be this cruel at al-most 30? Weren't people supposed to mature and become good hu-mans at some point? I could feel the ugly feelings of the past beginning to rise inside of me like a serpent.

"That's exactly what I said. Monn. Angela Monn." He spoke slowly and made direct eye contact with me as if to say, "Look at me! I'm telling the truth."

I closed my eyes. I did not want to look James Hawthorne in the eye. I didn't want to look at him at all: not today, not tomorrow, not ever. I wanted to go back to yesterday—no, to last week— and pretend that none of this ever happened, to *make* none of this ever happen. I wanted Angela to be alive. I was going to call her every day and make sure she was happy and not let anything bad happen to her.

But wishing wasn't going to make that happen. It wasn't going to make the persistent, rhythmic pounding that seemed to emanate from deep within my skull go away either. Who in the hell had shot me? I didn't have any enemies. I didn't get close enough to anyone for them to either like or dislike me. It had to be Angela's killer. Was Mrs. Monn in danger too?

Damn it! This was happening. I was lying in a hospital bed with my head bandaged. I needed to get back to work. My best friend was dead, and I was trapped in a room with James Hawthorne. I tasted tears as they slipped down my cheeks. I didn't want to feel sorry for myself, but sometimes I just couldn't help it. It was times like these when I really could have used a mom. But I had managed to kill mine about 25 years ago.

"I'm sorry." It killed me to say that to him. I could not look at him, for fear he would find my words insincere. "Can you please just tell me how long I've been here?" My voice was barely above a whisper, since even the slightest movement of my head brought about a brand-new variation of the relentless drumbeat. I prayed I didn't have a concussion.

"Not long really—only a few hours. Apparently, you were knocked unconscious when the gurney toppled over on top of you." He replied evenly. "I suspect they may have put something in your IV to help you relax a little. I heard you were fighting them at first."

Strange. I had no recollection of that at all. The full impact of his words hit me then. If I had only been here a few hours, he had been dispatched to the body—I winced inwardly again at my own slip—before he knew I'd been shot. I needed some time alone to think, to figure out what was going on. I closed my eyes, hoping he would take the hint and leave.

I had met James Hawthorne and his fellow five thugs on my first and worst day of high school. Maybe I'm being unfair calling them all thugs. I mean, he became an FBI agent so he couldn't be all bad—unless he was one of those bad guys who put himself into a top-level position to unleash his evil without anyone knowing about it. But then again, maybe some of that group were just high school boys being boys. I know at least one of them was my worst nightmare—had continued to occupy my worst nightmares throughout the years—and the things he did were not normal for a boy of any age. What a paradox. While that day has haunted me for over ten years, I would never have met Angela if it hadn't happened. Angela. The only true friend I've ever had, and her mother has loved me as her own daughter from the moment I first met her. Maybe we must suffer first in life to get truly wonderful things. I can't help but wonder. But why do we only get to keep wonderful things for such a short time?

Before Angela, it seemed that no matter how hard I tried, I was incapable of forming a lasting relationship—something I desperately wanted; I guess something every girl with no mother wants or needs. I felt the need grow as I got older. My emptiness felt so big.

When I was younger, I fit in well with the boys in the neighborhood. I was a natural tomboy with an intensely curious mind from the time I was little. I helped the neighborhood boys build treehouses, did experiments, and took data. I preferred hanging out with the boys because it always seemed like they had so much more freedom. Of course, as an adult I can't help but wonder if this tendency toward all things "boy" was a misguided attempt to gain attention or approval from my father—who I firmly believed had only wanted a son, hence the barely disguised boy's name. My scientific mind only needed the slightest prompt to know how to design a treehouse from scrap lumber or how to calculate how far off the ground we could safely jump without breaking a limb.

They even tolerated it when I began to execute my experiments on them. How many donuts can you eat lying down? Standing on your head? How many can you eat before you puke? The boys loved the food experiments, and it seemed that I had an endless resource of money. I was too young to understand that my father owned the largest pharmaceuticals company on the East Coast and that I was being used—that everyone called me the "mad scientist's spawn" behind my back. I had fun with them until Tommy Leon jumped off our stone garden wall and said I told him it was safe. I did not. I would have never made an error in calculation like that. Nonetheless, my fate with the parents was decided that day. Stay away from that Neely girl or your kid will get hurt. You would hope that people would look out for the child with no mother, but instead, they acted as if I had something they might catch. The dead mother disease.

I had one brief friendship in seventh grade. Jenny Bowser. I will never forget her—or the end of our friendship. She was exceptionally cruel. She fully validated my distrust of people in general.

It became apparent to me that I didn't really know how to play or form a relationship. I only understood how to analyze. Facts felt safe. Emotions not so much.

But then Angela came along on that fateful day and saved me. I knew I would love her forever.

Chapter Eight

DANCING WITH THE DEVIL

Sunday, December 4, 2022. 8:06 AM
9 hours 36 minutes after

I must have dozed off. When I opened my eyes again, James was no longer in my room. The shade was open on the window, and I could see that it was bright outside. Smells of hospital breakfast wafted through the doorway, making my stomach growl. When had I eaten last? Making a quick assessment, I could see that I was hooked to too many machines to just get up and leave. I also noticed a jacket hanging on the hook that did not belong to me. My stomach fell as I realized the scrunched letters read FBI. So, he was still here somewhere.

Wasn't it bad enough that I had lost my best friend and then someone had tried to shoot me, too? Why, in the middle of the worst week that I've had since—I don't know . . . high school, I guess—do I have to also deal with James Hawthorne? I have spent the past 10 years trying to put him out of my mind. Well, not him specifically, but he was part of the gang that attacked me. I was old enough and educated enough to call them what they actually were now: a gang. And he was in my hospital room, of all places, at a time when I felt very vulnerable. Me and vulnerable were not a good mix. I had to do something to change the situation and quick.

I had an idea. I pressed the button to signal the nurse.

"Yes, can I help you?" A cheerful young voice responded.

"Yes, hello. I need to use the bathroom." That seemed as good a reason as any to get out of the bed. I had to find a way to escape before he came back, and I knew they weren't just going to agree to letting me walk out. I mean, why exactly was he here? FBI or not, this guy was trouble with a capital T and my scientific mind did not believe in coincidence.

"I'll be right in," she replied in a sing-song voice.

She did not come "right in." Irritated, I wondered what people do when they really do have to use the bathroom. Defecate in the bed? It was a good thing I had been lying.

What seemed like an eternity, but was probably only about 20 minutes later, the nurse came in and said cheerfully, "I hear someone has to use the bathroom?"

"No, I already peed the bed." I gave her a deadpan look.

The nurse's smile disappeared quickly. This was going to be another kind of visit—clearly not one she liked.

Exasperated, I said, "I'm just kidding. Although, thank God I have good Kegel muscles. I called 20 minutes ago!"

Now Nurse Hanley was just pissed at me for calling her out for taking so long and because I got to see that look, the one that said, "I do not want to change your soiled bed."

"Look, I'm sorry, okay? I'm not a good patient. I realize that. How about we get me out of here?"

She pulled her lips into a tight smile, letting me know that that suggestion sounded good to her too. Unfortunately, she was not the one in charge—kind of like me and my boss. I do the dirty work; he evaluates it and makes the calls. Not that I'm complaining. I still can't believe I made detective at 25. I know it was part of the diversity equity initiative, keeping the balance of men and women in the department, but I still wonder if my name was the tipping point—what gave me the advantage over other females. It would be ironic if it did, after the grief it caused me early in life. Regardless, I just wanted her to hurry, something she seemed relatively incapable of doing.

And as if I'd summoned him up simply by thinking of the words "grief early in life," James Hawthorne re-entered the room. *Damn!* He had on a fresh suit and looked clean shaven. Did FBI agents carry "go bags" with extra suits and shaving supplies? I'm sure he would have no problem talking a young nurse into using an unoccupied shower. He may be a lifelong enemy, but I could still admit he was undeniably handsome. I would be willing to bet those puppy dog brown eyes had melted a few hearts, but they had zero effect on me.

"Daniela," he began.

"I go by Dan now." I offered him no explanation, just stared hard at him. Let him wonder all he wanted. I owed him nothing.

"Okay. Dan. I was sent here because this is not the only group of teen 'suicides.'" He made air quotes around the word. "There is at least one more group in Maine—same MO—all previously obese, 18-year-old co-eds."

He had my attention. I sat up, noting that my head was not pounding nearly as badly as before. What had Angela stumbled into? She had only *pretended* to be two of the three things—but she had still lost her life. She seemed like the most likely place to begin the investigation. For the first time since I saw her address go across my computer screen, I felt something akin to hope begin to blossom in my chest.

"Based on what you are telling me, it seems reasonable to call Angela's death a suspected homicide, not a suicide." I said. "Wouldn't you agree?"

"Well . . ." He dragged the word out so long I was ready to shake him. "That's not necessarily true." He looked down at his shoes, like there were answers there.

I wanted to scream at him to get to the point. I wondered if he was always this evasive or if it was FBI training 101. Either way, I knew it was going to drive me crazy.

"We have a theory that someone on the dark web may be encouraging these girls to commit suicide, that they joined some kind of group that we have not yet been able to locate." James seems hesitant to say too much and pauses as if he wants to say more but either can't or shouldn't. Probably one of those "need to know" situations.

Wow. I wasn't expecting that. "So, you are telling me that there is a serial killer out there somewhere? And he—or she—is killing young girls by making them kill themselves?" As hard as I try to keep my voice neutral, I can hear the incredulity coming through.

"Well, I suppose for lack of a better explanation . . . that is one way of summarizing it. We have a team working on it. What else can you tell me about Angela that the media won't be able to tell me? I mean, other than the obvious—she wasn't 18 like the others."

I felt like James was trying to sidestep my summary of the situation and instead try to pry information from me. I'd heard the FBI could pull stunts like that. "Sorry Hawthorne, I'm not giving anything 'til I get something. And you cannot tell anyone about her age—not yet. Nor her real name. Please. That must be kept under wraps, at least for now." I hated pleading with him, so I used my one ace. "You owe me."

My words had the desired effect. James looked like I punched him in the gut. I could only mentally apologize for this one because from here on out, I had to do and say whatever was necessary to find Angela's killer.

"I will not divulge any information about Angela until it is necessary. Not because I owe you one, but because she is someone I knew too. She was always fair to me when a lot of people weren't. I owe her this too."

"You do not know Ang like I do—did." My voice broke as I corrected myself to the past tense.

"Which is exactly why I need you to fill me in on her. The fact that she was your best friend puts us at an advantage. Tell me everything about her that you can. There is something I am missing." He spoke with such urgency and passion; I sensed that this case was important to him too.

"I was an intelligence officer for the Navy before I went through the academy. But even with that training, I keep coming up empty on these cases. They don't add up. There is a missing piece I'm not seeing."

I could relate to what he was saying. Didn't I feel the same way just yesterday? I should be grateful that someone else believed these were not random suicides.

"There are a lot of things I can tell you, but I'm not telling you anything yet. We have some serious past trust issues between us. You can't just march in here now with your dazzling smile, expensive suit, and FBI jacket and expect to erase our history that quickly."

As soon as I said the words, I wanted to pull them back into my mouth. Why on earth did I say dazzling smile? I felt my eyes round. Where had that come from? I could feel the warmth in my cheeks as James flashed one of those smiles at my words. They should not have been words to smile at. I'm an idiot.

"Ummmm . . . Do you still need to use the bathroom?" Nurse Hanley looked between us, her words adding to the awkwardness of the moment.

I had completely forgotten about her and the reason I called her into the room. Now, I waved her away impatiently. "Please just find a doctor who can sign me out of here. I have an investigation to conduct."

I chose my next words carefully. I wanted to make certain James knew right now that he was not dealing with the same scared little girl from Noraville High that he helped to hold down while his crazed leader removed my clothes. Thanks to Angela, I was not a grudge holder, or at least I was trying hard not to be. I could try to forgive, but I would never forget. I did not plan to take any of his 6-Pack crap anymore.

"Special Agent Hawthorne," I said, intentionally using his complete title and drawing it out emphatically to put more appropriate distance between us. "Perhaps we can work this investigation together. I believe our dual resources would be beneficial in seeking a quick resolution."

Realizing the old grudge was not far from our conversation, James was equally careful in his response. "Yes, I think that is a good idea, especially since we still do not know who shot you or why you were shot."

Damn! How could I forget the whole reason I was lying in this stupid bed in the first place.

Why on earth would someone try to shoot me? Surely it wasn't me they were after? "Would you like me to see if I can find the doctor?"

Seriously? This was really too much. He was trying to be my savior now? He was about 10 years too late.

"Thanks, but no thanks. I'm pretty sure I know the best way to get out the door quickly. Can you please grab my jacket out of the closet?"

I seemed to have no alternative but to keep asking him for help. He must love all the vulnerability from me. *Enjoy it, bucko. Once I'm back on my feet, you'll never see this side of me again. You do* not *know who I am now.*

He raised his eyebrows at the basic, navy blue, police issue overcoat he pulled from the closet.

"What?" I said, an apparent edge in my voice. "Basic issue not good enough for you flashy FBI guys?" I was proud that I went through the ranks on my way to becoming a detective. I grew up rich. Money had never given me anything real. Besides, the jacket was warm, functional, and had a lot of life left in it. Apparently, he'd forgotten that I did not fall into the "girly girl" category.

He threw his hands up helplessly in a "no harm, no foul" gesture.

His presence was really getting under my skin and my head was throbbing again. I sure could use a couple of pain relievers and a nice hot cup of tea to dissolve those little lifesavers real quick right now. But the last thing I planned to do was ask Special Agent Hawthorne for yet another favor, and I had absolutely no intention of taking anything else to dull my wits.

Digging through the pocket, I found my cell phone: low battery but not dead yet, thank goodness. I dialed my father's office. Of course, I was automatically routed to a machine. Mr. Pharmaceuticals Magnate would never take a cold call from anyone—not even his daughter— without first weighing the importance. I left a message like everyone else.

"Dad, this is Daniela. I had a small accident and was briefly hospitalized. I have been treated and need to be released immediately so I can return to work. I'm in the middle of an active investigation. Can you please see that my doctor is notified as quickly as possible. This is very urgent." The message was brief but to the point, just the way he likes them. I was sure it would do the trick. I had learned over the years, exactly what I could—and mostly what I could not—count on my father for.

If there was one thing I knew with absolute certainty, it was that my father did not condone missing work. If I had an active investigation, he would feel that I belonged at work unless I was bleeding out on an operating table. The other thing I knew was that he would never question my assessment of the situation. I would like to think it is because he has immeasurable faith in me, but I think it is actually because since my Ecuadorian nanny, Margette, left, I've been solely in charge of myself.

James shook his head. "I remember when me and the guys first met your dad at the start of the trial. We were so scared of him. He seemed almost like God, you know?"

"What trial?" I hadn't heard about any trials.

Had one of them been in trouble and my father had testified on their behalf? Or was he talking about the mediation from when Jeremy attacked me? Did my father help that creep? It killed me to think he may have supported the people who hurt me.

"You know—the clinical trial. The one us six guys did."

Shaking my head slowly, I said, "I have no idea what you are talking about. I didn't know you guys were in a clinical trial."

When he didn't respond, I continued, "As kids?" My next words dripped with sarcasm. "I'd love to hear about it since I barely saw my father growing up."

"I'm sorry Daniela–Dan–I didn't mean to upset you. I assumed your family discussed things like that at home."

"You can't have a discussion with someone who isn't there, can you?" I blinked rapidly. This conversation was not going to go south on me. "I didn't really experience a family—not the traditional kind—until I met Angela. Growing up, I just had my nanny, Margette. My dad worked a lot."

I took a deep breath. Damn. It sounded pathetic. James's dad had been the chief of police in our town. I'm sure his dad worked a lot too, but he obviously still found time to spend with his family. There was really no way to sugarcoat the fact that my dad had chosen not to spend time with me, so I didn't try.

"We didn't really see him all that often either."

"It's okay. Once I met Angela, her family became my family. Really. It was fine."

I did not want to feel like he was taking care of me. I was losing control. I must have really hit my head hard when I hit the floor. This was not like me at all. James Hawthorne did not need to hear my non-family sob story. I still wasn't comfortable with the matter of how he happened to show up right after I'd been shot. There's coincidence and then there's just unlikely.

"I'm sorry. I'm pretty sure the trial was only for boys."

He really did sound sorry—probably sorry he had brought it up in the first place.

"I'm sorry too. It just hit me wrong to hear that my father conducted a clinical trial with boys. You'd think he would have used girls so he could have seen my face more than once a month."

I wanted to smack myself in the forehead the minute the words came out of my mouth. *Here I go again!* I tried to laugh it off, but it came out sounding too harsh. Overall, I felt like I'd been slugged in the gut.

Suddenly I had a thought. The words "clinical trial" reminded me of the photos I'd taken at Angela's apartment. I scrolled to unlock the screen of my phone again, going through my photos until I got to the photograph of the contract on Angela's nightstand. I zoomed in on the bottom on the contract and gasped. Neely Pharmaceuticals? Why had Angela never mentioned that to me?

"James?" I extended the phone toward him, just as the door opened between us, forcing me to withdraw my hand.

"Well, if it isn't our favorite detective!"

I wasn't sure if Dr. Jackson's entry into the room was good or bad timing. I was just about to show an FBI agent my father's potential involvement in my best friend's death. Was I ready for that? Dr. Jackson had helped me with a few cases I brought in over the past year. I decided I was glad to have her in the room at precisely that moment.

"I just got a call from the big man himself—it seems he thinks it is time for his daughter to get back to work. All work and no play . . . But what would we do without Dr. Neely? Now let's check you out and see how you're doing."

There was no animosity in her tone. My father was well respected in town. I had spent years trying to figure out what others saw that I didn't, but this connection I understood. I had frequented the halls of this hospital often enough to see his name proudly displayed at the top of the donor list. The way others revered him was still a mystery to me. I stayed in the city after college—close enough to visit but not too close as to feel the constant rejection from him. As my father, he had completely sucked. But, if he could get me released right now, that would make him a good dad for the day—at least until I could get more information about the contract in the photograph. I'm sure he didn't even ask why I was there, so he'd never know that someone had taken a shot at me—unless, of course, he had hired someone to do it. But that was crazy thinking, right?

Dr. Jackson checked my eyes for signs of a concussion and then checked my wound under the bandages. "You were grazed by a bullet. One inch more to the right and this would have been a different meeting. How's your head feeling?"

"Good," I lied. I had to get out of here and back to work.

"Okay then. No sign of a concussion so I can't see any reason to keep you. Be careful out there."

I remembered bending down to look at the small incision on Angela's arm. I wondered now if that had saved my life. If both James and my father would have been visiting me in the morgue too, had I not seen that detail. Maybe both had already been visiting me at the morgue. What *was* the incision for? And who had made it? The thought made me shiver.

"So sorry, Dan. I've been telling them to turn up the heat but with the weather outside, it is hard to keep the chill out of the air."

I was glad she had mistaken my shiver for cold. I didn't want anyone to know I was thinking about my own ass right now. I thanked Dr. Jackson and, after all the wires were removed, pointedly asked James if he would mind giving me some privacy so I could get dressed. That guy sure didn't know when to leave. Thankfully, someone had hung up my suit so I wouldn't look like sloppy seconds next to him. It annoyed me that I even cared. Everything annoyed me. Basically, I was now back to square one with the added pressure that whoever had killed Angela now knew that I knew—or at least suspected. My one and only friend was dead. Her killer was after me. I had nobody—again. I needed time to think everything through and process what had happened without wondering where James Hawthorne fit into all of it.

My lungs felt like they were being corseted for a Victorian ball gown; the ache in my chest was that immense. And now I had to go out and work side by side with my enemy to solve the death of my best friend who had left me a trail of evidence implicating my own father? Was this the "great life" Angela was always promising me? I kept waiting to feel some part of it. But she was really the only great part of my life, and now she was gone.

Stepping into the hallway, I said, "Hawthorne, I think we're going to need to talk to Angela's mom first. Would you mind driving? Not sure I'm quite up to it just yet."

I was tempted to tell him this might be the one and only time he would ever hear me admit to a weakness so he'd better savor it, but then decided that I didn't really know who I would be without Angela. Would I still be brave and strong Dan the Detective? Was that me, or me through her?

His raised eyebrows and nod of his head said everything he needed to say other than, "Please, call me James."

If anyone could shed some light on Angela, it was her mother. They had a bond unlike anything I had ever experienced. Of course, I had never experienced anything regarding a mother/daughter bond other than the affection Mrs. Monn had showered upon me. I could still remember that first time I met her. It was the absolute worst possible circumstances, but I still remembered it fondly. It was "that" day.

Meeting Angela's mom had felt like eating a big piece of warm apple pie. There was something about her that made me feel instantly so safe and loved. She hugged me when she picked us up at the school and then welcomed me into their home as if I were family. And even though she had to leave work unexpectedly to pick us up, she wasn't upset about it at all.

It had felt so strange pulling into Angela's neighborhood the first time. I had never even been to that side of town. It looked so different than where I lived. There were chain link fences in the front yard with cracked concrete sidewalks in front of them. The word "unsafe" came to mind, which was ironic considering the situation she had just removed me from. Open green lawns and a lot of ornamental landscaping was more in my comfort zone, I guess.

It made me realize what a small and sheltered life I had lived to that point. I went to school, I went to gymnastics, and I went home. I guess Margette did things like grocery shopping while I was at school. I'd never really thought about it before. We had a housekeeper, cook, gardener, a flower delivery person—all the hired help necessary to run a home efficiently, and I had Margette to tend to all my personal needs. Every so often, when I grew out of something, Margette would schedule a trip into the city, and we'd go to Macy's to get what I needed. But those trips were few and far between, and we always went with a list, methodically checking things off. The only time I can ever remember deviating from that list was for one delicious ice cream cone when the Ben and Jerry's Cow Mobile happened to be giving out free Boston Crème ice cream samples at Faneuil Hall one very lucky July day. In hindsight, I can hardly believe Margette let me get one. She had a tendency towards rigidity.

That day, after Mrs. Monn had given me some clothes to put on, I sat quietly on their old scratchy green sofa while Angela recounted what happened. She was very thorough and didn't exaggerate anything from what I had told her. I never felt like I needed to interrupt her. When shewas done talking, Mrs. Monn hugged me and stroked my hair. Two hugs in less than an hour---and I liked both.

"Daniela, my love, I am so proud of you for the way you fought those terrible boys," she murmured against my hair.

I don't know what I had expected from her, but it certainly was not that. The people in my life just weren't affectionate. I cut loose of one huge, gulpy sob that day before I could stop it and then I felt so bad.

"I'm so sorry!" I exclaimed. "I didn't know I was going to cry." I didn't want her to think I didn't appreciate the hugs.

"It's okay to cry Daniela. Never apologize to me for such a thing," she crooned. "You are safe here."

And for the first time ever, for reasons I cannot explain, I trusted her. I felt safe and loved by two people I scarcely knew. It felt so good to be cared for—to be loved and nurtured. No matter how scared I had been that day, it almost felt worth it for that moment where my whole body felt warm and fuzzy even on the inside, like I was melting from the inside out.

I thought now about what it must have been like to be raised by someone like her. She was the perfect mother for someone like Angela. How would my family have treated Angela? They would not have supported her decision to become a girl. I was certain of that. As badly as they wanted a boy, she would have been forced to live as a boy. Thank God she was not born a Neely.

Chapter Nine

HOME SWEET HOME

Sunday, December 4, 2022. 10:30 AM

12 hours after

We never made it to James Hawthorne's car. As we stepped into the elevators, I felt the vibration of my phone. I fumbled to remove it before the caller hung up.

"Dan, thank God. How are you dear?" Mrs. Monn sounded very distressed. "I just got here to see my girl and they told me you were shot!"

"I'm fine. I'm fine. Really. Just a scratch. Where are you?" I cooed, noticing James's eyebrows had climbed high on his forehead as he witnessed my telephone exchange. I glared back at him. I did not show this side to many people and certainly not to men.

"I'm downstairs with my Angel." Her voice broke. "I can't lose you too."

"I'll be right down," I assured her. "I'm fine. I promise. Just stay where you are."

Naturally, Mrs. Monn would want to be with her daughter. Where else would a mother be— especially a mother like her? I seemed to have lost all track of time, logic, and reason.

"So, you are close with the mom too?" James asked. I knew he had overheard her concern in the enclosed space. I put aside my own feelings and only focused on how Angela's mom would be feeling. That is what Angela would want me to do. I could do that for her.

"Yes. She is the only mother I've ever known. I love her." It didn't matter that I hadn't met her until I was 15 years old or that an event he had precipitated had brought about my meeting her. All that mattered was that she and I still had each other right now.

He was silent for a moment before saying, "I'm glad you have her. She seems like a nice lady."

"The best." My voice cracked a little. I coughed and cleared my throat. "Angela's body will be showing increased signs of decay. I am going to encourage her to leave quickly. This is not a good place for her to stay."

He nodded. "Meet at her house?"

"I'll text you when we leave." We exchanged phone numbers, and I gave him Mrs. Monn's address. He looked up at me in surprise.

"She still lives there?"

"They take care of each other there. She has friends who supported her through something that was not popular back in the day. They never judged her or Ang." I said. "It's run down, but not dangerous. If I thought it was dangerous, I would get her out of there."

"Rare," he says before turning away, before suddenly turning back. "Oh, Daniela? Here."

He extended his hand toward me. I took the protein bar from him. "I always keep a box of them in my bag. Seems there's never time to grab a decent meal."

I wanted to say no, to be offended that he was offering it, but I was too darn hungry not to take it.

"Thanks. I owe you."

Mrs. Monn was standing next to Angela's body, staring intently at her. Death begins to do things to the human body after a few days that no mother should have to see. Even though Angela was safeguarded somewhat by the extreme cold of her bedroom, she was still beginning to display some undesirable effects, such as skin marbling, epidermis slippage, and odor. Thank God her eyes had finally been glued shut.

I fumbled in my pocket, hoping to find the Vick's still there. It was. I moved toward her, kissing her on the cheek and quickly said, "Here, this will help a bit." I swiped a dash of Vicks under each nostril before she could protest then did the same to my own nose.

This was one of the first tricks Jake taught me. Smell can affect our ability to assess accurately.

Right now, I had no doubt it would affect our ability to grieve properly as well. I took her by the arm.

"Mrs. Monn. Do you have any last words you need to say to Angela?"

She turned to me, her eyes wide. "What do you mean?"

"Angela has gone home now. She wouldn't want you to see her like this," I said gently. "If you have anything you need to say to her, let's say it and leave her in peace."

The eyes that looked back at me were blackened with grief. "I know. I just keep thinking it is the last time I'll see her and then I can't make myself leave."

"She is never going to leave us," I assured her, and as soon as I said it, I knew it was true.

Angela had made too big of an impact on my life to ever be gone from it.

We turned into each other's arms, and I finally felt safe. Safe enough to release the tears I had been holding in. Tears that said I would miss Angela every single day of my life. Tears that promised her I would find her killer. Tears that rejuvenated me. I steered her away from the body, and we walked toward the exit.

I could see Jake across the room, working on another body. I wanted to ask him about the incision on Angela's arm—I was certain I had not seen it at her house—but this was not the time or place for a question like that. It was apparent that the autopsy had been completed in my absence. I wondered who had been present. I had so many questions and was eager to read the report as well. But first, I needed to get Mrs. Monn home and ask her a few questions.

"Hey Jake, could we talk later?" I asked. "I would appreciate if you would hang on to the report until we talk."

He acquiesced with an upward tilt of his head. Good old Jake. He probably did the autopsy by himself. He was such a good man.

"Mrs. Monn, did you drive here?" I asked.

"No. My friend dropped me off," she admitted. "She was concerned about me driving.

I was glad she had friends like that. She would need them in the upcoming months. "How about if I take you home now. We could talk in the car."

The fog that was in my brain only moments before was completely gone. I'd read about things like this in my psych class—how a parent can overcome unbelievable obstacles for a child but apparently it was true in general for a loved one. I felt a surge of gratitude that she and Angela had given me the opportunity to experience life on this level of love.

"Thank you, Dan."

She followed me out to my car like an injured puppy. She looked so exhausted I wasn't even sure she could or should carry on a conversation. I decided to keep it simple, to just ask about Angela's recipe books on this visit. I could come back as often as needed. She would need me as much as I would need her. And I wasn't ready to bring James Hawthorne to her house.

"Dan, please tell me that my girl did not take her life. Please." Her pleading tone nearly brought me to tears again. "I tried to be the mom she needed."

"Mrs. Monn, you were always the mom she needed. Always." It killed me that she doubted herself. "I do not believe Angela would take her life and will investigate this case fully to find out exactly what happened and what went wrong," I promised her.

She nodded. I wasn't sure if she believed me. I guess if I was a mother, it might be hard for me to believe. I was only her friend, and I felt like I had failed her.

I quickly shot off a text to James, telling him to meet me at Angela's house instead before I rounded the Beast and got in.

We rode along in silence for a few minutes before I dared to ask the big question. "Do you happen to know where Angela keeps her recipe books?"

She smiled to herself. "Sure Dan. They are still on her shelf in her room at home. You know, a mom looks through things like that when they miss the little girl their grown child used to be." Then she grimaced. "I guess now, I'll be looking through them because I'll never again see the woman or the child . . ."

Her voice trailed off, sounding sadder than I've ever heard her.

"How wonderful that you have them," I reassured her. "I guess since you've read them, you know that they aren't just recipe books—they are also journals."

Again, she smiled, seemingly reassured by my words. "Yes. They are primarily journals. I always knew. But her father didn't," she replied. "There was more journaling than recipes as she got older because the recipes became her secrets, so she stored them in her head."

We laughed together. Angela was very protective of her recipes. Her thought was that you would know how to make it if you were someone in her "inner circle" because she would teach you. Otherwise, you needed to make up your own recipe.

"I don't want to be invasive," I began, "but I was wondering if I could borrow her recipe books? Obviously, the police do not know of their existence, and I thought there may be some clue in them to point us in the right direction."

It killed me to ask this question, but it was essential to solving Angela's murder and my discomfort was not important at this juncture.

"You know my Angela. She has always been an open book with the people she loved." She smiled when she said this. I could tell it was hurting her to say this in the past tense because she said it so awkwardly. "What a shame her dad never knew her. I wonder if I'll tell him."

It appeared that her thoughts were all over the map just as mine were. While I didn't think he deserved to know—his only request was that Angela never try to contact him or his new family since he had built a new life in Canada where everyone lived as the sex they were born into— there was this tiny cruel part of me that hoped he would suffer when he found out.

I could never understand how he could act like she didn't exist. She was incredible. But he did—completely. And now she was dead, and neither he nor his precious boy born to be a boy or girl born to be a girl children would ever know their amazing half-sister who would have moved Heaven and Earth for them. I privately vowed to get their information so that I could somehow share with them the wonderful sister they had missed out on because of their father's bigotry.

We pulled up in front of her house. The old neighborhood looked the same, surprisingly no worse for the wear over ten years. I walked her to the door, each of us using the other for support. "I'll grab the books and then leave you to rest." I promised.

"No worries, Dan. You're all I have left now, you know." She bravely tried to smile, but the ends of her mouth refused to turn up. She turned to go gather the books for me.

Her comment reminded me of something Angela had said to me once a very long time ago. "All of the important things in life are already decided. We are just preparing our lives around them." She had said this when I was trying to decide what I would do with my future.

"Do you think it is coincidence that I was the one who volunteered to stay after school and was walking right by the doors the day you were running from the 6-Pack and needed to get in? It had already been decided that we would be friends—that we needed each other."

"By whom?" I had asked, completely mesmerized by the conversation.

She had shrugged her shoulders. "Some call it God, some call it other things. It is a higher power of some sort. But if we are to be happy, we must follow what burns inside of us. That is why I am a girl. And also, why I am happy." She finished her speech with her typical smile.

"And me?" I had asked. "Nothing burns inside of me. I'm nothing." Even as I said this, I felt a fire burning inside me—a fire that wanted to help other people who felt like me: people with no voice.

She had smiled knowingly at me. "I saw you the day Officer I Could Care Less took your statement, Dan. It lit a fire in you. Even if only for a minute, you were tired of being treated like you didn't matter. And you made a statement that day. You said, 'If I were a police officer, I would treat everyone like they mattered. I wouldn't judge people according to where they lived or what they looked like.'"

She was right. For a few minutes, before Officer I Could Care Less (I never learned—nor cared to learn—his real name) had known I was a Neely, he had judged me for living in the Monn neighborhood. He had thought I was Margette's child because of my coloring. He had questioned me extensively as though I was lying, until he discovered I was a Neely. It had infuriated me that people would be mistreated simply because they were different or lived in a lesser neighborhood.

"You're a cop, Dan. You were born to be a cop. Maybe that's why you have to endure so much now, so you'll always be a fair cop."

As soon as she had identified what I was, I knew she was right. And I didn't want to be just a cop, I wanted to be a detective. I wanted to always make certain that the truth prevailed. I wondered now how she knew things like that. She was so insightful. I missed her so much.

Mrs. Monn returned with two books, each with Angela's beautiful calligraphic writing on the side in fuchsia: Recipes. *Genius.*

"Here you go, Dan."

I took them carefully. These were now all that was left of Angela. I would treat them with the respect they deserved.

"This is all she had?" I asked. It didn't seem like much. I thumbed to the last page. The date on it was 2014. Nonetheless, there could be a clue contained within.

"It is all she had here. She may have more at her apartment or at work." "Work?" I asked, surprised. "That doesn't seem too likely, does it?"

She shrugged. "She spends—sorry, spent—more time there than anywhere else."

I felt bad for reminding her to use past tense and tried to distract her now. "May I ask you one more question before I go?"

"Of course, dear. Anything." She smiled warmly at me, squeezing my hands.

"Did Angela ever mention to you that my dad's company was involved with the clinical trial she was participating with?" There. I said it.

Mrs. Monn looked thoughtful. "No dear. I'm sure she would have said something if it was your dad's company. I'm pretty sure it was a competitor of his."

"Thank you, Mrs. Monn. We will talk soon. I promise." I kissed her soft cheek and was overwhelmed by the love I felt for her. I always knew I loved her, but this felt so deep—like it was from the bottom of my soul. Maybe it was because she was the only person I had left.

Chapter Ten

LOOKING FOR ANSWERS

Sunday, December 4, 2022. 1:00 PM
14 hours 30 minutes after

James was waiting for me at Angela's apartment. As much as I tried to tuck away my feelings and put on my detective hat, the sorrow was eating at me in a way that seemed to affect my ability to function effectively. I knew we were going to need to look at this from every angle to catch Angela's killer before chief pulled the plug on me. I wasn't sure how tuned in he remained over the weekend but every time my phone vibrated; I expected it to be him. If he knew, I doubt he anticipated my release from the hospital yet. For the first time ever, I was praying that a lot of crazies walked into the precinct to keep everyone's mind off me.

I'd heard the press release on the drive over. No doubt my chief was pulling his hair out over that as well since they were my cases. I wished I could get the media to stop using the words "teen" and "pact" in the same sentence. There was an organization called TeenPact that was losing their mind over the negative publicity currently flying around with their name part of it. They are nationally known for teen-oriented programs on leadership, citizenship, and government and did *not* appreciate having their name affiliated with suicide in any way. Perfectly understandable. I didn't want it attached to my friend either.

I knew I would need fresh eyes on the scene. I would have to look past everything that was familiar to me in her happy little apartment—everything that screamed typical Angela—and look for anything that was out of place. I made a mental note to pull the feed on the security cameras and see if anyone had visited Angela in the days leading up to her death. Of course, I would see Mr. Smithers, carefully delivering her flowers, but with any luck, I would see someone else too.

Again, we decided to take the stairs over the elevator. Maybe that is a cop thing. I always got this uneasy feeling just before elevator doors opened, no matter where I was; like something or someone bad was waiting on the other side of the open doors.

I led the way with James following closely behind. Reaching the top of the stairs, I stopped suddenly and sighed deeply, bracing myself for what lay ahead. Thank God for Mr. Smithers. I owed him a huge in person "thank you." How long would it have taken before her mother or I had questioned her absence? I wondered why they didn't question it at the bakery. That was another thing to check. I pulled out my phone to make note of the work question and was rammed from behind.

"Whoa! Sorry! Face in phone."

"Definitely my fault," I said quickly. Jeez, why did I stop right at the top of the stairs? James's head had literally rammed right into my butt. How humiliating! Where was my head? I sure knew where his was. I almost laughed.

"Well, I don't have a head wrapped in gauze," he replied, supplying me with an excuse. "So it's on me to be more careful."

I didn't know what to say. Kindness often made me uncomfortable. It was the great oxymoron of my life. I didn't trust people because I felt they were fake and unkind but if they were kind and appeared honest, they made me uncomfortable. Go figure.

"I just wanted to make note of the fact that her work didn't question her absence and wondered why," I said after a lengthy pause.

Raising his eyebrows and nodding his head, James said, "Excellent question."

While we were speculating, Mr. Smithers opened his door, just a crack.

"I know you," he said to me.

"Hello Mr. Smithers. It's good to see you." I had never been more relieved to see Mr. Smithers. "I wanted to thank you for reporting Angela missing. She really loved receiving your flowers every day."

"She was a sweet one." He took one step further into the hallway. "Got a little weird lately, but she said she was on some diet program and them damn diets can do weird stuff to your head, you know? My Alice, God rest her soul, damn near went insane once with them Pheng Pheng pills."

That was more words than I had ever heard come out of Mr. Smither's mouth in the entire four years I had known him. He must have really cared about Angela. But then again, how could he not?

"Mr. Smithers, this is Special Agent James Hawthorne of the FBI. He's assisting me on the case."

Mr. Smithers gave James the once over. "FBI, huh?" I could see his mind working that over.

I tried to keep him distracted before his mind got carried away with him. "Did you happen to notice anyone unusual coming in or out of Angela's apartment during the past week or so?" I figured if anyone would notice her comings and goings, it would be him.

"She kept to herself mostly. She told me she was getting ready to find herself a soulmate. That was next on her list," he said. "Do you have any idea how hard that young lady musta worked to lose all of that weight? She was a determined one."

She had discussed her HEAP with him. They were closer than I realized.

"That last flower I gave her was a Hawthorne Sprig. She would've liked that one. You know, it means 'hope.'"

It felt like I'd been punched in the gut, the sorrow once again flooding my body and making me want to sob out all the tears I'd been holding in. Yes, she would have loved that. And the irony of the flower name did not escape me either. They really did have a lovely little friendship going on through the flower exchange. I never even thought about the language of flowers beyond my unholy fascination with lilies because of my mother's name. But then again, it was the lily thing that originally got Angela going on her flower shelf, so it had served its purpose in some small way.

"Well, thank you for your time." I put out my hand to shake his.

"Hang on. Hang on. Don't rush me now. You young folks, always in a hurry."

He shook his head with disgust, still giving James the side eye. I could tell he wanted to say more but was hesitant because there was an FBI agent present.

"Was there something more, Mr. Smithers? Special Agent Hawthorne is an old friend of both mine and Angela's." Lie. Lie. Lie. I think. Maybe he was Angela's friend. Didn't he say earlier that she didn't judge him when most people did? I couldn't imagine anyone judging him or for what, but maybe he truly had been friendly with Angela over the years, and I just didn't know about it. I was beginning to wonder if Angela's life was much fuller than I realized.

"Well now, there was one young man came a knockin' on my door a while back, looking for Miss Angela. I didn't tell him he was in the wrong place. I told him she moved. I figured if she wanted him to know where she lived, he would know." He harrumphed as if that settled the matter.

"Did you mention him to Angela?" I asked.

"Sure did, but she didn't pay it much mind. It was around the time she was having troubles with her diet and not thinkin' too clearly so she just thanked me was all."

"Thank you for the extra information, Mr. Smithers. Did you have anything else you wanted to tell us?" I made certain to be more respectful this time. Generally, this was something I prided myself on, making certain that elderly people felt respected. I was so not on my game.

"Just that I guarantee that young lady did not kill herself." He said this with complete confidence.

"Between you and me, I don't think she did either, but I've got my work cut out for me."

I gave him an apologetic smile. Sometimes the media latches onto things and it is hard to undo the opinion they create, even within my own ranks.

"One last thing, where does the super live? I want to get a look at the security feed." I motioned to the camera in the hallway.

Mr. Smithers shook his head, giving me a look of pure disgust. "That thing? It's been broken for years. They just hope it will scare people away because it's there."

That statement put an instant fury in my belly. When Angela had rented this place a couple of years ago, that security camera had been one of the top selling points. "We care about our tenants!" the online ad had read. Ha. Does anybody care? Or did Angela live in the land of throwaway people? The very thing I had promised to change when I became a cop.

This time I didn't hesitate to enter Angela's apartment. The bedroom door had been left open, allowing the residual odor to permeate the house. I grabbed the stolen tin of Vicks Vapor Rub out of my pocket and put on a new dab, holding it out wordlessly to James. I didn't need the additional reminder of how badly I had let my friend down.

Once inside, I momentarily distracted James by asking him to check Angela's medicine cabinet for any additional prescription medications. As he did, I quickly searched for her recipe book, hoping to tuck it inside my jacket without his knowledge. I'd had pockets sewn into all of my business suits for just such things. There were a few things a woman could manage that a man could not. With my breasts creating a distracting mound, the jacket hung easily over any slim items I slipped into that pocket. A female detective must have her own secrets if she is going to be successful in a male-dominant profession.

Unfortunately, my search turned up nothing. I felt certain that her childhood habit of journaling in her recipe book had most likely continued into adulthood. It was not something we had ever discussed beyond the time she told me, but Angela was a planner, and planners keep records. I was eager to take a look at Angela's more recent journaling, hoping to find some clues about her state of mind in the days before her death. Maybe her mom was right, and she'd kept it at her bakery.

"There were some interesting meds in her cabinet," James reported. Of course, I'd already known this, as Angela only had one bathroom, and I had used it whenever I was over. "I took a picture of each so we can research their prescribed uses."

I debated telling him what the drugs were prescribed for. How could he not know? He had gone to elementary school with Angela. He knew she was born a boy. What the heck did he think they were for?

As I pondered these questions, I noticed his glance had stopped on our photo on the bedside stand. That picture—again.

"It is so hard to reconcile that the woman in the photo with you is Angela," James stated flatly. "I know people change from high school, but that woman is beautiful."

"Yes, it *is* Angela, and she was *always* beautiful." My voice broke. I swallowed thickly and took a moment before I could proceed. "Few people took the time to see her inner beauty— especially men. That's why she had to do this stupid trial in the first place."

"What trial? Who was critical of her appearance?" He couldn't keep the eagerness out of the question. Finally, he thought he was going to get some information out of me, but not yet.

Sighing deeply, I replied, "She was never unhappy with her body or how she looked. The weight loss trial was just another step to complete her plan." It was becoming obvious that I was going to have to explain a lot of things about Angela to James. It felt so wrong sharing personal details of her life with him. But the professional in me knew I had no choice.

"And what plan was that?" James was all ears.

"I promise I will tell you everything. Right now, I just need you to know that Angela was the best person I've ever known, and the happiest. She did not kill herself." Really, what more did he need to know about her? "Angela saved me once. I didn't save her, but I can at least put her to rest the right way," I said, dangerously close to losing my composure. It was very hard to be in her apartment, surrounded by all things Angela but not actually being surrounded by Angela.

"Were you . . . in love with her?" He asks this question tentatively—without malice, but I can feel that it is a question he has wanted to ask for a while.

"I loved her, yes, but not in the way you are asking."

My heart ached. I did not want to have this discussion with him, but I understood why he was asking. There was a time, when I first knew her, that I had wondered what my feelings for her would have been if she had lived her life as a male. Would we have married eventually? It was a brief but confusing thought. But Angela was not a male and I was not attracted to females. Angela believed we were destined to be friends. She was the boy who was born to be a girl, and I was the girl who was supposed to be born a boy and struggling to figure out how to be a girl.

A lot of other people had wondered if we were a couple in high school, especially after I officially started to go by the name "Dan" instead of Daniela in my sophomore year. That had been Angela's bright idea, of course, to stop putting other people's opinions of me before my own and embrace my name instead of acting embarrassed of it. Between my boyish appearance, my name, and mean girls like Jenny Bowser, I'd been through my fair share of bullying by the end of my freshman year. It had been a very effective change after the initial shock and repercussions wore off. I remember the first days well.

If I had thought I had received confused looks about my identity before the change, after that change, they were almost ridiculous. The funny thing is, I got this weird feeling that some people were almost afraid of me—like there was this unspoken question hanging in the air that they were afraid to ask. And all I did was decide to embrace my name—be comfortable with myself but not change my gender. The whole situation with my name made me realize how difficult life must be for people like Angela and how truly screwed up and chaotic the whole system is about accepting people for who they are. We say we accept transgender, but what does that really mean? How do we *show* them we accept and respect their choices? Why do they make people nervous? Gender preference is not something to be feared.

"Why'd you change your name?" Marcie had asked, catching up to me in the hall after third period. Apparently, she had decided it was okay to talk to me after Jenny moved to Maine at the end of freshman year.

"I didn't change my name. Didn't you call me Dan last year?" Marcie's face turned red. "Well yeah, but I was just joking."

"Well, I'm not joking." I said, turning to walk away. I wasn't going to be late for class just so

Marcie would have gossip to spread.

"Wait! So, does that mean . . ." Marcie tried to ask.

I kept walking. Marcie was not trying to befriend me. She was the same old Marcie, looking for some good gossip. I wondered how she would spin my response.

It didn't take long to find out.

By the end of the day, Angela and I were officially a couple according to the high school rumor mill. The funniest thing about the situation was that my transformation seemed to make everyone forget that Ang used to be a boy. The fact that I was the "supposed" boy in our relationship made Angela happy. God, high school kids could be so mean and stupid.

That afternoon, Ang and I had met at our usual place, right in front of the bike racks for the walk home. She towered over me, having grown to an impressive 6 feet tall over the summer. She had always outweighed me by a couple hundred pounds and now was so happy she couldn't resist putting her hands under my arms and swinging me around.

"Dan, they are finally accepting me for who I am!" she squealed.

"Yeah, but they are calling me something I am not," I complained, feeling like a pathetic little rag doll. "Put me down. Now I really look like your girlfriend/boyfriend."

"Oh, get over yourself. You were born a girl. You have nothing to worry about. I'm transitioning. Do you have any idea how important it is to me to be accepted as female? This is who I truly am."

She beamed at me as we began the walk to her house. We had walked to her house together every day since "the event" with Jeremy and the 6-Pack, except during the winter months when the bus was the only viable solution. I was always expecting a repeat performance, but Angela was always promising there would be none. I looked at her, wearing her usual flowery dress with gold flats that she had no doubt spray-painted herself and flowing blonde hair and then down at myself in navy chinos, a light blue polo shirt with tennis shoes, and short brown pixie cut and realized I had helped to create my own misery.

She was so good at making me feel like a moron for complaining. Like when I had recently complained about my dad not paying attention to me. Ang was right there to remind me of the beautiful house I lived in, the private gymnastics lessons, the private tutoring, the unlimited online courses I was able to purchase so I could graduate two years early, the expensive colleges I had applied to without having to worry about how to pay for them.

I refocused my attention on how best to answer James now—how to fully satisfy his curiosity. "Angela and I knew we would be best friends from the moment we met. I think we had been dreaming of someone like each other for a long time." That was as true as it gets. "We both felt our friendship was meant to be."

I couldn't stop the corners of my mouth from pulling down, but I wanted to finish my thought. "Angela had recently reached a point in her life plan where the next step was for her to find her life mate—her husband. The one thing I'm certain of is that death was not part of her life plan."

His discomfort is obvious in the way he averts his eyes. "Dan, I want you to know—" "Please, let's not use Angela's apartment as a place where insincere sentiments are shared. I think we both know exactly where we stand with each other."

I hate how harsh I sound every time I open my mouth to speak to him. Or is it every time I speak to anyone and I'm only just noticing it with him? How many times did Angela tell me, "Try to relax a little bit Dan. Not everyone is out to get you." I feel sad now, knowing that every time she said that I had brushed her off, giving nearly the same response each time: "I don't think they're out to get me, I just don't trust them." I realize now that the sweet smile she gave me in response told me that she understood perfectly—that she had been trying to convince me to try to have a little faith in people, to trust.

But this time James didn't give up so easily. "Actually, I don't think we know where we stand with each other, but maybe it is time that we did. It's going to be hard to work this case together with skeletons from our past hanging over us."

I felt my eyes widen before I could stop them. I'll admit it; I was shocked. I've always thought of James Hawthorne as spineless. I know that doesn't really make sense given the fact that he became an FBI field agent. I guess my feelings are based primarily upon one incident, but that incident has both haunted and formed my life. "The first time you are alone, I'll be waiting." How many times have those words run through my head in a dark alleyway? Haunted my nightmares? Forced me to keep an extra gun in the nightstand next to my bed?

"Maybe you're right, but not here. Angela's place is a happy place. Let's go somewhere and talk after we're done. My house is not far away—I'm only about 8 miles away over in Chestnut Hill. How far is your hotel?" As soon as the words came out of my mouth, an involuntary shiver ran through me. I couldn't help but remember the feel of his hands on my arm as he held me down. Did I want to be alone with this man anywhere? That was a long time ago; he was a kid then. I silently admonished myself for such thoughts. They don't let bad people become FBI agents, do they?

James looked sheepish. "I haven't gotten a hotel yet. I got into town and spent the night at the hospital with you, so your place would be great, if you don't mind."

I must admit, his embarrassment was a comfort to me and helped to ease my concern.

"My place makes sense," I reassured him. "Let's see what we can find here." I just wanted to complete the search and get out of Angela's apartment.

We continued our search of Angela's apartment, carefully looking for anything that might be out of place or point us in a different direction. This part, at least, didn't feel intrusive. Angela would have welcomed anyone into her home at any time. She was an open book.

I pressed the messages on her landline answering machine to see if the bakery had left any messages but there were only solicitations. She had often talked about taking out the landline and saving that $30 a month but had to have the backup to reach her because of her business. I figured now was as good a time to call the bakery as any.

"You've reached Angel Cakes, I'm sorry I can't come to the phone right now, but I'm busy dishing out little slices of heaven. If I can help you with your next heavenly concoction, please leave your name, phone number, and best time to call back. And remember everything in life is better with a slice of cake!" Angela's familiar voice on the answering machine made the saliva in my throat too thick to swallow.

I returned the phone to its cradle, taking a moment to squeeze my eyes tightly before turning back around to face James.

"I got the machine. This is a busy time of the year at the bakery. How about we stop by in person?" My voice was raspy with emotion.

James nodded his agreement. "How quickly will they release the evidence to you? We could stop by the precinct on the way."

I pulled my lips inward. "About that . . ." I took a moment to think about how best to say this to James without pulling him into my web of deception with my chief.

"You want me to go?" He already put some of it together—the fake ID I'd told him about. What he probably wasn't thinking about was my chief's reaction to my getting shot. I was pretty sure he was going to want me to go through the usual departmental evaluation process after an injury, but I simply could not take the time to do that right now. If he didn't know I'd been released, I still had that ace on my side. I was breaking rules all over the place, but I had no choice. The situation called for it. It called for acting with emotion—something new to me. Angela would be proud.

"That would be great. But there is something I should show you first." It was all or nothing time. Either I trusted him, or I didn't. I dug my phone out of my pocket. 8% battery left. I could not forget to plug it in again or I would be without a communication device soon. I scrolled through the pictures until I got to the photograph of the contract Angela had left on her bedstand. "Take a close look at this," I said, handing him my phone.

"I wondered if you had changed your mind from earlier," he said as he accepted my phone. I was glad he hadn't pressured me. I heard his sharp intake as he used his left hand to magnify the screen.

"She left a copy of the contract?" He looked up at me, the expression on his face so eager he looked like a little boy who'd just found out he was getting a puppy for his birthday.

"Yes, and that is truly wonderful. But look again. Magnify the screen and look at the bottom line." I knew that happy, eager look was going to disappear quickly.

"Neely Pharmaceuticals sponsored the weight loss trial?" He seemed as genuinely shocked as I had been a couple of hours earlier. "What if this is the trial all of them were in?" If I wasn't so upset at the implication of my father's company, his rapid change in facial expression would have been comical.

"I don't know," I admitted. "Angela never once mentioned to me that Neely Pharma was running the trial. She told me that it was run by a company called Lily Legacy. I assumed it was associated with Eli Lilly Pharmaceuticals, although now that I see how Lily is spelled, I can see that it is not the same. But she knew from the start—from the minute she signed the contracts—that it was my dad's company. I don't know why she would keep that from me, but she must have had a reason."

I couldn't imagine what that reason was. The strange thing was, I had not felt the presence of a secret between us when we spoke of the clinical trial. How could that be? Could secrets exist between two people who loved each other? Apparently, yes.

"We definitely need to put our hands on that contract and take a deeper look," James said, "but I am encouraged by the fact that there was no contract at any other home. Maybe Angela was participating in a different trial—a copycat?"

The copycat theory was one I had considered from the start, but I found it highly unlikely that someone would spend an entire year working on killing someone. That really felt like a stretch. No.

We were missing some important piece of the puzzle and there was no way to find it without good, old-fashioned police work.

"No, I don't buy the copycat theory. There has got to be another explanation." I felt certain about this.

We took one last look around Angela's little apartment—quite possibly my last visit to my friend's apartment—and walked out the door, firmly reattaching the crime scene tape behind us.

Chapter Eleven

ANGEL CAKES

Sunday, December 4, 2022. 3:30 PM
17 hours after

I watched the cute strawberry blonde behind the counter. She was very friendly and blushed just often enough to be adorable. She was exactly what you'd expect to see behind the counter of a place called Angel Cakes.

"Hey, Sofie. How are you?" I had no idea how much Sofie knew so I wanted to tread carefully.

"Hey Dan. I'm good! We've been swamped! Need a part time job?" She laughed. I could see why Angela had made her the assistant manager. She kept this place running like a clock while Angela was gone.

The lighthearted laugh told me she didn't yet know her boss was dead, unless of course, she had a weird habit of laughing at inappropriate times, like me, which was unlikely. For the first time, I could see how badly that probably threw people off.

"Ha. No thanks! BPD keeps me plenty busy." I tried to make my words lighthearted, but they sounded flat, even to my own ears. I'd better get to the point and get out fast before I blew it. "I was just stopping by, hoping to pick up a book from Angela's office."

I was really going out on a limb here. For one thing, I didn't even know if the book was there.

For another, I didn't know if Sofie would be comfortable letting me rummage through Angela's office without her here. I was banking on the best friend factor trumping the assistant manager.

"Oh, Ang isn't here. She decided to go on a little trip. I'm hoping she met someone. A while back, she was talking about someone named Sam, so maybe with him. I'm surprised she didn't tell you!" Sofie held up a finger, puts her phone to her ear, and I hear her say, "Angel Cakes. This is Sofie. How can I help you?"

I watched her cover the mouthpiece of the phone and tell someone to make sure the Hoffman's strudels come out of the oven in 2 minutes, before returning to the phone with a cheery voice, "Yes, of course we have Lemon Crèmes today. Come on in!" Excellent multi-tasker. A good person to take over? Who will run Angel Cakes with Angela gone?

"I've been tied up with cases, so we haven't talked as much lately. Look, I'm sorry to bother you. You sound busy. I just need to grab a book quick." All I wanted was to get out of this bakery. It screamed Angela. It was her lifelong dream, happening successfully right in front of me—without her now. "Be right back," I said as I hedged back toward Angela's office, taking the decision away from Sofie.

Angela's office was incredibly organized. Of course. I sat down in her office chair and spun around, inspecting the room. I'd been in it many times, but I was always in a rush. I'd never taken the time to fully appreciate the cozy comfort of the room even though Angela had made certain to express her appreciation with an expansive sweep of her arm every single time I came. "I have all of this thanks to you!"

She was forever grateful for the money my father had invested in her bakery. I say invested, but he had really just given the money to her. All I'd had to do was ask. I never would have asked him for something for myself but asking for Angela was easy. Her dream was important to her and that made it important to me. I wondered now if I had been living vicariously off her happiness. I never really tried to find any of my own. I was always too busy, always in the middle of a case. Had I become my father?

The wallpaper was an elegant pastoral toile in tones of muted rose and cream. She had a farmhouse desk in distressed cream and a cream bookshelf enclosed in glass with a lock. Now there was something I wouldn't expect to see in a million years. A lock? But maybe that is where

Angela kept the company lock box as well? I really didn't know. But I could clearly see the word Recipes in her fuchsia calligraphic lettering on the side of two binder style notebooks. They did not teach me to pick locks when I became a police officer. I wondered if that was really part of FBI training or if that was just for TV. Now was the time to find out.

I got out my phone and thanked my lucky stars I remembered to plug it in on the way to Angel Cakes. Even though it was only a few miles, I was up to 14% charge—enough to text James.

Dan: I have a situation in the office that requires an adept hand and a couple of fine point tools.

James: I just happen to know an adept hand who carries such tools in his wallet. What excuse shall I use to get in?

Dan: She's busy. I don't think you'll need an excuse. Just ask her where the bathroom is. I'm just past it on the left.

James: On my way.

James had the cabinet open so quickly it was unnerving. I had no idea it was that easy to pick a lock. I suddenly appreciated the alarm system I'd installed in my home. I quickly grabbed both binders, sinking one into my inner jacket pocket, since I had told Sofie I was only after one.

"Tricky. I like it." James nodded his head, impressed with my ingenuity as he watched the binder disappear like magic, his gaze briefly lingering on the curve of my breast.

"What I lack in looks, I make up for in brains," I quipped.

"Hmph. Definitely not a true statement," he replied.

I was left trying to decide if he was calling me ugly or dumb. Or both. Or neither. But I opened that can of worms, so I deserved it. Like I said, I had no communication skills. Shrugging my shoulders, I said, "Let's get out of here before someone catches us."

"Thanks again Sofie." I said, lightly touching her arm as we walked past her to the door.

"Hey Dan, hang on. See you soon, right?" She hurriedly excused herself from her customer and turned toward me. "Angela said you would be picking up the Christmas strudel and also a caramel apple pie for someone named Jeremy?"

My breath caught in my throat, rendering me speechless. I could understand her comment about the Christmas strudel. It was my dad's favorite and Ang always made it to bring for the holiday. But Ang *planning* for me to pick it up meant. . . No. I refused to go there. And did she just say I was supposed to pick up a pie for *Jeremy*? Shaking my head at my ridiculous overreaction, I took a moment to calm myself before responding. "Just the Christmas strudel. The order for Jeremy must be for a customer. Better double check."

"Would you mind if I get back to you on that?" Sofie was pink cheeked and flustered—trying hard to put on a calm front but she was far too busy to be dealing with me right now.

"Sounds like a good idea." I quickly said goodbye and escaped the bakery, still feeling weak in the knees at all she had just said. Sofie's comment could mean anything. And I really needed to get over my unhealthy reaction to the name Jeremy. Unfortunately, I had not been able to speak to Angela before she. . . I couldn't say it. I couldn't even think it. Just *before*. She may have had plans to go on the trip Sofie was talking about. Everything Sofie just said may have been perfectly normal and planned—planned like Angela always planned.

"Everything okay?" James asked.

I didn't realize I was standing, resting against the exterior brick of the building with my eyes closed and head bowed. I snapped my head up, ready to fire back a hostile retort but what I saw in his eyes stopped me cold. His big brown eyes were filled with compassion. Haltingly, I told him what Sofie had said to me.

"I really don't know what to make of that either," he replied with honesty. "I can't imagine how hard this must be on you Daniela. Please let me know if there are things that hurt too much to handle. Maybe it's time for us to call it a day."

I could feel the sincerity in his words and appreciated them. James Hawthorne had surprised me many times throughout the day, and most of them were good surprises. Maybe Angela was right, and it was time for me to work harder on forgiving. The one thing I was sure of, it was time to call it a day. I was both emotionally and physically exhausted. The stress of the day had really gotten under my skin and my head was throbbing under the wad of gauze. I was beyond the acetaminophen the doctor had recommended. Now I needed a glass of wine, four ibuprophen, and some food sure wouldn't hurt either. The bakery smelled delicious. And I still had so many more things that I wanted to know before the day was over, specifically, information on the other clinical trial James had mentioned earlier.

Chapter Twelve

JOUSTING WITH JAMES

Sunday,

December 4, 2022. 6:48 PM
20 hours 18 minutes after

James looked ill at ease in my home. There was something about that fact that made me feel satisfied. I wondered if the sweet smell of lilies that perpetually filled the air made it worse, feeling too feminine to him. The flowers weren't really a feminine touch. I wish I could say I had thought of that, but really, they were just a continuation of a lifelong habit. The auto delivery of the flowers was a housewarming gift from a friend of my mother's, ironically someone I'd never heard of or even met. I guess everyone knew about her obsession with the flowers that were her namesake. I didn't mind. Any little piece of her that I could incorporate into my life, I did.

I felt ill at ease having him there too. I did not invite men to my home. But I had to remember that he was not really a man; he was an FBI agent. Although I was not much of a drinker, I once again thought about the ibuprophen and wine and considered that a glass of wine might not hurt our ability to start a conversation either. I got out some plates for the pizza he grabbed on the way over, thankful for his choice of mushrooms and peppers. I could use some vegetables. I'd been forgetting to eat again. I could hear Ang chastising me.

Even though I was agile and strong and had gone through Academy training, nothing changed the fact that I was only 5 foot 2 inches and struggled to keep my weight over a hundred pounds. Though I felt confident that every pound of that was solid muscle, it was not enough solid muscle to take down a large man for long. I prayed the James I'd invited to my home was nothing like the high school James. At least now I carried a gun.

"Could I offer you a glass of wine? One will keep you below the legal limit." I rolled my eyes inwardly at myself. This is exactly why I don't even try to entertain. I am stiff and awkward. I had no experience with social situations growing up. My spare time was either at the gym, taking online courses to graduate early, or in my blue room staring at the walls and planning this incredible future of mine that has unfortunately ended up being a rather lonely one.

James laughed. "I would love a glass of wine."

"Do you have a preference? White, red, or sugar?" Although I said this with a deadpan face, if he had chosen a sweet wine, I think I would have fallen over. Something told me that he had also been raised to appreciate the natural flavor of the wine. The two weeks Ang and I spent in Italy after her graduation taught me everything I never knew about the true flavor of wines.

I couldn't help but smile every time I thought of that trip. Mrs. Monn must have secretly saved for years. She had paid both our passages, as if I were her daughter too. Ang and I settled into an adorable little apartment in the hillside of San Gimignano in the Tuscan Valley. We each had a two- week rental of a Vespa. What a magnificent method of transportation in Italy. Mine was orange, and Angela's was turquoise. We zipped all over the Tuscan countryside on those things. They were great fun. We also took a few day trips on the wonderful Italian rail system. The fast train could take you from Firenze to Naples in just a few hours. We swam in the crystal waters off the coast of Praiano and walked the ruins of Pompeii. We marveled at the beauty of the Sistine Chapel and hiked the Renaissance Ring.

The Italian people treated us very well. Maybe because I closely re-sembled an Italian woman with my petite frame; thick, dark hair; and olive skin. Or maybe they just treated all people well, the way we wish

Americans did. I don't know. I do know I would go back there in a heartbeat. I have nothing but good memories.

My reverie was broken by James' response. "I'll have white, thank you." He smiled at me.

My face heated as realization of my smiling face dawned on me. I wanted to tell him outright it had nothing to do with him, but I held my tongue. I guess it was okay for him to think I smiled at him.

I could see him looking around the room, taking in the simple décor. "Your home is beautiful. They must pay detectives well in Massachusetts."

I knew he was talking about the location and not the actual interior of the home. Nobody would call my decorating skills beautiful and real estate in the Boston area was ridiculously expensive. I was very fortunate to live in this neighborhood, which by Boston standards was considered beautiful. The house was simple: 3 bedrooms, 2 baths, kitchen off the garage, living room, small dining room. Anywhere else, it would most likely be considered middle to lower middle class, but in Boston and more specifically, in Chestnut Hill, the price tag had been considerable.

I looked around my modest living room, trying to see it through his eyes. What did it say about me? I was not a person who placed a lot of value on material things. Angela said that was because I had always known anything and everything material was available to me at any time. That could be true, but I'd never really asked for anything much growing up. All I'd ever wanted was the love of a parent.

I'd picked this home because it had two features I simply couldn't pass up. First, it had an incredible rooftop patio that provided a sparkling (albeit distant) view of the city lights at night, and secondly, it came with a one car garage. With the mountains of snow that mother nature dumped on Boston each winter, the garage was worth its weight in gold in my book. I was closely sandwiched in between two similar homes, but the all-brick facade gave them each a unique and stately appearance.

Although his voice had a teasing tone to it, his comment fed my insecurity that people would think I was 'on the take' since I lived in such a nice area on a detective's salary, and it made me instantly defensive.

"My mother had a life insurance policy. My father saved it for me. This," I spread my arms wide," is all I have of my mother. I would trade it in an instant."

His face colored. I could feel his embarrassment. I wasn't trying to embarrass him. I was trying to let him know *I* wasn't a jerk.

"Anyhow, thank you for the compliment. I appreciate having a nice home to come to at the end of a sometimes-bad day."

"You know Daniela—Dan—since high school, every time I open my mouth to speak to you, I put my foot in it. I wonder if there is any way we could put the past behind us and start fresh?"

"I'm trying James. Really trying. More for Angela than for you or me," I answered honestly. "But you must know that I have spent ten years looking over my shoulder, waiting for the promise of that note to be carried out. I don't know if you wrote it or were just delivering it for Jeremy, but it has haunted me for a long time now."

"Dan, I did *not* put that note in your locker, nor did I write it," he insisted. "I found it when you dropped it—you know, after you slugged me. For a petite girl, you are strong as shit."

"Oh, come on now. I did not slug you. I pushed you. And that was only because I was afraid. You guys were there every time I turned around for almost two months before I finally snapped." I remembered every detail of that day—of all the days leading up to it—like it was yesterday.

It had been almost two months since "that day" and the 6-Pack had made a full-time job of harassing me in the hallways at school. To be fair, the primary culprits were Jeremy and Caleb, although sharing lunchtime with all six of them sitting at one table across the room from me made it impossible for even one bite of food to go down my throat. If I was being called skinny before, I wasn't sure what I was being called then since my clothes hung like sacks on me. Naturally, all the evidence had conveniently gone missing so there was no way to prove a crime had been committed. I would just stare at their huge bodies and relive "that day"—and wonder if I would even be alive now if all six of those bodies had crawled on top of me. I imagined that evidence would have disappeared too, and I would have become an official unsolved murder.

But I was probably letting my mind run away with me. I didn't really know anything, right? But there was no mistaking the look in Jeremy's eyes that day.

"I'm the one who went to my dad and told him about the other shoe. Jeremy was arrested *because of me*."

James's shocking words pulled me back from the past. It felt like someone threw a glass of ice water in my face.

"What? *You* helped *me*?"

I dropped to the couch. James Hawthorne had turned on his friend. He was never a bad guy?

Chief Hawthorne was not a bad cop? I'm finding this out ten years later? "Why? And why didn't you say something?" I asked, my head in my hands. I had wasted so much energy hating him for so long.

"Would you have believed me?" he asked.

"Angela would have made me believe you," I said. "She was good like that. She believed in everyone."

"I guess I was too afraid. But I'm here to help now. Everyone knew who my dad was, and I didn't want to be in the middle of a scandal," he admitted. "I broke free from the group after that. I was uncomfortable with them for the whole last year of the trial, but I was afraid to speak up."

There it was again, the "trial."

"So, tell me more about this trial you keep mentioning." I had to change the subject. I couldn't bear to think about Jeremy Richards for one more minute for fear the nightmares would begin again. And I did want to know more about the trial—the first one my dad had run.

"Hmmm. Where to begin . . . I don't really know how people were chosen for the clinical trial. I only know that there were six boys chosen, and we received our first shots when we were still in utero."

I put my hand up. "Hold on. Back up." I couldn't believe what I was hearing. "You're telling me that your mother took part in a clinical trial that gave shots to you while you were still in her uterus? Why? What was it for?"

James shook his head slowly. "We were never given a lot of information about the trial itself, but we went in for shots when we were little kids and then when we got older, we had to take supplements every day. The only thing I know is when we checked in for our monthly appointments, the lady always said, 'and you're here for the VITAL project?' We used to make fun of her English accent behind her back."

Yes, I could see young boys doing that.

"Where were your appointments?" This all sounded like something out of a Sci-Fi movie. I wanted to laugh because I felt a strange sense of dread in my stomach.

"At Neely Pharmaceuticals in the main gymnasium off the second-floor elevator." He said it like I should have known, which got my hackles up.

"And what happened at these appointments?" I could barely wrap my head around what he was telling me. There was a second floor gymnasium? Did that mean there was also a first-floor gymnasium? How did James Hawthorne know more about my father's company than I did?

"Each one was like a mini physical. Height, weight, vision screening, dental check. But on top of that, we performed physical and mental acuity tests as well." James looked uncomfortable, as if the memories were not good ones.

"Please, be more specific." I hated the pleading whiny voice that came out of me. Any mention of my father and I was instantly an insecure child.

"Well, for example, we would do sprints and some lifting. And then we might play a little game of one-on-one or something like that."

"But *why*?" I kept thinking about all the time these boys got to spend literally playing with my father—time I never got to spend with him. Did he create the trial just so he could pretend like he had sons? Is that why he was able to completely reject me? Because he had six superhuman boys he got to play with monthly?

"Honestly Daniela—Dan, I don't know why. I just know that all our parents were very invested in our success too—well, most of them were. Jeremy's mother had some mental health issues, but other than that, we all got together regularly. We did everything together. I suppose that is what made the group of us seem so formidable by the time we got to high school—so egocentric. We just didn't have the time or need to interact with anyone else."

I could see how being involved in something like that could form an almost "team" atmosphere. I mean, I had become part of a team during my years with gymnastics, but we remained individuals too. For example, the older girls didn't hesitate to let me know when my eyebrows resembled Bert from Sesame Street and told me to shave those caterpillars because they were an embarrassment to the team (Who knew? They looked just like Margette's.) Why did theirs become an evil team? That part I just didn't get.

"How did you know about Jeremy's mom's mental health issues. Isn't that something that is generally private? I mean, I wouldn't have any idea if my dad or Margette had mental health issues."

"Well," He hesitated.

"Come on Hawthorne. You're in my home, asking me to let the past be the past. You've got to open up and be honest with me." I suspected my use of his last name was the deciding factor. We were backpaddling—almost back to Special Agent Hawthorne.

"She actually struggled with alcoholism," he confessed. "She came to several of the gatherings drunk and said things that were very embarrassing to both Jeremy and his father." "What kind of things?" I could see that he felt very uncomfortable talking about Jeremy's family, but I felt compelled to know. For so long, I had thought of Jeremy as nothing but pure evil, but what if he had been just a troubled kid? Maybe I could go forward being less scared of a troubled kid.

"Well, once she started drinking, she would say really off the wall things. But the one thing she always repeated was 'Anyone want to know the price of a perfect boy? One baby girl.' It was such a weird thing to say, and nobody knew what she was talking about, but it made Senator Richards so angry that he even slapped her once. After that, she stopped coming."

Suddenly, I knew exactly what he was talking about. I knew why Jeremy's drunken mother said those sad words. But I didn't know if James needed to know—whether or not it was in any way pertinent to our investigation. I wanted to try to keep her secret if possible. The loss she had suffered had taken her away, and in her place, left a raving drunk who blamed Jeremy—the innocent child.

My God. That poor woman took her life my sophomore year of high school. But how could I pity the mother and not the child? I suppose that would make anyone evil. But whose fault was it? Was it my dad's fault because of the clinical trial? Exactly how many lives was my father responsible for?

I thought back to that night when I'd discovered the Richards' secret. It was the end of my freshman year of high school---my very first sleepover. I'd been so excited; completely innocent to the mysteries that would unfold before me. I learned so much about Angela that night. I learned that she had been born a boy but knew she was a girl from the time she could remember. She told me about the first time she had been called Monstrosity.

"It was Jeremy Richards," she said. "I remember the first time he said it because I didn't know what the word meant. I was 5 and he was 8. We were both at mom's café and he was eating with his dad. I was waiting for mom to get off work, coloring at a table."

I heard him ask his dad why the little "mon"-strosity was in the restaurant. He thought he was so clever using my last name like that. "Won't it scare the customers away?" he asked. Both he and his father laughed. They were looking directly at me when he said it, so I ran into the back and told my mom, asking her what it meant.

I had felt sick hearing that story. Jeremy was cruel even as an 8-year-old. "What did your mother tell you?" I asked Angela.

"She told me it meant that Jeremy was not a nice boy—that he was someone I should always stay away from. So, I avoided him, and he handed the name out to everyone. Eventually I looked it up and even though it was kind of stupid, I had to give it to him—it was a pretty good play on my name." Angela said all of it so matter of fact. Like it didn't hurt her. But it had to have hurt at some point.

"The key is to fake it 'til you make it, Dan. Maybe it would help if you were doing something that made you feel more in control of your own life," Angela had said to me. "Look at me. When I hurt, I bake. As a result, I'm going to be an incredible baker and have an amazing bakery someday. That's why I don't mind being fat. I mean, would you trust a skinny baker?" She laughed, and I laughed with her. Although I did know that many afternoons, Ang would make cookies or cakes, I thought she was just helping her mom out. I didn't know that she ever hurt.

"Want to know a secret?" she asked.

Did I want to know a secret? One of Angela's secrets? Of course I did! I wanted to know everything about Angela. Sometimes I wished I could morph inside her body and just become Angela. Before I met her, I thought that being smart was a great superpower, but now I realized that being loved was the greatest superpower of all.

"You know you can trust me," I replied evenly, keeping all excitement out of my voice.

"I do know that Dan." She smiled at me and gave my arm a quick squeeze. She knew me well enough by now to know that physical contact made me feel uncomfortable. "My recipe book isn't just for recipes," she said. "Sometimes, I journal in it too. When my feelings are too big, and I don't have anyone to talk to."

"But you have your mom," I protested.

"Yes, I always have my mom—but don't forget that my mom works. Even when I was little. They used to let me stay in the break room while she worked after Dad left until I was old enough to stay alone."

How strange that I had never wondered about the hardships of her life. I saw this secure, confident person so I never considered that life was hard for her too. Her life was probably a hundred times harder than mine with all she'd faced. She was born a boy. Her dad rejected her so completely that he moved to Canada. Her mom worked full time, even in the summer when she was home all day long.

Even though my dad wished I was a boy, he accepted that I was a girl. He didn't abandon me or anything. And I got to spend my summers at gymnastics camps or swimming in my pool. And Margette was always there.

"What do you journal about?" I asked her.

"Just life, when it gets too big or I'm too excited to wait til mom comes home. You know, I can't call her at work. She doesn't have that kind of job." She explained all of this to me without an ounce of self-pity.

"That's cool," I said. I didn't really know what to say. I was thinking about how I handled emotions. I just pushed them down—all of them. I didn't think about how I felt about anything. I just did was I was supposed to do.

She laughed. "Well, I don't know if I'd call it 'cool,' but it works for me. My recipe books have been something I've cherished since I was young—maybe because mom worked at the restaurant, and it made me feel closer to her. Whatever the reason, they became my comfort, so it felt natural to journal in them too."

"Are you going to let me read them?" I asked hopefully.

"Absolutely not!" She exclaimed. "Not unless I'm killed in a car accident and since I don't drive, I think I'm safe. I'm going to live a long life and enjoy every minute of it!"

That was the plan—her one plan that got terribly disrupted.

I think that once she met me, Angela had told me a lot of the things she would have previously written in her recipe book. But I had been somewhat unavailable during the past couple of years while I was work-ing long hours. First, trying to earn the coveted role of detective and now because being a detective required long hours. I had jokingly blamed my lack of availability on her more than once, but she took it all in stride.

"You might have less time for me now Dan, but you are 100% more available to me." I always got a big warm smile with that statement, letting me know I had become a good friend to her.

But right now, I wanted more information on the clinical trial that James and the other boys had participated in all those years ago. I needed to know if my dad had a hand in turning Jeremy into the monster he had become. I also wanted to talk to Mrs. Monn again to see if she knew anything about what had happened with Mrs. Richards back in the summer before my sophomore year of high school—before she killed herself.

"Are you still taking the supplements, James? Is the trial ongoing?"

"Honestly, that would have made sense, but no." James said earnestly. "They said the supplements were phase one of a three step trial process and that when we turned 19, phase one was over."

"Are you still in touch with the rest of the guys in the group?" I couldn't resist asking the question. After all, Angela had been my best friend in high school and remained my best friend even after college and joining the force.

"No, the guys and I were not seeing eye to eye before our senior year. Then, after the incident with you, I stopped hanging out with them altogether. One more thing. Something I never told anyone else. I also stopped taking the supplements after that. It just seemed like those guys were developing some serious issues and I didn't know if it was from their family or from the trial, you know?"

Well, that was interesting. "Are the supplements being sold on the market today?" I had to know if more potential predatory monsters were being created.

"Honestly Dan, I don't know anything more about the trial. Nobody ever contacted me again, which I thought was pretty strange to be honest. I mean, I spent 18 years of my life involved in a clinical trial and then the results just don't matter anymore?" He shook his head. "That doesn't make a lot of sense to me."

I considered his words thoughtfully. "Did you ever think about the possibility that you are still being monitored? I guess it depends upon what they were tracking but look at the job you are doing. It is a federal position—very easy to monitor if they are tracking things like intelligence, agility, or strength."

The extreme inward slant of his eyebrows told me instantly that he had not considered this and did not like the possibility. "I think I'd rather believe that I am finished with the trial and the people involved with it," he said with more vehemence than necessary.

His reaction told me there was more there, that maybe he wasn't as "done with the trial as he'd like to be" but I decided to leave it alone for now. After all, I knew more too . . .

"James," I said. His name rolled off my lips with more ease than it had a half hour ago. The ibuprophen and wine had worked their magic. There was a definite benefit to not drinking often. When I finally did have a glass of wine, it had the effect of a deep tissue massage. "I need to hear you say that you were not going to rape me that day."

James's face went white. He clearly did not expect that sentence to come out of my mouth.

"Daniela . . . Dan . . . I'm sorry!"

He sounded so frustrated that he kept calling me the wrong thing that I said, "Call me whatever you are comfortable with. It's just a name." That was definitely the wine talking.

"Daniela, I would never rape anyone. Never. I swear. I'm not a violent person." He was leaning toward me with his eyebrows forming a desperate peak over his strong, straight nose. "I don't even know why Caleb Hiery dragged you out there that day."

I looked into his soft brown eyes. I saw goodness there. Maybe it was the wine, maybe it was Angela's spirit speaking to me, but I decided to believe him—even if only for the evening. "That's right. You weren't in chem class, were you?" I said slowly as I thought it through.

"Nope. Jeremy just told us to be out at Trouble Triangle at 3:10 pm sharp. He said if we were late, he'd beat the shit out of our dogs."

When I barked a laugh at that strange comment, he said, "He knew they were weaker than him—and that we each had one: part of the program." He shrugged. "We all loved our dogs."

Of course. "Do you have a suitcase or anything?" I asked. He frowned. He was having hard time keeping up with my change of topic. Relaxed Dan was making him ill at ease. Now that was funny. I giggled.

"I have a 'go bag.' We have to have one in our car all the time; never know when the case will take us away," he admitted, looking uneasy.

I knew it! Nobody looks that good on a whim. But I couldn't afford to focus on how good James Hawthorne looked, not while he was half sitting, half laying on my overstuffed sofa amidst the billowy pillows. That was dangerous territory for me, and we had a job to do. I suspected part of what I was feeling was my soul crying out to be comforted and he was the only available person.

I poured another glass of wine for James. "I have a guest room. You're going to need to spend the night. We are going to clear the air between us once and for all." I wasn't going to leave him any choice. I knew it was selfish, but this was for me too. Angela would understand. I had to have his full cooperation to solve her murder, and if I could put any part of my own angst to rest in the process, I had to do it.

"Okay," he said, taking a rather large and indelicate gulp of his wine. Me telling him he was staying the night at my house was probably the last thing he expected to pass through my lips.

We locked eyes, each reliving the last part of that terrible day. I wondered if he remembered it as vividly as I still did, if he knew I would remember it forever.

"I ate my lunch sitting in a stall on an open toilet that day," I admitted. "Jenny Bowser and her friends came in and I listened to them laughing about how Mrs. McCullough had called me Daniel because I looked so much like a boy."

Even now, almost eleven years later, I still felt my cheeks grow hot. I was 15 again. I started my story for James.

Jenny and I were friends during seventh grade—the year everyone made fun of her for looking like a dog. I suppose similar situations is how friendships are formed throughout life. For one whole year, we were "that little boy and her ugly dog." But then Jenny spent the summer at the Cape before eighth grade and came back with boobs that changed her from Jenny Bow Wow to Jenny Bow Wowser. And after she and her new popular friends played a mean prank on me on the school bus, I became Dan the Man—a name that stuck. It didn't help that new teachers always struggled with my absent middle name. They always wanted to knock that 'a' off Daniel and make me Daniel A Neely. My appearance was no help.

Of course, Jenny always hinted at something she had "seen" when at my house, insinuating I had a penis lurking beneath my clothes. Anything to gain attention. That was Jenny—an attention whore. And so, on my first day of high school, I was once again indoctrinated as Daniel Neely, or more commonly known as Dan the Man.

I paused. James reached across and put a hand on my arm, reassuringly. I was momentarily stunned into silence. His hand felt so warm and comforting—almost like Angela, except the feeling didn't stop at warmth and comfort. I suddenly felt something much more. My eyes flew up to meet his, opening wide. I held my breath to calm myself. Logically, I knew what this was. My body's response to my bereavement. But it still surprised me.

"Go on, Daniela," he encouraged.

I cleared my throat; thankful the touch had not affected him the same way. I shivered now as I felt myself slipping back into that classroom so long ago.

By the time I got to chemistry class, I was feeling some of my old anger toward Jenny. The way I dealt with anger was through academic excellence. If I was smarter than everyone else, at least I had that one thing.

"Who can give me a definition of chemistry and tell me the role it plays in our lives?" Mr. Osteen was the senior chem teacher and jumped right in after taking roll. I'd heard great things about him and had high hopes that I would finally learn something in his class. I was the only freshman.

Jeremy instantly wagged his hand in the air. I was familiar with him. Everybody was, not only because his father was a senator, but also because I had heard of 6-Pack. I knew they were a group of six super smart, super athletes who had powerful parents. Everyone talked about them: Jeremy, James, Caleb, Josh, Bart, and Thomas. They were an intimidating group.

Without waiting for Mr. Osteen to call on him, Jeremy began his recitation. "Chemistry is many things; one of those things is a reaction between two people—and I think we all know what that role plays in our daily lives."

Ha, I thought. *You are so hilarious.* What a dumb and egotistical answer. But pretty much everyone else laughed. He'd known they would. Everyone wanted to be on the Richards' bandwagon. Jeremy was accustomed to having people fawn all over him. He might play the dumb card, but rumor had it that he was a very smart guy with a full scholarship to MIT on the table.

I don't know how Mr. Osteen kept from rolling his eyes as he said, "Yes, certainly that is one definition. But does anyone know the scientific definition?" He looked hopelessly out over the classroom, having had many of the kids in class in previous years.

.Before I realized what I was doing, my hand was in the air. I had been conducting scientific experiments since before I started school. And with my dad being a scientist, if I didn't know what chemistry was, both of us would be sorely disappointed in me. "Chemistry is the study of the transformation of matter. It is used in the development of pharmaceuticals, in agriculture, and in modern day forensics to name a few."

My voice began to shake toward the end as I noticed all eyes on me—the senior eyes. That was one of the disadvantages of taking online courses. I was rarely in class with kids my own age anymore. I felt both exhilarated and terrified. But I was also tired of being made to feel like I was "less than" because of how I looked. And I was sick of arrogant jerks like him, thinking they knew everything because he had an important dad. We are not our parents. We have to earn our own way in this world.

"Excellent, Daniela!" Mr. Osteen was far more enthusiastic than he needed to be. Either he felt bad for his misguided greeting to me as a new student in a senior chem class — "Welcome to our class Mr. Neely! Are you new to Noraville?"—or he was openly applauding the underdog because he too was tired of the arrogance of the 6-Pack.

A slow but steady clap brought my attention back to Jeremy. "Bravo, Dan the Man," he said, careful to maintain direct eye contact with me.

Ah, so this was Jenny's Jeremy. She would have told him that. I wondered why she was still so cruel to me.

I fought to contain the chill that wiggled down my spine. There was more laughter from his minions before he continued. "It takes a real man to best me." Jeremy threw his hands up in the air and gave me a charming smile, but I heard the unmistakable warning in his words.

"Let's move on." Mr. Osteen continued his lecture, but I knew all was not forgotten nor forgiven as Jeremy stole glances my way and dipped his head with a sly smile.

After school, his good old buddy Caleb Hiery grabbed me by the arm and steered me back behind the school to Trouble Triangle. I'd never seen it before, but I'd heard about it. It was a spot where the two buildings intersected, and the trash bins obscured the view. I thought it was mostly used for drug transactions, but I knew that wasn't why I was being taken there. It was not a place I ever hoped to visit, especially not with a member of the 6-Pack. Nonetheless, I did visit it that day.

"And well, you know the rest," I said, unwilling to rehash any more details. "If it wasn't for Angela . . . She was my angel that day. She could have chosen to not get involved. We weren't friends. We had never spoken before. But she saved me, and she protected me for an entire year after that."

I closed my eyes, remembering her kindness, her generosity, her willingness to get involved even though we had never spoken a day in our lives.

"Do you understand now how much I owe her?"

"I think I am envious of the level of devotion the two of you have for one another. That is so rare," James said.

His use of the word *have* made me want to kiss him. Wait, what? Uh, no! I did not want to kiss him. I closed my eyes and shook my head to clear the thought.

When I opened my eyes, James looked confused. "Dan, what about that story caused what happened afterward?"

"You tell me," I shot back, but I knew he wouldn't have an answer. I had always wondered the same thing, but Jeremy was too much for either of us to figure out.

I had had too much in one day. I needed to get this man settled in his room, catch a few hours of sleep, and then, I had a date with a recipe book.

Chapter Thirteen

RECIPES FOR LIFE

Sunday, December 4, 2022. 10:30 PM

24 hours after

Angela's voice rang out so loud and clear in her entries. It was as if she was sitting next to me. But she wasn't sitting next to me. Her body had been lying in a morgue for close to 24 hours now. Swallowing hard against the thickness in my throat, I read on, desperately searching for clues.

Angela's Recipe Book

September 19, 2021

"My Angel's heart is filled with joy; now, no longer a boy."

I just woke up with that crazy line in my head! Ha. Maybe now my fully female brain could ace an English class because that is the most poetic thing I've ever written in my life! Hopefully I actually wrote it and I'm not suddenly remembering something that some famous person wrote years ago but I guess there aren't really too many boys who became girls and wrote books to tell about it.

*** Lili Elbe, you have been my inspiration! ** I feel these words in my soul.*

My journey is finally complete.

I did it. I had sex as a woman—finally—at 24. And the slimeball I was with had no idea. Joaquin. Highly unlikely that was his name. If he was Spanish, then I am Christie Brinkley—and I currently outweigh her by about 150 pounds.

Speaking of which . . .

Slimy Joaquin, who did deliver the promised orgasm, so THANKS for that!!! . . . also created another hiccup in my happily ever after plan.

I heard him call me a whale. Yup. Overheard him on the phone saying he spermed another whale. Perfect example of beauty only being skin deep because he sure was easy on the eyes. I wanted to tell him he actually just screwed a man to emotionally scar him for life but I knew his look of horror would hurt me more than him, so I just let it go—and besides, THERE IS NO PART OF ME THAT IS MALE ANYMORE!

I know I'm overweight.

I've been overweight my whole life.

Food makes me feel better when nothing else does.

I think mom started using food to make me feel better when I was a little kid when dad couldn't accept that his perfect little boy preferred girl things.

It's funny—or not really—but if a little girl prefers boy things, playing with trucks and tractors, showing an interest in hunting and fishing; she is considered a super cool girl. But if a little boy prefers dolls, loves pink and sparkly things, playing dress up and shows an interest in cooking with mommy; nobody thinks that is cool. It makes people so ill at ease. I've always wondered why.

I was actually a really cool kid too—just not comfortable being a boy. I knew it as soon as I could talk. Why was that so hard to understand? Why was that so hard to accept?

Mom has always supported me. She has loved me exactly how I was every day of my life. She taught me to love myself that way too. She wrote the book on unconditional love.

I hope I can be that kind of mom someday.

Geez. Dad. What would Dad say if he knew that I just had sex as a woman. He would hate me even more than he did when he left.

He would be furious if he knew his support money paid for my puberty blockers and estrogen treatments. But hey, it was meant to support me and it did. It allowed me to be who I was meant to be.

Enough about Dad . . . He's ancient history. Haven't spoken to him in 20 years now.

I want to get on with my life—with my HEAP—and it looks like it is going to happen faster if I lose some weight.

I know I can do it.

I'm invincible.

Today, I have to celebrate with something heartier than a pastry. We are having **Angelic Eggs Benedict!**

For the sandwich:

2 organic eggs, poached Salt

Pepper

1 freshly baked croissant (see September 16, 2014, for recipe), cut in half Canadian Bacon

Avocado Spinach

For the Hollandaise Sauce

½ cup of butter 3 egg yolks

1 tbsp fresh lemon juice 1 tsp dijon mustard

salt pepper

Heat ½ cup of butter in microwave for one minute (make certain to cover).

Pour into blender and add egg yolks, fresh lemon juice, Dijon mustard, salt, and pepper to taste. Blend.

To Assemble the Sandwich

Place spinach, avocado, and lightly seared Canadian bacon on each half of croissant. Add lightly poached egg to each half. Drizzle hollandaise over each side. Salt and pepper to taste.

I know, I'm eating away my disappointment. But that is what I do. And this sure is a delicious meal.

September 23, 2021

No recipe today—just great news! I can hardly believe my luck.

It's like the gods are shining down on me, letting me know they want me to be happy.

I knew they did. Mom was right.

I've already located my next step through a clinical trial!!!! And it's completely free! Right in my price range!

The internet is an amazing place. It basically hands you life on a silver platter.

There are a few technical difficulties such as . . . I'm not 18 and I'm not in college anymore, but honestly, if I can overcome the obstacles I've already overcome in life, I feel like these obstacles are almost a joke.

I already contacted two online places promising to get me fake IDs. Neither one is on the [scary] dark web and it looks like it is only going to cost me around $80. If I get picked, I will be signing up for a research study to see how a new implant helps with weight loss.

Criteria for study: need to lose at least 100 pounds, female, 18 year old co-ed.

I could stand to lose 150, but I'm not trying to get skinny—just become more visually pleasing to achieve my goals. Too bad I wasn't born in the Rubenesque era. I would be beating the men off.

I wonder if I will be as shallow as men appear to be. I've been so focused on accomplishing my goals, I haven't given much thought to who I might be attracted to most.

The hardest part is going to be my job of course. Those random bites, licks and tastes are still my biggest nemesis. No diet ever works because of the BLTs. Sigh . . . fingers crossed.

I can't wait to tell Dan!

September 30, 2021

They want me!

I'm going to be part of the 'TUC Clinical Trial'

They didn't say what the TUC stands for, but it sounds about right for what will be happening—they're gonna tuck that fat away!

They barely even looked at my fake ID, even though I was sure I was going to get arrested on the spot.

I guess I'm nothing more than a test subject to them.

The orientation was long and weird. There was a lot of talk about 'confidentiality' since the results of the trial would determine if the product was viable. We signed a LOT of documents.

I noticed the Neely Pharmaceuticals Logo was at the bottom of each page.

I wondered why Dan wouldn't tell me about a clinical trial like this if her dad was behind it.

But really, her dad never has talked to her much. I'm not sure they speak at all now except on Thanksgiving and Christmas.

No matter. If I'm going to fully accomplish my happily ever after plan, this weight loss feels right as my next move.

So...onward! No secrets or BLTs shall pass my lips.

October 10, 2021

I got the implant today.

It was quick and didn't hurt at all.

It felt like I got a shot in my arm.

It is hard to believe this tiny little microbe is going to make much of a difference. I hope I didn't get my hopes up for nothing.

There was so much excitement in the waiting room. I could tell that every girl there had high hopes for a different life.

I remembered feeling that anxious before my gender surgery.

I looked at each of them deeply, wondering what suffering they had been through.

Life can be so hard, especially if you don't have a parent on your side. It doesn't matter if you are a boy or girl or skinny or fat. Kids find a reason to terrorize you. Teachers don't realize how mean kids can be and sometimes it is the goody two shoes kids—the popular kids with super involved parents who kiss the teacher's butts. They can be the meanest of the mean.

I wanted to tell this group that I had already overcome much worse—that they could do this—but I realized they would look at me and see the truth; that I looked exactly like them. Unless I wanted to get into a heavy discussion about the fact that I was born a boy, my words would mean nothing. And there were no guarantees about their reaction either. As much as I wanted to shout it to the rooftops because I am proud of who I am and what I've gone through to get here, I learned from my dad that people want you to be who you were born to be. If someone who created you—who loved you from the first moment they set eyes on you—cannot accept a change like that, it doesn't seem too likely that the average person is going to, no matter how many 'true to yourself' videos they've watched. There are still so many haters. It is best to just blend in this place. It's not like I'm going to become besties with an 18 year old.

When I went back into work afterward, the familiar sweet smells of the bakery did not tempt me like they normally do. I'm sure this is just the halo effect like when you're in a new relationship and tomorrow, I'll go in to bake the Petersen's wedding cake and have that big lick of leftover batter on the spoon in my mouth before I know it. But wouldn't it be great if that didn't happen?

It doesn't hurt to wish for a miracle, does it?

December 6, 2021

I've been on the program for eight weeks now and I can't believe what is happening to me. I've gone down two sizes in clothes already. I've been shopping at the Goodwill because I need so many new clothes and don't want to waste money. I've become a true believer—I believe this is going to work! I know my clothes are only going to fit for a little while now, so I buy cheap, donate, and buy cheap again.

I am no longer affected by the smells in the bakery at all, which is insane! I love baked foods! I do my job and then eat the meals that I'm told to eat, like 3 ounces of lean turkey, two slices of avocado, a small green salad with lemon juice . . . meals that would have been a starter for my appetite before. I didn't realize that my portions were so supersized before this. But still, I can't help but wonder how can one little implant do this?

Does it release a prescription drug into my body? Did they implant it into my 'craving' center? However it works, its like a miracle.

If I make it through the rest of the holidays like this, I will become the poster child for this implant! Ha . . . I guess I can't since I'm not actually who I said I was . . .

Oh well, I'll just stay focused on the positive. I've never felt more in control of what goes into my body. It is almost as if an inner voice is speaking to me. Wherever that voice is coming from, don't stop talking now! This is amazing!

December 25, 2021

Christmas dinner was kind of weird and kind of funny. We did the same thing we've been doing since Dan got her own place; me, mom and her dad all went to her house for dinner around 3. Sometimes it feels surreal to be sitting at the dinner table with the famous Dr. Markus Neely—like it should make all of us more important people somehow, but we're not. I'm just a pastry chef, mom still works at the Cozy, but at least she's the manager now, and Dan made detective last year. I tell myself he's just a person—not a particularly friendly one either—like the rest of us, but when he talks, it always feels like he is evaluating us.

"Are you excelling in your advancement within the department Daniela?"

Dan gets embarrassed but always answers politely. He is the one person she does not correct about her name. I think she's just happy when he tries to talk to her.

Tonight, I think he may have tried to compliment me but it came out as usual—awkward—and made everyone look sideways at each other around the table.

"Angela, I believe your girth has been greatly reduced."

Dan and my mom's eyes bulged but I almost laughed. Even writing it now makes me want to laugh. I should have said, "Why yes, Dr. Neely, I do believe my girth has been reduced. How is your girth?" MY GIRTH?! What am I, a horse? Who talks like that? Mad scientists, I guess. I mean, I don't have any proof he is mad, but he is definitely a scientist through and through. Sometimes it feels like he doesn't live in our world at all. I feel so sorry for Dan. She has never been loved by a parent. I've always had mom.

I would have loved to tell him I am part of his clinical trial–his TUC trial–and that it is amazing but since I do not actually qualify for the trial, I didn't say a word. I don't want to get kicked out now; not when I'm doing so good. All I said to him, and it was mostly just to put Dan at ease because it is not her fault he is her dad, was "Thanks for noticing Dr. Neely."

When he kissed Dan's head as he was leaving, he said, "I wish you continued success in all that you do." Merry Christmas to you too jerk. Geez. When he hurts Dan, I want to punch him. I don't even know if he loves her or if she is just an obligation he fulfills. I almost think

I'd rather have the jerk who hated me for being a girl instead of this guy who can't muster up any emotion at all for anything. Life must have been hard for Dan's mom. Everyone says she was really pretty. Lillian Neely. Her name has a nice sound to it. Dan must have inherited her goodness from her. Dan is tough on the outside, but that's all fake. She's just afraid of being hurt.

January 6, 2022

I went for my three month weigh in today. I've lost 34 pounds. That is impossible but it happened! What is even more insane is the questionnaire I had to complete. It took an hour! The questions were so odd. It asked me things like 'When you are scheduled to eat 3 ounces of chicken, how often do you want to eat beef instead? Ha ha . . . my options were occasionally, often, and never. God's honest truth? I have no idea. I think I could probably go without eating at all. I only feel inspired to eat exactly what is on my menu plan. Such a weird diet!!!

The questions went on and on. I was thinking, "Look at the numbers guys. I lost 34 pounds in three months. I'm not cheating. And why do you care if I want to eat beef instead of chicken?!"

I wish I could have seen some of the other girls this time, but I was the only one in the waiting room. It made me wonder if the other girls had failed or if I was the only one who had stuck to the plan. Or maybe they just scheduled us further apart now that each appointment was more involved. Hopefully it wasn't working better on me because I was actually older and I was screwing up their clinical results. I feel bad about that possibility, but I can't go back now. I feel better every day. I've started walking every morning before work. I feel healthier than I've ever felt before.

I am an amazing woman!

April 10, 2022

It's me! I'm sorry I haven't written in so long. My life has just kind of blossomed I guess. When I wake up, I feel like walking. After work, I have started running. I have hated exercise my entire life but now I love it. I don't know what is happening to me. It's like this little voice in my head says, "how about a little walk?" and before I know it, I'm walking and enjoying it! I guess part of it might be the healthy eating; not that I ate unhealthily before but running a bakery does put a lot of yummy sugary food into my mouth on a normal basis. I also wonder if there is some type of mood enhancer in this implant. I mean, I've always been a positive person, but now I absolutely love life.

I had my six month weigh in yesterday with another crazy questionnaire; a variation of the first, and just as long. I logged a total of 68 pounds weight loss. Six months ago, I would have told you that is simply not possible, but here I am—68 pounds lighter. They told me that at my next weigh in, I will need to meet with a counselor so I should plan 2 hours. I can't imagine why I would need to meet with a counselor because I am happy, but I will prepare. They wished me good luck on my finals as I left. It gave me a jolt and reminded me that I am Angel Adams and I am a first year college student. Duh.

June 16, 2022

I've met someone!

I'm still trying to decide how I feel about him.

We kind of noticed each other as we were running along the Charles River during my evening run a few weeks ago.

At first, we just waved but this week, we met up at 6 and ran together three times. Before tonight, all I knew about him was his name.

Sam. It's a good name, but a good name doesn't make a person good. Tonight, he brought some sandwiches from the Panera down the street in a cooler. I thought that was a really nice gesture. He asked if I wanted one after our run and we ate sitting on the open gate of his truck. I opened the bread, took out the turkey (I think I could measure 3 ounces in my sleep now), the avocado and the lettuce and ate those things, trying to be as inconspicuous as possible about my diet. I've always hated those girls who picked at their food and didn't want him to think I was one of them. I pulled off chunks of the bread, throwing it to the ducks and pigeons while we talked. But then he asked me if I had a gluten intolerance so I felt compelled to be honest with him. I let him know I was participating in a clinical trial for weight loss and had already lost 80 pounds. He pulled back like I'd slapped him. It seemed like he was kind of disgusted but I'm hoping I misread his reaction. Then, because his reaction made me very uncomfortable, I tried to joke with him and said, "It's not like we know anything about each other yet. For all I know, you used to be a girl!"

The look on his face told me he did not think that joke was funny at all. He said he was pretty sure I'd know if he was a freak. A freak.

I think that sums up how he would view me.

God. All of the roadblocks. I thought the pathway to my HEAP would be direct.

When I went through the counseling before surgery, Tina warned me that not everyone would be accepting of the change I was making—and I knew that; I mean, look at my dad—but I just never factored it into my HEAP. I never thought about how difficult it might be to find that guy who could look at me and see 'woman' and want to build a life with me that way.

I can't stop thinking about the entire conversation with Sam from the time we sat on his tailgate until he said the word freak. It has played on a loop in my head pretty much all day. I can't pretend it didn't happen— that I didn't hear the words. That they didn't hurt. 'Freak'. How did I tolerate it for so long?

I know one thing for sure. I could never hide the truth. It is too important to me to be loved for everything I am.

July 10, 2022

Today I had my 9 month weigh in. Everything is going according to plan and I only have 10 pounds until I reach my personal goal weight. I barely recognize myself and wonder for the first time if people think I'm pretty. I think I might be. I have been looking at my reflection in storefront windows when I walk past to my bakery. It gives me butterflies in my stomach to know that it is me in the reflection.

Ironically, the questionnaire today asked a lot of questions about my mood and feelings as opposed to diet questions. And the counseling session was surprisingly negative. The lady kept telling me not to be surprised if I started feeling agitated and overwhelmed. Her questions were making me feel agitated and overwhelmed! She said a lot of people who go through extreme weight loss like this in a short period of time can become consumed by anxiety. I told her I felt wonderful, but she insisted on giving me a prescription for Xanacan, a new anti-anxiety drug. She wants me to have it filled to have 'on hand' in case the panic hits. I figured that if I debated this with her, she might suspect I was older than 19 (which I supposedly turned last month) or that I was anxious, so I just smiled and accepted the prescription.

I wish I could have told her the only thing I have new concerns about has nothing to do with my weight.

After the sandwich incident, I decided I didn't want to run into Sam again so I started running at the high school track in the evenings. I made a firm decision that I don't need anyone in my life who thinks trans people are freaks. He could have said a million things—or nothing at all and just laughed at my weak joke—but that response told me he was not the guy for me. I regret that I told him the name of my apartment building but haven't heard anything from him yet.

The trial is almost over and I'm ready to complete my HEAP—and NOT with a guy like Sam.

September 19, 2022

It's hard to believe that one year ago, I made the decision to lose weight and today I am 100 pounds smaller. I'm proud of myself for this accomplishment in a way that surprises me. When I created my HEAP, losing weight was not part of it. But now that it has happened, I feel so incredibly happy and full of energy every single day. Maybe everyone wants to effortlessly look their best. And this really was effortless. This implant will change lives. I wish I could shout to the rooftops the impact it has had on my life, but I've had to be very discreet about it. Only Dan knows what I did. Everyone else thinks I'm the diet champion of the century. I wish I could figure out why they are only testing it on 18 year olds. I want to tell them what a tremendous impact it could have on the lives of 20 somethings . . . but I'm sure they have a specific reason and when it is released to the general public, everyone will benefit. Some of my longtime clients have come into the bakery and asked me, for me. "Where's Angela these days?" So I guess it is not my imagination that I look nothing like my former self.

I'm trying to map out a way to meet nice guys . . . and figure out how to detect open-minded guys. Guys who will love me for me and get on board with my plan. I think I'll dig into the surrogate fund and splurge on a new wardrobe now that I'm at my final size. Of course I could lose more but I'm good with the way I look now. Dan has had enough grief in her life over being skinny. I'll keep a little bit of meat on my bones, thank you very much, not to mention the loose skin that I know will never leave me—but that's okay. I love that skin too. It is a reminder of where I've been.

I have my final meeting with the TUC team next month. I'm hoping they will answer a few questions now that it is over. The whole thing has felt so secretive. I always wonder why nobody else is there. I can't be the only one remaining in the trial, can I? My guilt over that possibility builds daily.

October 10, 2022

So, I guess I should've read the fine print. But I was too excited and too busy trying to con my way into the study. I'm not done. It is a two year study. I don't have to lose any more weight—that part is up to me and I can tell them I'm done whenever I'm done—but I have to keep the implant in for 'up to two years' per my signed contract. I asked the TUC reps to please explain to me their reasoning and for the first time since I began, I did not like their response. They said, "We do not have to explain our reasoning. You took part in a free clinical trial and agreed to keep the implant for up to two years."

My only commitment is to go back every three months, so I'm not going to make a big deal out of it. It was my fault for not reading the contract and honestly, would it have mattered to me if I'd known? Honestly, in the beginning, I would have thought it would take at least two years to lose a hundred pounds.

There is a part of me that would like to contact that slimy jerk from Romeo to the Rescue and when he gets to my apartment, say to him "Remember me? The whale you spermed?" and then kick him out the door. And I would also like to go back to Charles River and walk up to Sam and say, "Guess what, I am one of those freaks you cringed over. I used to be a boy." Yikes. Does being skinny make you mean? I've never had hateful thoughts like that before. I guess those things bothered me more than I acknowledged at the time.

Maybe I'm just upset because I wanted to be done with this part of my plan and move on to the next. Maybe they were right about the anxiety setting in. This is the first time I've felt any negativity in over a year. And I've always been a positive person. I guess I should fill the prescription just in case.

November 24, 2022

What a day.

Today started like any normal Thanksgiving. I got up early and made my famous pumpkin gingerbread pudding; the one I bring every year to dinner at mom's. Before it was done, I was literally dying to go for a walk and could barely wait 'til the bread pudding came out of the oven. The minute it was out of the oven, I was out the door like a dog who has been waiting all day to pee. Seriously. I felt so overwhelmed. It wasn't until I was several blocks from my apartment that I realized I was still in my pajamas with no jacket and no shoes on. I wasn't even cold!

I ran back home and the front door to my apartment was still open too. Geez. Where was my head?

The whole thing freaked me out a little but I decided it was probably because of all of the extra hours at work I put in during the past week. Everybody and their brother wanted holiday pies and it seems like nobody bakes anymore. Believe me, I'm not complaining. It won't be long now 'til I can afford an apartment in Jamaica Plain. Business has been so great!

I've heard that lack of sleep gives you brain fog. That must be what's happening. The thought of people who had seen me made me laugh.

But when I got to mom's house and told Dan what happened, she didn't laugh. She was worried.

Especially since it was only 34 degrees this morning. She kept asking me if I was sure I was okay.

I told her I was absolutely okay. But the truth is, I wasn't absolutely sure.

November 27, 2022

Well, I really blew it this time and someone saw me.

When I stepped out of the elevator, I overheard Mr. Smithers in 2A telling Candi Johnson in 1B that he saw me—checking my mail in my birthday suit on Saturday morning. I could tell by the look on her face she didn't believe him, which actually made me feel bad for him. Because . . . you won't believe this . . . he was telling the truth.

"What is wrong with young people these days? They think they can do anything they want and there will never be any repercussions?" Mr. Smithers is never going to forgive me—already proven by the fact that there was <u>not</u> a fresh flower in my vase this morning.

I love Mr. Smithers. He was my first friend. He has been putting one fresh flower in the vase outside my front door for over three years now. He's kind of a gruff, lonely old man and the flowers seem to be his way of communicating with me. He always acts kind of annoyed that I don't know what the flower means; but he is always ready to explain it when he sees me. Honestly, before I met him, I didn't even know flowers had meanings. How lame is that? I'm an artist. I should know things like that. I think he is lonely since his wife passed. There are so many lonely people in the world. It is so hard to find ways to reach out. I love that he figured that out about me—that I would love flowers—just by seeing the little shelf of flowerpots and vases by my front door. It is very kind. Dan and I just need to find a very young version of Mr. Smithers. ☐

It is so nice to know someone is always thinking of me.

Sometimes, that flower is the brightest spot in my day. My best friend works long hours and so do I but there is always a perky little flower at the door to say, "Welcome home Angela! I was thinking of you today!"

But today, he was feeling very unforgiving. Who could blame him? What on earth made me do such a thing? I can remember stepping out of the shower, drying off and then thinking I should check the mail, so I did. I just forgot the step in the middle where I put on clothes or a robe. I really must apologize. But how do you apologize for something like that? For the first time in my life, I'm not sure an apology is enough.

It is like I have no control over my actions. I really need to get some rest. Fingers crossed he forgives me.

Chapter Fourteen

THE CRAZY WALL

Monday, December 5, 2022. 4:00 AM
29 hours 30 minutes after

Angela's last fourteen entries kept me up all night. She had completely abandoned using it as a recipe book during the past year. That timeline matched up with when I became detective. Was that a coincidence? Was it because I had been too busy for her, and it had to become her confidant? Or was it simply because she no longer desired food? Either way, her bakery had not suffered as a result. She had too many tried and true recipes that she had developed over the years. Maybe a baker didn't need to keep creating new recipes in an established bakery. What would I know. Food held very little importance in my world. It was a necessity only.

I couldn't stop the connections that were pinging back and forth in my brain. By 4 am, I was at the kitchen table, creating an evidence board. I could finally understand why it occasionally got the name "crazy wall" because I really felt kind of crazy when I was creating it. Maybe that term came from someone who also had a murdered loved one; not that there was any solid proof that my loved one was murdered—yet—but with every note card I completed, I felt more certain.

Name of the case? Why fight it? The Virgin Suicides—at least for now, even though Ang was definitely not a virgin. Cops in general had discovered long ago that it was easiest to just go with the name the media chose because that is the name the general public could identify with. It never felt right to me, especially now, letting the media choose our case name, but I had more important things to worry about than the name of the case.

I created the first five cards:

Victim: Angela Monn. Canadian American Female; 6 feet 1 inches, 178 pounds, blonde hair, blue eyes; cause of death: overdose of Zanacan, suspected homicide

Victim: Kayleigh Obrien. Caucasian American Female; cause of death: overdose of Zanacan

Victim: Jasmine Patel. Indian American Female; cause of death: overdose of Zanacan

Victim: Siena Atkins. African American Female; cause of death: overdose of Zanacan

Victim: Namie Wako. Japanese American Female; cause of death: overdose of Zanacan

I needed to access my database to fill in the height, weight, and physical description information for the other four Massachusetts victims and ask James about the Maine victims, but I was raised with good enough manners not to wake a guest in my home at 4 am. In my distracted state of mind last night, I had accidentally left my computer bag sitting on the desk in the spare room that was really my office with a pull-out sofa. I just couldn't bear for him to sleep in the real spare room—the room Ang would have crashed in if we drank too many glasses of wine. It was decorated in pinks and ivory with satins, ribbons, and laces just for her. She was such a girly girl, and I loved that about her. Maybe the me I wanted to be. But I was blue through and through—the bedroom of my childhood formed me whether I wanted it to or not. Almost instinctively, I picked out blue clothes, which worked well for a detective anyhow.

As I was writing the cards, it suddenly occurred to me that each victim represented a different ethnicity. That was an odd coincidence and a detail that had escaped my notice until now.

The cards were stacking up:

TUC. 2 year weight loss clinical trial, Victim 5, Angela Monn was experiencing loss of control during the last days.

Also, had the women in Massachusetts cleared all social media sites like the women in Maine?

If so, we would need to contact friends and see if they had shared posts to examine the dark web angle.

I made a side note to check with the other victims' families to see if any of them had displayed symptoms similar to those that Angela had experienced prior to the death. What happened to these young women?

Two more cards went up:

Romeo to the Rescue Sam from Charles River

I needed to check with Mrs. Monn to see if Angela had made any contact with either of them directly before her death. I was furious and frustrated about the fake security camera in Angela's building but wanted to canvas the area to see if maybe a nearby building would have security footage that would show the guy who came by Mr. Smither's house, although I didn't have an exact date and didn't know how I would identify whether it was Romeo or Sam. I guess the FBI has facial recognition software for things like that. But first, we would have to establish exactly who lived there to rule all of them out. It sounded like a process that might take more time than I had.

And then, because my gut—both my women's intuition and my detective's instincts—told me to, I added two more cards:

Jeremy Richards/Jessica follow-up

Neely Pharmaceuticals

get information about clinical trial all phases

**who ran individual clinical trials? **

It pained me to write "Neely Pharmaceuticals" on a card, but both James' comments and Angela's diary put my father's company undeniably right into the middle of this mess. I wished my last name was not Neely. Another nail in my coffin leading to removal from the case. I was really under the wire to crack this one.

There was only one remaining card to write. Who the hell shot me? And why?

I couldn't figure out what possible involvement I had in these cases other than being the detective assigned to them. It wasn't like I was close to solving the cases. Why would someone shoot *me*?

"Wow, you're up and at it early this morning!"

James's voice made me jump, nearly spilling coffee all over my crazy wall.

"Actually, I never made it to sleep last night. Grab a cup of coffee. I've got a lot to tell you."

James looked fresh as a daisy at 4:29 am. How the heck was that possible? This guy's grooming habits were going to drive me nuts.

My kitchen was modern but not spacious. James had to walk all the way around my mahogany pedestal table to get to the coffee pot. Returning to my side, he leaned over the table next to me.

"So, tell me what kept you up all night." James had poured his coffee and was ready to begin.

I looked at his earnest face. I could see no traces of malice there. I vowed anew to try hard to work side by side with him and put the past behind us. I don't know why I was shot or if it had anything to do with Angela's death, but my focus had to be on her, not me.

"Well, first, I need to ask you for the information on the 'suicides' from Maine." I used air quotes to indicate I no longer believe these were suicide cases.

"Sure," he said. "Let me grab my computer."

Handing me his cup to hold while he was gone, I quickly grabbed a coaster from the drawer and hurriedly smoothed my hair and rubbed water under my eyes. I couldn't even imagine what I looked like, but I knew it was nothing good.

Returning with his Mac, he picked his coffee back up, giving me a questioning look. The coaster stood out like a sore thumb against the butcher block counters. In my traditional, slightly English country kitchen, I had stark white coasters with bright red print that read '**confidence is your best color; wear it often.**'

"Angela," I stated, letting him know that conversation was over, although the memory of her giving them to me reignited in my mind.

I'd frequently complained that no color looked good on me, that my complexion was kind of strangely olive and looked gross with both my hair color and my eyes. I had received these coasters for my next birthday.

"Here we go," he said, opening his Mac. He started to laugh. "Is your Wi-Fi name really Dantheman?"

"Yep. Password is the same plus @2. That was my address growing up: 2 Whitley Place."

"Yeah, I know where you lived. Everyone knew where Dr. Neely lived."

I snorted. "Ha! Believe me, Dr. Neely didn't really live there. Only me and Margette lived there. And even I didn't feel like I lived in the *house*, just the bedroom. The house is like a museum. It's hard to explain."

"Does your dad still live there?"

"I guess he still has people taking care of it. I know he rents an efficiency closer to work. I have only stopped by the house a few times since I left for college. My dad has asked me to always call first to make certain I don't alarm the caregivers. My guess is the only people who visit regularly are the cleaning people and the flower delivery people, still faithfully delivering a dozen lilies weekly."

"If nobody lives there, why would someone deliver a dozen lilies weekly? And don't the caregivers know you?" he asked.

"It is something my mother had scheduled when she was alive. Her name was Lillian, but she went by Lily. Apparently, she was obsessed with lilies, and the weekly delivery was never stopped after she died."

"You don't find that strange that 25 years later, flowers are still getting delivered and nobody even lives there? *And* you have to get permission before you enter?" he asked incredulously, as if there had to be something more to this story. "Come on Dan. Does that sound right to you?"

"I was taught to respect my elders—to never question them. That's how I've lived most of my life. Also, I think my dad is a man of habit. He continues to do what he has always done," I explained. "Although I must confess, now that you say it out loud, it all does sound rather unusual: calling before going over, fresh flowers in a house nobody lives in..." I contemplated my words and decided not to get sidetracked with things that had nothing to do with the case. "I guess maybe I too have turned into a creature of habit."

But now I couldn't stop thinking about it-- why I needed to notify my dad in advance before I was going to stop by the home I grew up in. It was so odd.

"And you get them delivered here too?" He gestured to the flowers on the sofa table, visible through the dining room, their smell pungent in the stale morning air. His question was a distraction from my questioning thoughts.

"They are delivered here but not by me. The delivery is a gift from a family friend. The flowers are my only remaining connection to my mom," I said, but even as the words left my mouth, I could feel the strangeness of the situation. If someone chose to honor my mother for that long---25 years and counting---wouldn't they have made some attempt to meet me by now? I was an adult. Lilies were not cheap. "It is a bit odd, isn't it?"

"More than a little, I'd say."

His comment made me feel defensive. "You know, my dad and I rarely speak. Chances are, he has sublet the home to somebody, and I know nothing about it. I don't really have any attachment to the house. Even the bedroom wasn't really mine. It was the boy child's bedroom."

I hadn't thought about my bedroom—my home—in years, and I was surprised to find myself choked up. I had no idea what happened at the house. And the real reason I didn't go back was because I felt *so* attached to it—as if by being there, I would somehow find my lost mother within its walls—and I couldn't bear to face those feelings alone now that Margette had gone back to Ecuador to be with her family. Even that thought about Margette hurt. I thought I was her family too, but I had not heard from her since she walked out the door nine years ago.

All this emotion was probably just because I was exhausted, no doubt. I cleared my throat and took a deep breath, trying to regroup.

"Oh! I didn't know you had a brother."

James meant no harm by his statement, but it hit me wrong.

"Why *would you* know whether I had a brother? I don't know if *you* have a brother."

James looked surprised. "I'm sorry—I didn't mean to be intrusive or insensitive. And for the record I don't have a brother. I guess I forgot to mention nobody involved in the trial had any siblings. Once, when I asked Dad why, he said the trial was only for boys and we had to be only children."

"But what would have happened if someone accidentally got pregnant or divorced and had children with another spouse?" I was playing devil's advocate, but I needed to know if he knew what was going on or was playing dumb.

"They wouldn't have been able to be part of the program anymore." James was matter of fact about it, like it was no big deal. But it was a far bigger deal than he realized. I felt compelled to tell him.

"Well James, would you call it a big deal if a family was forced to give up a child at birth and then when that child located them as a young adult, took away $400,000 in college funds because she sought them out?"

James looked at me as if I'd grown horns. But everything I'd just said was the truth and had happened.

I decided to just be out with it. "Did you know that Jeremy Richards had a twin sister that the family gave away at birth?"

James's eyes bulged. "No way! I know Jeremy's parents could be over the top, but they would never give away their child. They were basically good people."

"Were they though?" I gave that question a moment to sink in. "Do good people raise a kid like Jeremy? Think about what you told me Mrs. Richards used to say."

James looked everywhere in the room except at me. It was clear he didn't know what to say.

He probably knew good sides to Jeremy. Everybody has good sides.

"Think, James. Think about Mrs. Richards' drunken comment. 'What is the price of one perfect boy? One baby girl.' Not only did they give her away, but they also gave the adoptive parents a huge sum of money to *take her*. And when that child—Jessica—later came to them to meet her biological parents, they took back her entire college fund of four hundred thousand dollars. Does that sound like good people to you?"

James was silent. I mean, what could he say to that? And now that I was older and thinking about it within the context of the clinical trial, the whole situation looked a lot different to me too. There might be more to it than I originally thought.

"James, I met her. I know for a fact she exists." I could see that this information made a difference to him. "Mrs. Monn brought her home for game night. She helped her. She was always helping people out. Jessica was a new waitress and struggling. Turns out she was struggling because she had never been a waitress before. There's a whole story there I'm not going to get into, okay?"

What I didn't tell him was that I had been upset with Jessica's arrival and that's part of why it made such an impact on me. I cherished my time at the Monn house, and it was the very first time Margette had ever let me sleep over. She was so rigid with her rules. I didn't want my sleepover derailed by some neurotic stranger, and Jessica was a basket case when I first met her. It sounds so selfish now, but I had only been part of the Monn family for less than a year and I was admittedly jealous. Poor Jessica. I now know she wanted the same thing I did—her mother.

I jotted a quick note to talk to Angela's mother about Jessica. Although Angela had said nothing further about Jessica in the part of her diary I'd read, there was at least a chance they were connected somehow. Angela always told me to trust my gut. She said I had an excellent one for intuiting things.

"What if..." James began.

"What if what? Go on." Was he thinking the same thing I was thinking?

"Well, I was just thinking about what you said. I remember how devastated Jeremy was when his mom died. Did you know he dropped out of MIT? He had a full scholarship."

"And..."

. "What if Mrs. Monn's good deed put her own daughter in Jeremy's crosshairs? Being number one: the biggest, the brightest, the strongest, the richest—all those things meant everything to Jeremy. If anything threatened that, I can't even imagine how he would react."

"My thoughts exactly," I said. "But I can't help but wonder if my imagination is running away with me based upon my past with Jeremy Richards. Hearing his name at the bakery earlier really messed with my mind. Really." I meant it. "But we shouldn't rule out any leads." I pondered for a minute before I continued, "I know I'm overly tired and overly caffeinated and can't quite find the right link yet, but it is there on that board. I know it."

James nodded pensively as I spoke.

"Oh, and for the record, I do not have a brother."

"But you said—" he started.

Part of me enjoyed making James squirm, but I caved.

"My parents had planned on a boy, and nobody ever got around to making any changes to the room. I grew up in a room decorated with vibrant shades of blue and little quotes hand painted on the walls such as 'Little boys are made of frogs and snails and puppy dog tails.' It's quite beautiful. I lived in it but never thought of it as 'my' room. I always thought of it as the 'boy child's' room."

"It still looks like that?"

James sounded so incredulous, and the situation had become so tense that I almost laughed, but I held it in. James did not know me well enough to understand my weird habit of inopportune laughing to relieve stress and anxiety.

"Yep. Looked like that 'til the day I moved out, and I'm sure it will look like that forever. The whole house is like her museum." I was getting a lump in my throat dredging up old memories, so I quickly diverted the subject.

"So . . . I read Angela's Diary, and it had some illuminating facts in it—facts that further point to homicide."

My words had the desired effect. I thought James' eyebrows were going to shoot off his forehead.

"You read Angela's Diary? Without me? I thought we were doing this together."

I shrugged. "I told you Ang was my best friend. I wanted to make certain there was nothing she would prefer to keep secret. Besides, I couldn't sleep."

For the first time, I saw a look I couldn't really decipher on James' face. Maybe disappointment, but also maybe distrust. It was suspicion at the very least.

Although it gave me a twinge that I wished it didn't, I ignored the look. I reminded myself that all I cared about was catching Angela's killer.

"Before you start asking me what it says, I need that bio information from the Maine victims to complete my board."

My palmed hand indicated he should look at what I had created while he slumbered peacefully in the room next door.

James glanced at the board, briefly sat his MAC down to refill his cup of coffee— grumbling "I'll never get through this without more caffeinated reinforcement"—and then proceeded to dictate stats as I jotted them on notecards.

Victim: Abigail Johnson. Caucasian American Female; cause of death: overdose of Zanacan

Victim: Arya Khati. Indian American Female; cause of death: overdose of Zanacan

Victim: LeTonya Jackson. African American Female; cause of death: overdose of Zanacan

Victim: Kiko Tanaka. Japanese American Female; cause of death: overdose of Zanacan

By the time I was writing 'overdose of Zanacan' on the last card, my hand was shaking.

"You know, I heard you graduated a couple of years early and I knew you made detective early too, but you are kind of intense to work with. Are you sure you are okay?" I wasn't sure if James sounded overwhelmed or concerned. "I think you need this more than me," he said as he offered his cup of coffee.

But my hand was not shaking for lack of sleep nor lack of caffeine. It was shaking out of pure adrenaline for the exact duplication of the 'suicides,' which I was pretty sure were not going to be called that any longer after I showed the details of my evidence board to James. I waved the coffee away.

"I know I'm intense. I don't know how to be any other way. This is my life. There is nothing else in my life other than my work. I used to have Angela, and clearly, I was a terrible friend since her body lay rotting for days without me even knowing she was dead. Now, all I have is finding her killer."

He nods, hearing my pain and self-loathing and watches as I put each of the four cards under the posted cards that corresponded with the ethnic backgrounds.

"There is a definitive pattern in these cases. There is no way it is a coincidence that there were four victims in each location who just happened to be this ethnically diverse—especially not in Maine for God's sake! Everyone is Caucasian there!" My voice had risen an octave or two by the time I got to the end of my diatribe. "The question is why a killer would choose women so diverse? It goes against everything I've ever learned about serial killers. Do they have a common denominator I'm not seeing? Other than their age?"

James took a closer look, and I could see that his curiosity was now piqued too.

"I'm going to need to go back and talk to each of these families," he said, more to himself than to me.

Then, after further examination of the other cards I had pinned on the board, he asked, "Romeo to the Rescue?"

"Yes." I stated firmly. "That lead definitely needs to be checked out."

"Well, do you mind telling me what or who it is?" I could tell James was trying very hard to remain patient with me even though he was accustomed to taking the lead on cases like this.

"After Ang had her sex reassignment surgery, she wanted to see if it was true that she could experience all of the pleasures that a woman typically feels, so she went online and hired a company called Romeo to the Rescue."

I could see a flush creeping up behind the white collar of his somehow impeccably pressed shirt, but James asked the tough question. "This is my first case involving a sex reassignment surgery. Honestly, I wasn't even sure the rumors about Angela were true. Kids can be mean, and once you're labeled, that's who you are, even if you're not." He says this to me with a straight face, as if I didn't live that life too.

When I don't respond but just give him a look like he just said something extremely stupid and obvious, he finally gets it and apologizes.

"Look Daniela—I'm just going to call you that, okay? I'm not being sexist—I swear. I promised myself that if I ever got the chance to talk to you, I would make it up to you by never slipping up on your name and now it's hard to call you 'Dan' after practicing 'Daniela' the whole drive down here."

Despite my intentions to not be charmed by James Hawthorne, that admission got to me. He practiced my name for 3 hours? I couldn't help myself. I smiled.

"So, can you explain to me exactly how this guy Romeo would have been helping Angela? I mean—did they just remove her penis or . . . What exactly happened? Is there any chance he discovered what had happened and went crazy on her?"

James's level of discomfort was so high we might as well have been talking about when he started having nocturnal emissions. I wondered why this discussion was so uncomfortable for him—for most people—but I also knew Angela's confidence and determination had affected my opinion of the discussion. And in the end, it was just medical science after all.

"The surgery was basically a penis inversion. They didn't remove her penis; the only thing they actually removed were her testicles, and they saved the skin from them for the outward things, you know—labia, vulva—to make it pretty, like a girl. They made a cut between what everyone has in the far back and her urethra and inverted the penis to create the vagina."

With James staring at me, I was oversimplifying a bit, but now even I felt uncomfortable. He looked incredulous.

I waited for him to say something, hopefully not too dumb.

"That is unbelievable. I had no idea something like that could happen. Would she be able to enjoy it? Or have kids?"

"Well, yes to kids, but not in the traditional way. Science hasn't gotten as far as uterus transplants yet, but there is hope that will come in the future. Angela planned to use a surrogate for her family. Also, yes, she would technically be able to enjoy it. Before inverting the penis, they use the head to create a clitoris for that purpose."

I have never felt more self-conscious saying the word "clitoris" in my life, but now I felt blood spring to my cheeks. Geez. This was a work colleague. What was wrong with me?

I took a deep breath and continued. It's important James understand this—for Ang's sake. "That is why she hired Romeo to the Rescue—not a person—a company that specialized in deflowering young women with a promise of making their first time good for them too. You may not know this, but most 'first time' experiences are terrible for the woman. We are just faking it to make the man happy. Angela didn't fake anything in her life and didn't plan to start with her sexual experiences."

"And was it? Good for her too?" Although his neck was now crimson, curiosity had gotten the better of him.

"Yes. It was. She got what she paid for. She had a wonderful experience, until she was walking back from the bathroom after cleaning up and overheard the pig—sorry, the *guy*— making crude comments about her on his cell phone, calling her a whale." I felt sad just remembering that conversation. It hurt *me* when people treated Ang badly. "But he definitely did not know she had undergone a gender reassignment surgery."

"Wow, that must have really hurt her." He sounded sincere.

"Well, that shows how little you knew Angela. It didn't hurt her. It just showed her that she had a piece missing in her HEAP, so she got busy filling in the missing piece. Angela was completely comfortable with her size, but she felt that if the first man to see her naked body was disgusted by it, chances were pretty good that other men might be too. So, she systematically attacked the problem like she always did."

"HEAP?"

"Happily Ever After Plan. Maybe I should make a card with that."

Tears clouded my eyes as I wrote it down on a card and put it under Angela's growing tier.

HEAP

Happily Ever After Plan

"And what is TUC?"

"It is the clinical trial that Angela was involved in. I am assuming it is the same trial the other women were involved in as well, although I have no concrete proof of that fact. Angela's contract is the first piece of evidence we've put our hands on." Then I remembered something important. "I completely forgot to ask you—were you able to check out the evidence bags? Do you have the contract and prescription bottle?"

Suddenly, James hung his head sheepishly. "I was dreading having to tell you this," he said. "It appears that the evidence must be misfiled. They were unable to locate it."

My heart leapt in my chest. "Are you serious?" In all the years I'd been with the force, I'd never had a piece of evidence go missing. Not since my assault. And now? Was history repeating itself? I hardly knew what to say.

I was so thankful I had the wherewithal to take photos. They were only of the top copy, but it was something and something was better than no evidence at all. If I hadn't answered the call, there would be nothing now—just like the other victims. I couldn't help but wonder if anyone else had left anything that had magically disappeared too.

"James, do you know if the women from Maine were involved in a clinical trial that was associated with their weight loss?"

"Yes, they all were, but there is no information available on the name of the trial, who ran it, where they checked in. . . . Literally, nothing. And we cannot get any medical information without a subpoena, and we cannot get a subpoena without a legitimate reason for one. Thank God for Angela. She might blow this case open."

I bristled at the seemingly callous comment about thanking God for Angela. After all, she had to die to blow open this case. But then I smiled.

"Yes, she might. She was good like that—always getting to the bottom of things and making them right."

It eased my pain, just a tiny bit, knowing Angela could have a huge impact, even in death. The world thought it would change her, but it couldn't. She was born to change the world . . . just not in the way she had hoped.

Chapter Fifteen

DIVIDE AND CONQUER

Monday, December 5, 2022. 8:00 AM
33 hours 30 minutes after

James and I each had a list. We were going to divide, gather information and reconvene at my house, hopefully later tonight.

Although I had dreaded the extra work I would have when my partner went out on two weeks disability because of his rotator cuff tear—he *had* to be able to effectively shoulder his gun—I was now grateful. The last thing I wanted to do was have to explain my relationship with James to him. O'Malley could get carried away with the teasing sometimes. He was a good guy, a great detective, and he had a lot to teach me; but his nasally Boston accent and constant taunting about me getting blown away by a strong wind got on my nerves sometimes.

James was headed to Maine to meet with each family to dig a little deeper now that he had more information from Angela's crime scene. His goal was to see if there were any additional similarities: did the parents know who ran the trial, where the meetings took place, were there any friends who might have social media posts from before they deleted their accounts, was there any evidence of loss of mental control? When dealing with suicide victim's families, it was important to treat the families with the utmost care and respect. They were already beating themselves up enough blaming themselves for not seeing it coming.

We agreed that his conversation with each set of parents would also include asking if anyone remembered a reference to Romeo to the Rescue. We both knew we couldn't rule out that possibility, especially since Angela had mentioned the creep in her diary. Even though it was a long shot, stranger things had happened. It was just possible that we had a couple of crazies create a company out there targeting a specific type of woman. You see all kinds of whackos in this field of work.

The first thing I had to do was get my butt into the station. My chief had left four messages on my phone since 6 am. Someone had told him I got checked out of the hospital. I prayed that he trusted me enough not to pull me off this case. I felt like I was making steady progress with James, and we were heading in the right direction. On the way there, I returned O'Malley's call. He had also called a few times over the weekend—most likely because he heard I got shot.

"Your momma." Senior Detective Thomas O'Malley answered the phone. I would give a hundred dollars to hear an 'r' come out of this guy's mouth, but he was Boston born and raised and proud of it. For some reason, his poor grammar didn't get under my skin.

"Not my momma. She's six feet under." Our standard greeting---tasteless, but I'd learned that joking with him about this eased the pain somehow.

"What the hell you got yourself into?" He asked.

"What do you mean?" I asked, not wanting to say more then he knew. Turns out he knew everything. How that guy found out everything going on in the precinct while he was out on medical leave of absence was beyond me.

"Angela's dead," I croaked, barely able to say it.

"Yeah, yeah, I heard. You know kid, life happens. And death happens too. There ain't shit you can do about it." This is O'Malley's way of saying how bad he feels that my best friend has died. "My question is, who the fuck shot you? And why?"

"I didn't really get shot, O'Malley. I was only grazed. It's nothing." I tried to move past my shooting so we could focus on what was important: Angela. "The question is, who killed Angela?"

"Aw kid, way I hear it, she killed herself." He sounds sympathetic.

"No, O'Malley. She didn't. I promise you she didn't." I said this with much more volume and force than I intended. "Please, just listen and then you can decide."

I quickly went over the details of the case, leaving the name 'Neely' out of my description of the pharmaceutical company. As I spoke, I noticed a black Escalade keeping a steady pace behind me. The front plate looked like it was from Maine. Maybe they had different laws on tailgating there.

Annoying.

"Any thoughts?" I asked him, hoping he would say no. I really did not want to discuss the case with him. One partner was enough, and I felt like James and I were finally on the same page. My eyes remained trained on the Escalade, still following after a sharp right turn. I knew a tail when I saw one.

"Sounds like a straight up hate crime to me." He said with conviction.

"But we don't know if any of the other victims recently had a gender reassignment surgery," I said firmly.

"Do you know that they didn't? Seems to me that's the first thing you check out. It ain't the kind of thing people advertise; you know what I mean?"

Of course he was right. That should have occurred to me immediately after Angela's death. Maybe I *was* too close to the case. And why didn't James think of that? Maybe because we had each always thought of Angela as a female. It was nearly impossible to consider her any other way. So . . . was *he* too close to *me*? That thought gave me a little thrill that it shouldn't have.

"Thanks O'Malley. I knew you would have all the answers—as usual, wise guy. Now I'll just go blow away."

"See you kid. My wife's giving me a dirty look because I woke her up. Better go take care of that." He cackled.

I ended up feeling glad I checked in with O'Malley. I couldn't allow my ego to be so fragile that I stopped learning from the guys with experience, and O'Malley was one of the best. I was lucky to be placed with him and even more lucky that he cared enough about me to check in with me after he heard I'd been shot.

I took another peek at my rearview mirror. Didn't that clown know I could see him following me?

My next call was to James. I shared O'Malley's theory with him.

"You know, that is definitely something we should check. It is not the type of information a parent would feel the necessity to share about their recently deceased child—especially not one who took their own life. I don't know why I didn't think of that. Wouldn't it be terrible if these were all hate crimes identified through the dark web?"

I shivered when he said it. How exactly had Angela gotten her fake ID? Wasn't the dark web where you bought things like that?

"That's exactly how I felt when he said it. It is on my list now too," I said. "First, I'll check in with the chief, then I'll go by Neely Pharmaceuticals to talk to my dad, and then I'll give a call to the four families and see if I can schedule with them. There are several new questions for us to ask them and these are conversations that should happen in person."

"Couldn't agree more. After I contact each of the families here, I'll see what progress we've made on the dark web connection. Let's update after each family visit and discuss fully at the end of the day."

"Sounds perfect. We'll call in some food," I said without thinking. It was how I would typically handle a day of evidence gathering, but it was presumptive to think he would do the same. We had gotten comfortable quickly.

"How are you doing without any sleep?' he asked.

"It's not the first time. I'm fine," I said, although my eyes burned like fire. "I'm eager to solve this one."

"Sounds good. Talk soon." He ended the call.

I had meant to tell him about the black Escalade before the call ended but I was at the station by then anyhow. What could anyone do to me here?

Chapter Sixteen

CHECKING IN WITH CHIEF

Monday, December 5, 2022. 9:15 AM
34 hours 45 minutes after

"Well, look what the cat dragged in." The chief looked at me intently, as if trying to ascertain that I was fit for duty. This is one time I wished I didn't have my long hair tied back to expose the wound on the side of my head. I also wished I didn't need the gauzy bandage, but unfortunately, head wounds bleed ridiculously. "I'm only gonna ask you this one time Neely and you better give it to me straight. Is that your daddy's company you're going to check out?"

Interesting question. So, at some point, the documents had been at the precinct. Good to know. I wondered if he knew they were currently missing. I could feel the heat rise in my face; grateful he didn't mention my injury. "Well chief, yes and no. It is his company, yes, but (1) we don't know if they are involved in any way and (2) there are many sub departments within the company that my father may not oversee. Theoretically, he may not even know about the things I'm going to check out. There is a board with governing shares that makes decisions too."

"Yeah, yeah, yeah. And my father was Abraham Lincoln," he said, disbelief dripping from every word. "You get one chance to check this out. If your daddy is involved, you let me know asap and you get assigned to a different case—got it? No funny business here."

"Of course, Chief." And I meant that too. The last thing I wanted was to prosecute my own father for murder. No matter how absent he had been from my life, he had never done anything to harm me. He seemed kind of a sad man, to be honest. And Angela liked him. He got points for that.

"I know this girl was your friend, and you shouldn't even be on the case, but since we've got ID that says she ain't who she is, I can buy you some time," he said.

I could feel my eyebrows shoot up in surprise before I could stop them.

"What, you think I got this job just because I got a pretty face?" He shakes his head, amused at himself. The Chief must be pushing 60 but you can tell he has always had a "pretty face." He's still got a thick head of dark hair graying at the temples, slate blue eyes the color of a stormy sky that tip down slightly at the corners, and a cleft in his chin. His overall appearance has always reminded me of Russel Crowe.

"You've got 48 hours to convince me that she wasn't the fifth suicide victim, you got it? We got all the evidence we need to close this case up already. I'm extending this courtesy to *you*, not your daddy, because *you* earned it. You gotta show me something solid." Done talking to me, the chief shrugged his shoulders, waiting for me to leave the room.

"Thank you Chief." If there was one thing I'd learned since joining the department, it was that a little respect went a long way. Each member of the force put in long hours and put themselves in harm's way every single day. The simplest call could turn ugly on a dime. That scrawny guy who seemed harmless, verbally harassing people on the street might have a big knife or gun in his baggy jeans. Not only did they earn the respect, but they deserved it.

"Chief, could I just ask you one more thing?" I knew I was pushing it. He had already done me a huge favor and I should have just walked out the door. But I had the feeling that he was one person who might give me an honest answer to a question I'd been wondering about for most of my life. Chief was a straight shooter.

"What is it now, Neely?" He looked exasperated. He was making a point of looking every which way except at the gauze on my head. I could only assume the doctor had written a full release.

"Chief, why does everyone act differently when my father's name is mentioned? Here, the hospital . . . pretty much everyone acts like he is someone special. And he's not." I knew that sounded a little bit like a spoiled kid, but I was just stating the truth.

Chief rubbed his thumb and forefinger together. "Money talks kid. You ever look at the donor list on the annual newsletter? Let's just say your daddy is a very generous man."

"Is that how I got this job?" The question came out before I even knew I was thinking about it.

"It didn't hurt you none when it came down to the final list, but you earned your position fair and square with good police work."

I needed to hear that. "Thanks Chief. I won't let you down." I excused myself and headed out of the building, scanning the street for the black Escalade. It was nowhere in sight. I knew I did not imagine that I had been followed to the precinct. Ill at ease, I wondered why it had followed me and where it had gone.

For now, I needed to focus on Neely Pharmaceuticals, a place I had rarely visited in my lifetime, a place that had provided me with a bountiful physical life and an empty emotional one. Mentally, I went through a list of questions I needed to ask of my father. But I guess the first question was would he even let me in his office to talk with him.

Chapter Seventeen

MARCUS DANIEL NEELY

Monday, December 5, 2022. 10:30 AM
47 hours left

The guard at the gate seemed to know me, but I'd almost swear I'd never seen him before in my life. If he didn't know me, he had been well trained to expeditiously cross reference visitors to the family members. I chose to take it as a positive sign. Maybe my father was looking forward to seeing me and had notified him. A girl could hope.

The numerous levels of security it took to get inside of the facility made me feel good too. It *should* be that hard to get inside of a facility that made and distributed drugs. A bit of pride swelled in my chest. This was my family's business.

By the time I'd reached my father's office, I was mentally giving myself a slap, wondering how I could think that my father, apparent pillar of the community and loved by all, could be involved in anything homicidal.

"Good afternoon, Daniela. How can I help you today?"

He didn't act like it was the slightest bit strange for me to show up for a visit after, you know, my whole life. My chest constricted as I hoped he would comment on my hospital visit. But he only continued to meet my gaze levelly, not even tempted to glance at the gauze. My chief had a harder time averting his eyes.

Marcus Daniel Neely. My father. He really was an impressive looking man. He was incredibly tall—although I'd never even wondered how tall really, I would now guess he stood at least 6 foot 5 inches because he was well over a foot taller than me. He had sharp green eyes that seemed to pierce right through me. I imagined that if I held two fingers behind my head and said, "How many?" he would be able to guess accurately. His full head of hair still boasted quite a bit of a rust color that reminded me of a summer sunset beside his whitened temples. It was no wonder people held him in such awe—his very appearance demanded it.

I couldn't imagine what genetic mutation caused my coloring and stature. The few photos I had seen of my mother had shown a tall, blonde lady with blue eyes. I'd learned in bio class that there was a 1% chance of me popping out with these big brown eyes. I seemed to defy nature . . . But I couldn't go down that rabbit hole today. I felt like enough of a failure for not being born a boy, and there was no room for self-deprecating thoughts on this case. Angela needed my head focused on her, not me.

"Hey dad. Thanks for seeing me on such short notice. I really appreciate it." My voice was quivering. I laughed.

"My God Daniela, you and that laugh. What are you nervous about today?"

Well, at least he knew me well enough to understand that weird quirk. My shoulders relaxed a little.

"Dad, I need to talk to you about some clinical trials that took place at Neely Pharmaceuticals."

"Daniela, I believe you know that I cannot discuss the work we do here. All trials are confidential." The deep frown on his face also held disappointment, as if I were a child asking to stay up past my bedtime on a school night.

"Dad, I am here out of respect for you and in my official capacity as a detective. There are five young women who participated in a weight loss clinical trial who are now dead. The fifth victim, who was found two days ago, left a copy of the contract sitting on her bedside stand. The trial is apparently being run by Neely Pharmaceuticals." I watched him closely as that information sank in.

Either he had an exceptional poker face, or he genuinely did not know what I was talking about. "Daniela, I assure you that no such clinical trial is taking place here. I would have immediately been notified of any mortality rate on any trials."

"Are you in charge of all clinical trials? The person who would be notified of any problems?" I knew this, at least, was a question he could answer.

"I facilitate all trials," he replied evenly.

"Meaning?" I ask.

"Meaning exactly what I said."

Here was the man I grew up with. He was unbending in his ways. There was one explanation and one only. If I didn't like it or understand it, that was not his problem in any way. Angela had suggested to me several times that my father had Asperger's Syndrome. I looked at him now and considered that possibility. If he did have a disability that he had no control over and I was holding it against him, that made me a terrible person. But I just didn't see it. I decided to try a different tact.

"Dad, do you believe that Angela—my friend Angela—is a person of integrity?" As much as I hated to betray Angela's deceitful methods to get into the trial, I couldn't see any other choice.

"Of course. Angela is a person of the highest integrity. And she is also an excellent baker. I very much enjoy her raisin scones. I send my assistant out for them every Tuesday."

This news momentarily stunned me. I couldn't picture my dad eating something as delicious as a raisin scone. I could better imagine him eating, say, cardboard? Goodness. I really did not know the man at all. Or maybe I was just unable to see him as a person—a person who might enjoy scones.

"Dad, Angela left an entry in her diary outlining her participation in a clinical trial through Neely Pharmaceuticals. Does that ring a bell?"

My dad shook his head and looked at me disapprovingly. "Daniela, I am sure I raised you better than to read another person's diary. Why would you do such a despicable thing? Please give it back to her at once."

"Dad, no offense, but you didn't do much of the raising. That was Margette's job." The insult came out before I could restrain myself.

"Remember? But yes, you are right—*she* did raise me better than that and I wouldn't have read it except for the fact that Angela is dead."

I let the words sink into him and then into the room. The silence seemed to last forever.

"Dad?"

"That's impossible. I'm sure I would have heard if something had happened to Angela." He staunchly refused to believe me. As if I would make up something so heinous.

"Yes, you probably would have Dad. She is currently being called Angel Adams by the media and I'm sure you've heard of that death—the 5th Virgin Suicide?"

"But why would they call Angela, Angel Adams?" He still looked disbelieving, but I knew he was putting together the name Angel with the name of Angela's bakery.

Drawing in a deep breath, I laid it out for him, not allowing him to interject until I was finished. "She got a fake ID with that name on it. She was too old for the trial, so she faked her age and name."

I knew I had to tell him the rest. It was so odd that my own father didn't know after all the years Ang had been my best friend, that she used to be male, but then again, he wouldn't even know if I had changed my gender.

"Angela was born Adam Monn. She was born into a boy's body. From the time she was very little, she knew she was supposed to be a girl. Her mother supported her and loved her. She never cared whether Adam was a boy or girl. She just called him her little Angel. When Adam began to wear dresses all of the time, his father became very angry, saying his mother was creating a freak. He said she was mentally ill. He divorced Mrs. Monn and moved to Canada. When he left, Adam asked his mom to call him Angela because it was so close to Angel, the name she had always called him. Angela's dad has a new family now, a typical family where everyone is the gender they were born into."

Now that I had gotten through the hardest part, I paused. The silence in the room was deafening. My dad sat at his desk with his fingers steepled onto his forehead, as if in deep concentration, probably wondering how he had missed it, like I once had.

"Go on."

"In school, some of the kids remembered when Angela was a boy, and they called her monstrosity. You remember her last name was Monn."

"Yes, I remember," he said.

"Well, we never really talked much when we were little because you know, I was kind of a freak too. Everyone called me a boy."

His head jerked up. "They did? Why would they call you a boy?"

"Dad, seriously?" He looked genuinely shocked. Now I know why Angela always called him the mad scientist. Or maybe men just didn't notice things like that about their children.

Shaking my head, I continued. "Anyhow, when I started high school, she helped me when the 6-Pack assaulted me."

"Daniela! What are you speaking of?" He reared back, red faced, so quickly, that for a moment I feared his gorgeous leather chair might topple backwards with him in it.

"Come on Dad. You remember. When I was a freshman in high school?" After all these years, we were finally going to discuss it. Why he had let me down. How he had let me down. I wondered if he would cut off the conversation like always.

"I assure you that I have no knowledge of any assault by a '6-Pack.'"

I continued, my heart pounding so loud now I was sure he could see it through my blue polo. "Jeremy Richards and the other five boys who were part of the VITAL project, held me down, and Jeremy stripped off my clothes. He—"

My father stood up so quickly that the chair spun out of control and crashed into the full panel of windows lining the wall.

"You didn't tell me," he accused. He was staring so intently at me his eyes seemed to be shooting sparks. I never noticed before how beautiful they were.

I felt my eyes widen at his response. "Didn't the police tell you? Didn't Margette tell you?"

"No!" He said that single word with such vehemence it echoed through the room.

"Sit down dad. It is past. It *happened*. I *survived.*" My shoulders slumped. How could he not know? Didn't Margette have to tell him? I sighed. "Anyhow, we're not here to talk about me. I'm here to figure out what happened to these young women." I continued. "Angela completed her gender reassignment surgery last year and then decided to lose weight so she would have a better chance of meeting someone to complete her plans for her future."

He sat back down, almost immediately calm, nodding his head. "Yes, I recall Angela's reduction. She did a very nice job."

I was amazed at how quickly his demeanor could change and that he made no comment about Angela's sex reassignment surgery. I had fully expected him to grill me on it. Even if he was a killer, he was not a bigot. That singular fact made me like him more.

I remembered her diary entries about his comments. She always took his awkwardness all in stride. "Yes, well, she lost that weight through a program here at Neely. Well, not actually here at Neely, but the contracts had the Neely Pharmaceuticals logo on them." It felt like it took me a long time to get the story out.

"Well, I'm afraid that is impossible, Daniela. We are not involved in any clinical trials for weight loss at Neely. *That*, I can tell you."

"Dad, Angela was an incredibly detailed person. She would not make a mistake about something like that."

"I'm afraid she has," he said with certainty.

"No Dad, she hasn't. It is something called the TUC program."

I saw a look flash across his face—a look of recognition—when I said the TUC program, but he quickly made his expression neutral again. He was very good at it.

"Daniela, I cannot help you today. Thank you for the visit."

"Dad, this was not a social call. This is an investigation, and if you don't willingly cooperate, you know what happens next. They take me off the case and come in heavy." I was so frustrated. I could see that he recognized the name TUC. "Please, just look at this photograph."

He leaned closer and looked at the close up of the contract that I showed him with Neely Pharmaceuticals across the bottom. I heard him draw in his breath quickly.

"Can you please show me the entirety of that contract?" He asked.

"Actually, not yet. It is still in the evidence locker," I lied, not wanting to tell him it had been 'misplaced.' "We are investigating Angela's death as a homicide right now."

"As you should be," he said. "Please, show me the smaller version of the page."

I pulled the photo back up for him and he read aloud, "Lily Legacy. Yes. Of course. I should have known." I heard something that sounded like disgust in his voice. I'd never heard him express that kind of emotion before.

"Dad?" I wasn't sure what was happening, but it appeared that he had put something together, and I knew that I needed to know what that something was.

"Daniela, I will say one thing and one thing only: the TUC program is not a weight loss program. TUC, Thalamus Under Control, is a Department of Defense program. You've received bad information. Now, I've already said more than I should, so . . ."

He suddenly rose and strode around his desk. For one brief moment, I thought he might hug me. My heart raced. *Do it!* my whole body screamed. *Tell me you love me, and you are so sorry you never showed me that you loved me! Say you're happy I'm okay!*

But a lifetime of distance stood between us. Instead, he nodded and walked out of the room.

I walked around his desk, repositioned his enormous black leather chair, and sat down in his pristine office. Pressing my feet down hard, I pushed off, spinning around and around in his chair, pretending for one second, that I was his little girl who came to play at the office. The chair came to a stop facing his credenza. I found myself staring at a folding frame that held five 5 x 7 photos. I sat up straighter when I realized all the photos were of me. Me holding a first-place gymnastics medal out from my chest, me in a red and black cap and gown graduating high school, me in a maroon and gold cap and gown graduating college, me in full BPD attire being sworn in as an officer, and me shaking the BPD police commissioner's hand the day I became detective. The frame created a deep ache in my chest, a feeling I didn't have time or energy to analyze right now.

I closed my eyes against the feeling, tap, tap, tapping my toes in a sideways motion, rotating the chair toward the wall of glass and opened them to the wintry New England coastline. *What a view* I thought. *I could avoid my family every day in an office like this too*. Then, with a sinking sensation, I realized what I was really looking at: wintry clouds. Very heavy looking snow clouds. I hadn't had my TV or car radio on in days; my mind had been so caught up in the case. Suddenly I was worried about the forecast, remembering that James Hawthorne had driven to Maine this morning.

Chapter Eighteen

A MOTHER'S HEART

Monday, December 5, 2022. 12:00 PM
45.5 hours left

Hastily, I left my father's office and was relieved that the Escalade was still nowhere to be seen. I couldn't shake how closely it had followed me earlier. It had felt like a tail. Maybe it was my mind working overtime because I'd been shot. As hard as I was trying to push that fact from my mind—to put Angela first—it was ever present, nagging at me. Especially since I had no way of knowing if it was mere coincidence that it happened when I was viewing Angela's body—if it was tied to Angela's murder—or if someone had followed me there with no awareness of Angela whatsoever.

Maybe someone in a black Escalade with Maine plates. When I was working a case, I became completely oblivious to everything else around me. That single mindedness and the way I shut everything else out could be why my best friend now lay dead in the city morgue. Had I missed signs? I would never know.

Looking at the ominous sky, I decided to head straight for Mrs. Monn's house. That was one visit that I wouldn't put off. I knew she was suffering terribly, thinking her daughter had taken her life. The information I planned to share, that we were now considering Angela's death a possible homicide, would ease her pain, at least a little.

As I pulled up to Angela's childhood home, I was reminded of the first time I came here. Her neighborhood was what people in my part of town called a "fringe" neighborhood. Although I didn't fully understand that as a teenager, I could more accurately see it as an adult, especially as a cop. Her home sat on the outskirts of an area that was known for some suspicious activity, not an outright bad neighborhood, but not far from some bad things going on. There was a bail bondsman down the street along with a laundromat where I now knew drugs were trafficked.

I knocked, thinking that if Ang were alive, I would've walked right in. Life had already changed.

"Oh hello Dan. You know you don't need to knock." She embraced me warmly, as if I were her own child, not the one who had days earlier given her the worst news of her lifetime. Even though Angela's time on this earth was so short, she was so lucky to have such a wonderful mom.

"Hello Mrs. Monn."

Angela's mom had often insisted I call her Peggy, but my father forbade the impropriety. I was too scared he wouldn't allow me to go to Angela's house if he heard I was calling her mom by her first name. After so many years, "Mrs. Monn" felt as familiar to me as calling her by her first name. It was too late to change now.

"Could I come in?"

I fully embraced her. There were few people I felt comfortable doing that with. Now she would be the closest thing to Angela that I had, and she was always the closest thing to a mom that I had.

"Of course, dear. You are always welcome." She opened the door widely, then asked. "How is your head sweetheart? Any lingering pain or dizziness?"

"Nothing," I said dismissively. I had to get the attention away from me. I was not the important one here.

Despite the location, I have always loved the Monn home. It was so different from my own. It felt instantly welcoming. Mrs. Monn decorated in warm colors. Her house was full of reds, oranges, and yellows. And nothing felt too nice to sit on or put your feet up on. I could see how growing up in a house like that would make you feel happy every day.

"Could we sit down and talk?"

My heart was pounding so hard, I was sure she could see the buttons jumping on my light blue polo. I clutched the recipe books I'd brought to return close to my chest.

"Come in, come in." She ushered me through warmly. "I'll bet you haven't had lunch yet, have you?"

Although I had not eaten, food was the last thing on my mind with the deadline looming large, but I knew it would make her happy and my body did require nutrition.

"You're right. I have not had lunch." I smiled brightly at her.

"Go on into the family room. I'll make us some lunch and tea." Mrs. Monn always made a pot of tea. It was the cure all for everything in life, except, obviously, an overdose of Zanacan.

Relaxing, I noticed the older journals sitting out and began to thumb through them. What a gift to Mrs. Monn while she mourned her daughter. Angela was so good at pouring out her heart. I smiled as I read her first ever recipe: cherry tarts. She pressed her thumb in the middle of a biscuit and put cherry pie filling in the middle and baked it. She was five years old: so creative and sweet.

Then I read an entry that brought me to tears. It was written on September 3, 2013.

I met a girl today. A girl who I think might become my friend!! I've always wanted a friend—a real live friend who could talk back to me. Being with her made me feel stronger and smart. Prouder of who I am. And really proud of my mom.

This girl is kind of a mess. She is more lost and confused about being a girl than I can ever remember feeling. I've seen her around before, but we've never talked. It's not because I didn't like her or she didn't like me—it's just that neither one of us ever really bothered, like we each accepted we wouldn't have friends in school for some stupid reason.

This girl is super rich, but she is also really unhappy. I'm not sure she has anyone who really loves her.

At least I got the impression she didn't think she did. I know she doesn't have a mom—hers died when she was born. God, I wouldn't trade my mom for any amount of money in the world. She doesn't really have any of the amazing things I have. Gosh—it made me realize how lucky I am. When we tried to call her dad, we only got her nanny. Apparently, her dad is too busy and his job is too important to be bothered by his daughter. I know how that one feels, for sure! Well, my dad didn't necessarily think his job was more important than his daughter—he just refused to have a daughter. I'm not sure which is worse. Anyhow, her nanny was kind of strange and offered to pay my mom for helping. I don't know if it is because we look poor or because her dad said to, but it hurt my mom's feelings so her nanny is not one of my favorite people. It was all so weird.

Well, the whole story was so weird really. I stayed late to help organize the art room supplies because of course; I was the only volunteer. The art teacher had a baby over the summer so her boxes were still all over the place. My mom would've done the same thing—spend time with your baby instead of putting work first. (Of course that just makes me love my art teacher even more!)

I think most of the kids take art just for an easy A in high school, not because they care about it. But I care about all things artistic. I have to. Someday, I'm going to make some insanely beautiful cakes and pastries. It's all part of my plan . . . as you know! HEAP!! (Sorry about all the exclamation marks—I'm so excited! I have a friend! Ugh! I keep getting ahead of the story!)

I was just about to leave when I saw a half-naked girl running across the back field toward the building. No kidding. She didn't have any pants on at all. And she looked scared. Really scared. I could see a boy running after her, but she was a lot quicker than him.

I started moving toward the doors just as she hit them hard. Of course they were locked—it was after school hours—so I pressed the bar to let her in and she literally fell inside the building.

I dropped my backpack on her skinny little bare butt—it totally covered it. I mean, this girl is skinny. Not like me. I'm probably about three times as big as her—yes, I've eaten every recipe I've written in this book and loved every single one of them. You won't be laughing when I open my bakery someday! Nobody will!! But back to my story . . .

She said some senior boys were after her. I almost rolled my eyes at her since that was pretty obvious. What wasn't obvious was why. It was hard to imagine senior boys going after her. She wasn't exactly a head turner—as a matter of fact, she probably looked more like a boy than I ever did, albeit a cute one. How's that for ironic? (Please note that I did not use the word 'coincidence'—summer school English class paid off!)

Then she said it was the 6-Pack—that she had outsmarted one of them in Chem class by accident and he wanted payback. Before she even said his name, I knew it would be Jeremy Richards. It had to be. He is an evil boy. I knew this from my own past experience. And I was right.

I didn't ask any more questions; I just tore down the 'welcome back students' banner and wrapped it around her and we went looking for a teacher to help. At that point, I still didn't know we would be friends. I thought I was just helping someone in trouble because my mom taught me to always help people less fortunate than me. I'd say 'no pants' definitely made her less fortunate. But when we finally found a teacher (the teachers cleared out faster than the students on the first day—do they even like us?) who could help and he offered to call Daniela's mother (that's her name–I like it; it's kind of a mouthful and my tongue trips over it a little bit, but I think I'll get used to it), she said she didn't have a mother and started crying, I knew we were meant to be. I mean, who better for someone like her than my mom, right? My mom's love was always big enough for me—it never faltered, not even once from the time I first told her I was not a boy.

She never said, "Don't be silly, of course you are a boy." She just asked me questions about how I felt, and we went from there. I always knew she believed me–that she believed in me. My mom was exactly what Daniela needed too. So, I called her, and she picked us up and took care of Daniela like I knew she would.

I quickly wiped away my tears when I heard Mrs. Monn approaching, but the sympathetic look she gave me said volumes. The chicken salad on a croissant was delicious, and I wolfed it down like I hadn't eaten in a week. Once we had settled in with our tea and had gone though some strained small talk about some minor details, I told her I needed to ask her some additional questions so we could get to the bottom of Angela's death, which we no longer believed was a suicide.

"Oh!" Her hand flew to her mouth. Tears began to stream down her face. "I knew my girl wouldn't kill herself. Not after she worked so hard. She was happy."

"I know she was very happy too, Mrs. Monn. I want you to know that the questions I am about to ask are not necessarily tied to the case; they are just me double checking every possible link, okay?" The last thing I wanted was for Mrs. Monn to think my dad or the Richards were involved in Angela's murder.

"Yes, I understand, Dan," she reassured me. "I watch Forensic Files all the time. I know how this works."

That comment made me smile. I wished things were as cut and dry as they made them appear to be on TV. Solving cases would be so much easier.

"Do you remember right after our freshman year of high school? When Jeremy Richards' twin sister came over to play games with us?"

Mrs. Monn sat back quickly in her chair. "Why, of course I do, Dan. I am still in touch with Jessica. She has remained a friend. I can't imagine what she has to do with my girl's death."

I was afraid of that reaction. "I'm not insinuating she has anything to do with Angela's death. I was just hoping you could answer a couple of questions about her."

She visibly relaxed. "Of course, Dan. Anything you need to find Angela's . . . well, to help solve the circumstances . . ." She stopped.

She, like me, was unable to say the words. I understood. It made it too final.

More delicately, I probed, "Do you remember any more details about what happened with Jessica that summer? I mean, did she ever get her college money back or anything?"

Her lips were pursed as she nodded her head. "Yes, she did get her college money back and she did start college, but it was a semester late." Then she let out a deep sigh. "It was such a tragedy the way it all unfolded."

My interest was instantly piqued. "What was a tragedy?" There were a few things she could be referring to.

"Well, I have always tried to respect the privacy of others, but if you feel this information could help you find Angela's killer . . ." She winced as she said the words before she continued.

"Please," I said. "You never know what little tidbit of information might lead us in a direction that tells us something important."

Nodding, she began. "Mr. Richards would not budge about giving back the money. I never knew him to be a very kind person and that certainly reinforced my opinion of him." She didn't mention the terrible thing he and his son had said about Angela as a small child. "But Mrs. Richards contacted Jessica constantly once she had her number. She seemed happier than I'd ever known her to be. The two of them got together frequently for a while." I saw a sad look pass over her face. "Darlene was finally happy for a few months. Poor woman. She deserved it."

"Why only for a while?"

"Well, Dar—, Mrs. Richards could not convince her husband to return the money to Jessica. And I think she felt like she had to make up for what she did—giving her away, you know?"

I started to get a feeling for where this conversation was headed.

"She had completely stopped drinking—went through a 30-day rehab program and everything. And she reassured Jessica that she would make sure she got the money for her college— told her to ask for a delayed entry, which Jessica got with no problem. That girl is smart as a whip."

The way she kept pursing her lips told me that bad news was coming.

"I think she wanted to do two things: spend some quality time with her daughter and make sure nobody would question her mental capacity to change the terms of her will."

There it was—what I knew was coming.

"Mrs. Richards brought the money into the marriage, which is probably why Mr. Richards didn't divorce her all of those years she was a drunken embarrassment. But over the years when she was drinking heavily, he took complete control over the money and invested it in his name only.

Also, while she was alive, she couldn't do anything to the terms of the adoption proceedings. But dead was a different story. Nobody had control over her will. So, she put a clause into her will providing an equal share of her assets should go to her birth daughter, Jessica May Abernathy, upon her death. She said that anyone who contested it would be cut out of the will."

Mrs. Richards was a good person. Mrs. Richards was a good mother who had been forced to give her baby girl away and it had ruined her life. But who had forced her? Her husband? My father? And why? I still did not understand the *why*.

"Mrs. Richards took her life so Jessica could have her money back—have a good life." I surmised.

"Yes," Mrs. Monn admitted.

"Did Jeremy know?" I asked.

"Oh yes, the boy knew. He came to the café and threatened me."

My heart began to hammer in my chest. Why was this the first I was hearing of this?

"Threatened you how? Why didn't you tell me? I'm a police officer!"

Mrs. Monn placed a soothing hand on my shoulder. Dan, you weren't a police officer then, dear. You were a 16-year-old girl who had also been threatened by Jeremy Richards."

I let the truth of her words sink in.

"Besides, what could he do to me? An 18-year-old boy saying he would make me pay someday and actually having the ability to do so are two different things, you know? I understood it was his grief talking." She had taken the high road and allowed Jeremy to express his grief, a typically kind reaction from her.

But had he taken the high road? Or lain in wait? I remembered Sofie telling me about the bakery order for Jeremy. I had to follow up with her on that.

"That whole story is a great tragedy. I'm so sorry for Jessica—and for Jeremy." I decided to move on. "Do you remember anything Ang may have discussed with you recently that concerned you? Maybe a new boyfriend? Maybe one named Jeremy?"

"Well," she said, "she did tell me about a man named Sam who she met running—can you believe my Angela became a runner?"

Yes, I remembered reading that too. It was on my list to locate this Sam and see if he was the kind of guy who could put my friend to sleep permanently. Angela had gotten so lax with her entries in the end. I guess there came a point in time when you just lived them and jotted them down out of sheer happiness.

"Can you think of anything else?" I asked. "Did she ever mention a Joaquin or Romeo to the Rescue?" Angela and her mom talked frequently. I thought of the last message she'd left on my phone. "You're spending more time with the dead than the living again, Dan!" Oh, how I wish I could go back in time and change that.

A look of pure disgust twisted Mrs. Monn's delicate features. "That snake? No, she only saw him the once. That was enough."

Then she cocked her head to the side, as if contemplating a problem. "Well, I doubt that this has anything to do with what happened, but she did say she felt like she was 'out of control,' and for Angela, that was a big deal. You know what a planner she was."

Mrs. Monn had Angela's favorite pink blanket wrapped in her arms, twisting it as she spoke.

Her tea remained untouched on the coffee table, no longer steaming. Unconsciously, she raised the blanket to her face and inhaled. The gesture made my throat thicken with tears. I wanted to inhale Angela's scent from that blanket too.

Blinking rapidly and clearing my throat, I put my detective hat back on as best I could. "Did she say why she felt out of control?" I probed.

"Well, she had a few experiences during her last weeks—you remember one of them, she told us about it at Thanksgiving after your dad left—and she just didn't feel like she was in control of her own thoughts and actions."

Shaking her head, Mrs. Monn lowered her face into the blanket, and I knew she was thinking she should have done something more. I knew that because I felt the same way.

"We'll figure this out. I promise."

Although I wasn't supposed to make promises to the victims' families, this victim's family was my family too and I knew I would keep this promise or die trying. I moved beside her and put my arms around her, at last catching a little of Angela's scent from the blanket and my tears flowed with hers.

The first thing I planned to do was haul ass back to my dad's office. This time, he was notgoing to treat me like his little girl. This time, Detective Dan Neely was going to get some answers.

Chapter Nineteen

THE HEARTLESS

Monday, December 5, 2022. 2:30 PM

43 hours left

The same guard asked for my identification this time. All the "feel good" thoughts from before vanished in an instant. He had been advised to expect me previously with a photograph. Nothing more. No doubt I wasn't the only one that slick procedure had impressed. Bravo, dad. 25 years old and still looking for something "real" from my father.

The cute young lady at the lower-level desk informed me brightly, "a few staff members have gone home for the day. Early release from schools. Nor'easter headed this way, you know."

I pressed my lips together, feigning a smile I knew did not reach my eyes.

"I'll walk you up myself," she said, kindly ignoring my fake pleasantry.

"Thank you," I responded. This time offering her a real smile. It wasn't her fault I had to question my father about his involvement in my friend's death. Cap's words came back to me. He meant it. If my dad or his company was involved in any way, I would be removed from the case immediately.

She carried on a steady stream of chatter on the elevator and as we passed through the security stations. My mind was busy putting together all the pieces of the case that I knew about so far. I caught the word 'detective' at the end of her sentence with a questioning uptake. I knew she had asked a question but had no idea what she had asked.

"Oh, I—" I began.

"It's okay. You're just like your dad," she said.

She smiled when she said it, and I sensed no malice in her words but, nonetheless, I felt as though I'd been slapped. I was just like my dad. Not an aspiration of mine, but I suppose it was inevitable.

She gave two sharp raps on his door before opening it and stepping aside to allow me to pass through, pulling the door closed behind me.

"Dad? I have . . ." The words died in my throat, bewildered at the scene before me. My staunch father was reclining in his chair, shoes off, socked feet crossed on his desk. With the bank of windows behind him displaying the magnificent New England countryside, he looked the epitome of a relaxed man. I blinked, unable to believe it was him.

On his desk, he had a less than half-filled decanter of a golden liquid sitting beside a nearly empty, beautifully chiseled crystal glass, and as I watched, he removed the lid from the decanter and refilled the glass all the way to the top of the letter N etched into the side. I listened to the liquid softly crackle over the ice cubes. I wondered briefly where ice cubes had come from, then observed a silver bucket sitting on the credenza. Was this a typical thing to have sitting in your office? It was new to me, but then again, detectives didn't have offices like pharmaceuticals magnates.

This was a side of my father I had never seen—would not have believed existed. It hurt that I was only now starting to know him. But whose fault was that? His or mine? After all, my visit earlier in the day was my first. Angela had been after me to give him more of a chance for years.

I drew in a deep breath and exhaled slowly, determined to have a different type of meeting than the one we'd had a few hours earlier. "Dad," I said firmly. "It has become apparent to me that Neely Pharmaceuticals was involved in the clinical trial that Angela was participating in at the time of her death. I'm going to need detailed information on that trial."

"Daniela, there are things we do know and things we don't know," he began. As he spoke, he swirled the golden liquid slowly before raising the glass to his lips and draining it in a single tilt. "Sometimes, the things we don't know end up hurting us more than the things we do know—you know?" He chuckled softly when he said this line, although there was no humor in his face. This was very clearly not his first refill.

"Dad, you're not making a lot of sense. Can you just give me information on your TUC trials please?" I asked. I wanted to be exasperated with him, but there was something so vulnerable about him at that moment, I just couldn't summon up any anger. All my life, I had dreamed that he had a softer side. Apparently, he did. It lay at the bottom of a bottle of bourbon.

He chuckled again. "That's just it, Daniela. They are not *my* TUC trials. They were Lillian's. The whole project was hers. The VITAL project was her baby."

Now I strongly suspected he was outright drunk. Was he talking about *my mother?* She didn't work for Neely Pharmaceuticals. She was a patent attorney.

"Dad, are you talking about Lillian my mother? I think maybe you are confused. Do you need a ride home? We could talk about this tomorrow." Maybe he loved Angela more than I realized. I'd never seen him this undone before. "I know you've had a long day and Angela's death must have been a shock to you too."

"Daniela, there are some things about your mother that you don't know. Maybe I was wrong to protect you from the truth." He pulled the top from the decanter again and refilled his glass. "I would ask if you'd like a glass, but I know you can't drink on the job."

So, he wasn't drunk. He had the wherewithal to know I couldn't drink while on duty. I sat down and listened more intently to what he was saying.

"What truth are you talking about, dad?" I asked. Since we had never really had a "real" conversation that I could ever remember, I was pretty sure he had had no opportunity to impart any fatherly truths to me.

He watched the liquid swirl as he rotated the glass in his hand, seemingly mesmerized. I wondered if he had forgotten we were talking.

"Dad?"

He threw back the glass of bourbon all at once and sat forward suddenly, his green eyes blazing into mine. "When I found the ledger, I knew she was a monster. What kind of woman could kill her own babies because they were the wrong sex?" He poured again, rapidly. The ice was gone, and the bourbon went down quickly in a single draw.

"Who are you talking about? What are you talking about?" It seemed fair to assume that he was drunk now. But still, curiosity nagged at me. What secrets had he been hiding from me? Could there be a nugget of truth in his drunken deluge? Surely, he wasn't still talking about my mother?

"But what she did to you was even worse. Poor little Daniela. I thought your grandmother would take care of you. Would love you. But those terrible boys . . ." He put his face in his hands now, shaking his head. "I wasn't there for you."

My throat went dry. I was torn between the desire to comfort him and shake him. I both wanted to know more and didn't want him to say another word. He was saying crazy things. I didn't have a grandmother. Both my parents' parents were dead by the time I was born. My father had been a surprise baby, born to a 53-year-old mother. His parents each lived long lives but had passed years before my birth. My mother's parents had both died in a house fire when she was 19 and she had inherited a substantial fortune from them. These were things I had heard from Margette many times, a recitation of my family history. The things he was saying now were making me hyperventilate.

I worked hard to gain control of my breathing. In, two, three, four . . . out, two, three, four. I repeated this in my head until I felt in control.

I decided to throw him a bone. He was in no state of mind to continue this conversation or provide me with any information that would be useful to the case. "Dad, I always knew you were working hard to provide for me," I said. This was something I had told myself in my adult years. "You can't be two places at once. I understood. That's why I had Margette."

"But I wasn't. And she was. And you didn't," he proclaimed miserably.

Oh wow, this was quickly becoming an incoherent conversation. "Dad, I'm going to take you home now," I said, walking around his desk and taking hold of his arm. "Let's put your shoes on, shall we?"

To my dismay, my father began to cry. Fathers don't cry. Daughters don't even cry. I didn't know what to do, so I just kept on working. I picked up his shoes and put them on, one at a time. Of course they were Bostonians. He could afford any shoe he wanted, but these were his favorites, no doubt influencing my own love of Clarks.

I grabbed his overcoat from the closet and demanded, "Stand up dad." He stood. While I proceeded to thread his long arms into the enormous coat, he looked down at me, an occasional silent tear landing on my hand.

"I didn't know. I swear to you Daniela." The broken look on his face told me that he was saying a truth, whether it was a drunken imaginary truth or not. "I didn't know until I found the journal and then it was too late."

"It's okay dad," I assured him, not sure of what I was reassuring him. What journal? "I turned out okay, don't you think?" I flashed him my brightest smile. I've been told I have a smile that lights up a room. The only problem is that I only turn that light on a couple of times a year. I just can't find much to smile about.

I led my father passively through the security checkpoints and outside to the Beast. As we walked, I didn't try to engage him in conversation, concerned at what may come out of his mouth. I didn't think he deserved to be embarrassed at work. I was surprised by how defensive —how protective—I felt of him. It made me wonder if I loved him. I'd always assumed I didn't—that we didn't love each other. Maybe there were different kinds of love and I'd been searching for an ideal that didn't exist.

After I had my father safely buckled into my vehicle, I quickly checked my cell. One message from James. I knew this was neither the time nor place to pick it up, although I desperately wanted to. I felt surprised by how quickly I was beginning to count on James.

"Dad, do you want me to take you home or to your apartment?" I asked him. I'd never seen his apartment, only heard that he had purchased one close to work.

"I can't risk running into her. I'm too angry. Take me to my apartment," he said.

"Okay. No problem. What's the address?" I asked. Wait. "Running into whom? Margette went back to Ecuador Dad, remember?"

I didn't realize there had been bad blood between him and Margette. Maybe that's why she left so abruptly, and I never heard from her again. Maybe it wasn't me. Maybe it was him.

"Dad, you didn't short Margette on her pay, did you? She always did her job." I was concerned now, even though my concern was probably eight years too late.

He shook his head, leaning back against the seat and closing his eyes.

"Margette always got what she was promised. Everyone in her family did. Do you think it is coincidence that Massachusetts was the first state to legalize same sex marriage? It's us who suffered Daniela. We were the throwaway people. You and I."

I processed what he said but couldn't make any sense of it. I ran the various conversations through my mind, trying to link information but couldn't. Same sex marriage? Where on earth had that comment come from? I opened my mouth to ask him to further explain when I heard a soft snore coming from his open mouth.

The moment of true confessions was officially over. I would never see this side of my father again. I had learned information that was so discombobulated that it would take more than my scientific mind to figure it out. I suspected much of it had been garbled in his inebriated state anyhow.

My best conversation with my dad was once when he was drunk. That would be a great conversation starter.

When I reached my father's apartment, I realized that "efficiency" really was an accurate term for where he lived. This man, who could afford anything, had opted for a quaint little end unit, no more than 700 square feet with one open area that included a kitchen, living room and counter space that served as an eating area. His bedroom and bath were separate. It was sparsely furnished but surprisingly done in warm colors. His sofa was a striped coral and gold, and he had a beautiful oriental rug in earth tones. I could not place my father in this unit.

Quite possibly the thing that threw me the most was the absence of lilies. I thought that was a basic expectation of sorts. His bedspread was a chocolate brown chenille with russet throw pillows.

The man clearly loved earth tones. I wondered why our home had been completely done in neutrals: grays, creams, whites, beiges, and lilies of course. I felt ashamed that this was the first time I had visited my father's home—apparently his real home—since I graduated high school. Why had he never invited me?

I led him to the bedroom, removed his shoes and belt and put him under the comforter. He had removed his jacket and tie earlier and I didn't know him well enough to take off his pants. What a strange thing that was—I didn't know the man who was my father, who raised me, well enough to take off his pants so he could sleep more comfortably. I suppose there were stranger things in this world.

Suddenly, he leaned over the edge of the bed. I thought he might throw up, so I ran for a trash can and brought it back under his chin, leaning close. "I've got you dad," I said softly. I doubted he would remember any of this tomorrow, but tonight—for one incredible night—I had a dad.

But he didn't throw up. He leaned on one elbow and looked up at me. "I left the hospital that day to meet the decorator. I didn't want my new baby girl to come home to a blue bedroom," he said. His eyes never left mine.

"What happened?" I asked. I was scared to find out where this story was going, but knew I wanted to hear it. I had once overheard the nurses at one of my physicals talking about how my father had left the hospital after my birth and never returned—that he had abandoned me.

"I found the ledger under the crib mattress. It broke my heart. But I couldn't be selfish. You weren't mine. I had to let your grandmother raise you." He fell back on the pillow, as if saying it out loud had taken all the energy he had.

"Dad, I don't have a grandmother. You've had a little too much to drink," I said as I leaned over and lightly kissed his forehead.

"I know," he said, tears falling freely now. "I'm so sorry. I didn't know it would be that way."

"Get some sleep now, dad. There's a Nor'easter moving in. You probably won't be going into the office tomorrow."

I smoothed his thick hair back gently. I never thought about what a wonderful opportunity it could be to care for a drunk parent. I was probably the only strange person who would see it that way.

"I'll check on you tomorrow."

I turned off the light and locked up behind me. I left my dad's apartment, knowing I would never again meet the man I had just met. The moment was forever gone. I wondered if it had been orchestrated by someone up above. Thanks Angela.

Chapter Twenty

REUNION WITH THE DEVIL

Monday, December 5, 2022. 4:45 PM

40 hours, 45 minutes left

Snow had begun to fall in huge flakes that looked like dollops of mashed potatoes on my navy-blue jacket as I made the dash between my dad's apartment and the Beast.

I started to feel a little panicked at the reality of the nor'easter as I felt the winds kick up under my vehicle—the only negative to a Sequoia or other large SUV. Its height made it a bit precarious in high winds. A nor'easter would be about the worst possible scenario for James if he was going to try to drive back from Maine later. I couldn't deal with having someone else taken from me right now.

As soon as that thought went through my head, I rebelled against it. James Hawthorne was another investigator on the case, nothing more. *If something happened to him, it would have no effect on me* I told myself, but even as I thought it, I knew I was lying to myself. In only two short days, James had become someone I counted on. Maybe it was only because I'd lost Angela and he was in the right place at the right time, but regardless, I had to acknowledge that I was concerned about him.

I now had three messages from him. I needed a find a place to stop and listen to them. I remembered a little shopping center near the Monn's house on the other side of town. That seemed as good a place as any so I wouldn't have to wait until I got home. With this snow, the drive home could be slow.

I found the small shopping center. It was more run down than I had remembered: half convenience store and half pawn shop. This really was an interesting area. I put the Beast in park, letting it idle, got out my notepad, and pressed play on my messages, ready to take notes.

Message 1: 508-555-1212: 12:15 PM: "Hey Daniela, James here. I just left the home of Arya Khati. Her house was full of people. They are having a traditional Hindi funeral, so she has already been cremated and now they are in mourning for 13 days. They told me to come back in two weeks. No talking today; no exceptions. Any friends she might have would also be Hindi (according to the parents) and not allowed to speak to us yet."

I jotted down "Arya Khati: no cooperation, parents in mourning period of two weeks. Check back" and found myself thinking that if I thought my 18-year-old daughter had killed herself, I would welcome any person who had a different theory. But then again, I was not raised with religion and didn't understand its value.

Message 1: 508-555-1212: 1:22 PM: "Hey Daniela, James again. I just left the Johnson home.

Kind of weird people. Didn't really seem to know much about their daughter. I couldn't help but notice that both were also obese. Poor kid—never had a chance with genes like that. She still lived at home. Died at home. They didn't know she was on a diet if she was. They thought she might have been sick, or school was hard—that's why she lost weight, but never asked her. Was born a girl. They looked at me like I was crazy when I asked the question, but I can't imagine coming out to people like that, so other LGBTQ issues are still in question . . . We should follow up. Gave me her cellphone and I copied her contacts. She didn't have many. Hope we can check them out later. Hoping they will know something parents didn't. Weather is starting to look bad. How does it look there? Forecast is not sounding good."

Johnson: "Not transgender that parents were aware of, but other sexual preference unknown.

Got list of contacts from phone—may be a better source than parents who did not know she was on a diet."

I supposed it sounded preposterous to someone like James, who had two loving parents growing up, that this teenager's parents didn't know whether she was dieting, but my dad wouldn't have known. I thought about what would have happened if I had been found dead and James had gone to question my dad. Would he have been able to supply him with a single detail about me or my life? I didn't think so. Not all families are loving and involved with each other. Some just exist beside one another and thrive despite each other.

I moved on to the last message, hoping for better information. So far, it felt like he had wasted a lot of time driving back to Maine. That was the bane of good policework.

Message 1: 508-555-1212: 2:08 PM: "Dan, hey, it's James. I just grabbed some lunch (God I love street tacos! They were Sublime! Ha . . . Go there every time I'm up this way). LeTonya Jackson's family just moved our meeting earlier. Parents are both teachers and they're getting home early today because the weather has gotten worse here. Snowflakes are as big as quarters, never a good sign. I'm going to look for a hotel and settle in before the next meeting. Doesn't look like we'll be checking anything out together tonight. Hope the weather isn't too bad there yet. Hope we talk soon. Don't forget to eat!"

He called me Dan without sounding awkward! And he was worried about me eating! I had to decide how I felt about that. But, *s*peaking of eating, that chicken salad croissant that Mrs. Monn made me for lunch was no longer registering in my belly. I would need to grab a little something soon. Smiling that he knew me that well already and disappointed that I missed his call, I considered calling him back. My finger hovered over James's number on my call log. But he didn't say exactly what time they had rescheduled for. He could be with—

I heard a sharp rap on the window and nearly dropped my phone into the crack between my seat sand the door, barely rescuing it with my shoulder. I was so jumpy today. I needed sleep. My nervous system was on overdrive.

The snow covering on the window completely obstructed my view. It was crazy how quickly the snow had accumulated. Remembering the black escalade that had been tailing me earlier, I very cautiously opened the window about an inch, the accumulation of snow immediately spilling into my car and dumping into my lap. I made quick visual inspection, ensuring the doors were locked and that my service revolver was nearby.

"Hey, everything okay? I noticed your car idling here for a while," a disembodied voice called through the cracked window.

A cold chill, like icy tendrils, slithered down my spine, caused my breath to hitch in my chest. The air around me turned frigid, as if a gust of arctic wind had swept through the Beast, leaving me shivering involuntarily. Every hair on my body stood on end, prickling with fear and anticipation. I would know that voice anywhere. Jeremy Richards.

The sound of his voice—the knowledge that only a 2 x 3-foot piece of glass stood between us— sent a jolt of electricity through my veins, leaving me momentarily paralyzed in a mixture of dread and disbelief.

Quickly, I repositioned my finger on the window button, ready to roll it up at a moment's notice. In an unnaturally high-pitched voice, I answered, "Everything is fine. Thank you. I was just entering an address in my navigation."

"Just checking. Better get on home little lady—got a nor'easter coming."

Little lady? The last time we had met, he was challenging my manhood. Now I was a lady? I felt myself falling back into the worst day of my life. It was ten years ago, but still felt like yesterday.

It had been my first, and worst, day of high school. Caleb Hiery had approached me at my locker. Caleb was one of the 6-Pack. His father was a big shot lawyer in town.

"Hey Dan, how goes it?" I knew he said this far too casually, and my stomach was instantly in knots. He leaned against the lockers, blocking my way. I hated the way my locker was at the end of the hallway. It was so easy to trap me.

"Fine, thank you." I tried to sidestep around him, but he straightened up, continuing to block my way. "I'm sorry, but I have to go. Margette will worry if I'm late."

"Looks like Margette is going to have to worry today. I know someone who needs to talk to you." He grabbed my arm tightly, pulling me close, and steered me out the door.

I tried to make eye contact with every person we passed, but each looked away quickly.

Nobody wanted to be next.

Immediately I could see where we were headed—the small gravelly triangle behind the school, obscured from view.

As we stepped behind the trash bin, Caleb shoved me to the ground. I could feel the gravel cut into my hands and my right cheek. Thank God I was wearing jeans to protect my knees. Knees are important to a gymnast. Hands can be taped, and nobody had ever cared what my face looked like anyhow. My words of thanks were short lived. When I looked up, all six members of the 6-Pack were standing over me.

My chest tightened with panic. "What do you guys want? Why did you bring me here?"

They knew I was terrified. The waver in my voice gave me away. Who wouldn't be? Six against one wasn't exactly good odds. Pack mentality. I knew fear would spur them on. I had to keep a cool head.

"Well, seems to me that you questioned my manhood earlier today."

Unbelievable. Jeremy Richards took my answer to the chemistry question as an attack on his manhood? In what universe? But no answer was the best choice.

"So," he continued, sweeping his arm expansively around the group, "me and my guys here . . .We got to thinking . . . and decided to question *yours.*"

They burst out laughing as if he'd said something incredibly funny instead of incredibly stupid. My manhood? I wanted to scream, *I'm a girl!*

I began to get a picture of what was happening. I noticed James Hawthorne looked increasingly uncomfortable. I got more nervous. I knew his dad was the chief of police. They must be getting ready to break the law—with me.

I stood up. "This is ridiculous. I'm a girl. I'm leaving now."

I pulled my shoulders back, mustering all of the dignity and authority that I could into my 5- foot-2-inch frame and began walking toward the small crevice between the buildings and trash bins. *Please God . . .*

But the 6-Pack weren't taking orders from God that day. I doubt they ever did.

"Hey, bitch. I'm talking to you." Jeremy shoved me into Caleb, who shoved me into Josh Reynolds. Josh pushed me to the ground and kicked me in the stomach, as if I were a rabid dog.

With the six of them—Jeremy, Caleb, Josh, Bart, Thomas, and James—huddled over me and the pain in my gut screaming, I changed tactics. I had to get out of there.

"Okay, look, I'm sorry. I wasn't trying to upset you or emasculate you. I just want to get good grades. That's all. My dad is a chemist. If I don't get a good grade in chemistry, I'll be in trouble."

"Oh, look who's changin' her tune now, apologizing and using big words like she's as smart as seniors. I guarantee you're in more trouble now than you would be with your pill pushing daddy." Jeremy grabbed a fistful of the front of my shirt. "Hold her boys."

How did he know—

Caleb and Josh pinned my shoulders to the ground while Jeremy reached down and unfastened my jeans. I really did not like where this was going and desperately scanned my mind for any possible way out.

"Hey man, I think we got our point across." James Hawthorne looked like he wanted to run away but didn't dare disobey Jeremy.

"I just want to see what the little bitch has between her legs. Don't tell me you haven't wondered. Everybody does. I'm doing a bona fide community service here."

As he yanked on my pants, I began to scream, kick, and writhe with every ounce of gymnastics conditioning that I'd received over the past twelve years. Jeremy ripped off my right shoe and tossed it toward the trash bin. The only thing left to prevent ripping my pants off was my other shoe.

"Just let me go. I won't tell. Please. Just let me go!"

Even though I knew they fed off my fear, I had lost my ability to hide it. I was terrified. But Caleb and Josh held on tightly.

"Well boys, it whines like a girl and looks like a boy. Here we go . . ." My jeans and underwear came off together in one final jerk, along with the not-so-saving shoe.

Caleb and Josh seemed shocked and instantly released me. I scrambled to my feet, until I hit the wall. Two of the boys, James and Thomas, had the decency to look away. Then I heard a sharp intake of air.

"Damn, now, don't you look like a girl and all. Why've you been hiding under those clothes?"

I watched in horror as the front of Jeremy's jeans expanded. Dear Mother of Mercy. I decided to run for it. What would happen if they caught me couldn't possibly be any worse than what was about to happen.

I sprinted toward the tiny crevice to the right of the trash bin, for once grateful to be as thin as a rail, as if the devil himself was after me, because really, wasn't he? I cleared the crevice and placed my entire focus on the school doors with a speed that only pure adrenaline could fuel. My heart pounded so hard; I could barely even hear my own thoughts.

The doors will be locked.

There is a no re-entry policy after school.

`Still, I ran toward those doors as if they alone would save me, not knowing if the boys were directly behind me and not caring that I was half naked.

And somehow, miraculously, when I reached the school doors, one of them magically opened and I fell flat on my face into the corridor. Something heavy dropped on my butt, but it wasn't until I heard the click of the door reclosing that I felt I could draw a breath.

That was the first time I met Angela. She had saved me from Jeremy that day, but she wasn't here to save me now. I had to face him on my own.

Drawing a deep breath, I replied, "Thanks so much!" in that same tinny voice, praying I had adequately disguised it. I waited until he turned away to roll my window back up, too scared of making a mistake and coming face to face with him. When he finally returned to his SUV, I nearly cried in relief.

But glass and steel were not nearly enough distance from Jeremy Richards.

I put the car into drive and eased out carefully to not attract his attention. Glancing back, I saw a black Escalade in my rearview mirror in the parking lot. Did Jeremy drive a black Escalade? Was he driving the Escalade that had been following me? The memory of that 10-year whispered threat made me shiver once again. Was this a coincidence?

My phone call to James was going to have to wait until I got home. I needed to get as far away from Jeremy Richards as I could, and the drive was not going to be fast by the look of the weather.

Chapter Twenty One

REALITY CHECK

Monday, December 5, 2022. 6:30 PM
39 hours left

After a tense 50-minute drive home on snow-covered roads with aggressive Boston drivers, I was on complete sensory overload. I made a quick call to James that went straight to voice mail. Had he answered, I'm certain I would have spilled my guts about seeing Jeremy. I was still too upset not to. But on the machine, all I said to him was "I'm returning your calls. Hope the weather is not too bad there."

I had less then 40 hours left to figure out who killed Angela before my chief pulled me off the case, before her mother would have to forever believe her beloved child had killed herself.

I hung my wet overcoat and holster on the hall tree, trading my wet Clarks and socks for a pair of moccasin slippers that had often passed as shoes when I forgot to change them in haste. I had trudged through the weather too many times today, and the soft Sherpa inner soles felt so warm and soft.

I made a cup of hot chocolate to settle in with my notes and then, knowing I needed something to calm my nerves, tipped one, then two shots of Bailey's Irish Cream into its chocolatey depths. It wasn't something I typically did, but after coming face to face with the devil himself, it seemed a reasonable solution. I'd indulged in alcohol twice in two days—more than I'd had in the past several months. It made me wonder if any of the victims had felt that way in some capacity—had faced some part of their childhood angst and tried to drown it out with the Zanacan. Most people have past monsters to slay.

But not Angela. Angela would not do that. Period. Her entire personality did not change. She faced the hardest thing any person could ever face. She was born into the wrong body. And she faced it with grace and confidence. No. Angela did not try to drown anything with Zanacan. I *had* to find out who did this to her.

I added the information James had sent in his voicemails to the board but had little else to post. As I examined my notes, I realized the one important fact. The attempt on my life was specifically tied to Angela. I had visited one of the other suicide victims at the morgue and no attempt had been made on my life. What connection did Angela and I share that would make someone want us both dead? We didn't really move in the same circles. I was not involved in Angela's clinical trial, nor her bakery, nor her appointment with Romeo to the Rescue nor had I ever met Sam. Why me? I underlined the words several times.

Who wouldn't want me to be present during Angela's autopsy? Even if she had been murdered by Sam or the slimy guy from Romeo to the Rescue, how would eliminating me change anything? The next detective on the case would find the same incriminating evidence as me. I felt like that was the key—like there was something there holding the answer—but I wasn't seeing it.

Maybe a visit back to the morgue would be my best move right now. It wasn't that far, and I did have a good SUV for the snow. The only problem was that I'd just finished my hot cocoa and the warm glow I could feel on both my cheeks and from the inside out told me that driving may not be the best idea at the moment. I was a "lightweight" when it came to alcohol. It didn't take much to give me a buzz, especially since I was currently operating on an empty stomach and no sleep in almost 36 hours.

The ringing of my phone startled me.

"Hello?"

"Daniela—finally!" James sounded happy to hear my voice. I didn't mind hearing his voice either. It was hard to believe that in a few short days he had gone from enemy to friend to . . . whatever this was.

"How is the weather there James?" My own confusion over our relationship made me say something completely stupid. I knew exactly how the weather was there.

"It's terrible!" He laughed. "But I was able to get a room at The Kennebunk Inn for the night, so I'm good. I'm just disappointed to be missing out on that meal we were going to 'order in.'"

"Yeah, well, I doubt if anyone is delivering here tonight. The roads are covered. You know things start shutting down. I'll probably be having fine dining of grilled cheese and tomato soup." My stomach growled as I said the words. Genetics are only half of the reason I'm so skinny. Drinking on an empty stomach was so dumb.

"They hook you up pretty good at the Inn, so I'm a little luckier than you." An awkward silence followed before he said, "So . . . I was able to interview the last family on the Maine list, the Jacksons."

"Oh yeah? What did they have to say?" I felt like smacking myself in the forehead. This investigation was important. *Think, girl, think!* I needed to stop acting like a lovestruck schoolgirl. I barely knew James. Only yesterday, I thought he was trying to kill me. I exercised the luxury of rolling my eyes in the privacy of my own home.

With only 39 hours left to figure out who had killed Angela, I knew I had to become even more driven to follow every clue. It was not likely that Cap would give me an extension—nor'easter or not—and there was nobody else who would bother looking into the case. They would use the evidence at the scene and that would be that. Fifth Suicide, case closed.

"They said LaTonya found the notice regarding the TUC trial on a bulletin board at school and wanted to be part of it. Both parents were completely involved in and invested in their daughter's weight loss journey. She had struggled with obesity her entire life, trying one diet after another. Neither of them had ever struggled with obesity and it did not run in either of their families, which made LeTonya feel even more like a failure."

It was so sad to hear the pain these young women went through suffering from obesity.

"The parents' main concern was the expense," he continued, "but when they found out it was free if she met the criteria, they were 100% on board."

"Did they say what 100% on board meant exactly?" I had to know if their experience was similar to Angela's.

"LaTonya was at the University of New England, Biddeford Campus. She was given a diet to follow and had check-ins in Portland, which was about 15 miles away, every three months. She said the TUC trial was like a miracle. She never once was tempted to stray from the diet."

I sighed. So, it was the TUC trial. Ang's words exactly.

"Yep, that is what Angela said too. Please tell me they have a copy of the original flyer or her contract."

"No, the parents have searched everywhere—her dorm room, her car, her backpack, her bedroom. The contract is nowhere to be found," he said. "The parents are grieving heavily. They do not understand why she would take her life. She was finally happy after being so unhappy for so long. But she'd never wanted to be skinny, only accepted and loved, and she felt she had finally reached a weight where people saw her, not just her obesity."

That was exactly what Kayleigh O'Brien's mother had said: finally happy. It was a good thing the media hadn't yet caught hold of the suicides in Maine.

"And was she transsexual or did she fall anywhere within the LGBTQ spectrum?" I asked.

"Nope. Born a girl. Living as a girl. Loving boys. Which brings me to one notable thing. Her mother does recall her talking about someone named Romeo."

I felt like someone punched me in the gut. If one of those slimy little punks from Romeo to the Rescue was hurting these girls, I would—

"Daniela? Did you hear me?" James asked.

"Yes. I'm guessing the FBI has better capability to dive into internet things like that than a local police force, am I right about that?"

Although I wanted to be the one to nail these guys and fully prosecute them of the law, I also knew that I did not have the same unlimited resources available to me as James did.

"Yes. I'll order a deep dive immediately, specifically targeting the email addresses of the girls who have died. Her parents were also happy that we are looking deeper. I could see the hope in their eyes. I think they would actually be happy if their daughter was murdered. Suicide is so much worse. They think it means *they* failed *her*."

God, what a horrific thing—to be happy your daughter was murdered. But I completely understood the rationale and felt the same way. If Angela was murdered, it meant that some mad man took the decision out of our hands but if she killed herself . . . To think that Mrs. Monn thought she had failed Angela killed me. She was always there for her. She was always there for me too. I had to solve this to show her she had done nothing wrong. I couldn't bring back Angela, but I could save her mother.

"James, has there been any progress on the dark web angle? Were you able to get any of their laptops for your analyst? It is starting to make a lot more sense."

"Yes," he said. "I was able to get three laptops today. I turned all three over to my analyst before I checked in at my hotel. He'll be able to see what they deleted. Nothing is deleted forever unless it is burned or destroyed."

"I thought of something else today. As much as I only want this to be about Angela, I feel that we cannot ignore this any longer. I am tied to these murders in some way. Why did someone try to kill *me?*"

There was silence on the other end for what seemed an eternity.

"James?"

"Daniela, I've thought of nothing but that since I got here. That is the piece that doesn't fit in this puzzle. So, we have to assume it is the piece that will solve it as well—especially since nobody made an attempt on the life of a police officer or detective in Maine."

My stomach dropped. This is why James was sticking so close to me? And I thought it was something more. I was glad he could not see my heated face. I was an idiot to think someone like James Hawthorne would be interested in me. Even though I had finally filled out in all the places I was supposed to, I still had to have my work suits custom made because they didn't sell them for detectives this small. I was like a little girl playing dress up—and that is probably how he still saw me: a little girl. Detectives were supposed to be big and ominous. Nonetheless, this is what I was given, and Angela had taught me to make the best of it. But had she convinced me that I was more than I really am? Why couldn't I have been 6 feet like my mother or 6 and a half feet like my father? What kind of cruel freak of nature was I?

"I think I'm going to head back into the morgue, James. I have a feeling that there are some answers there," I said. "Right before I was shot, I noticed a small incision on Angela's arm. It appeared to be postmortem."

"I think that is a really bad idea, Daniela." James asked. "We don't need a repeat of the first incident. Besides, aren't the roads snowed over yet?"

'We' don't need a repeat? 'He' thinks it's a bad idea? What is he, my dad? His concern really got under my skin. Maybe it was because what I had felt for him felt false to me now. Maybe it was because it sounded fatherly and I'd managed without one until now just fine, thank you very much. Or maybe it was just because I was in an agitated state from running into Jeremy earlier still—a fact I had still not shared with James. Regardless, his comments were all I needed to make the final decision to go to the morgue.

"Thanks for your concern, James, but I'm a big girl who has managed just fine without you for a very long time. I'll let you know what I find out."

Furious, I hung up, grabbed my purse and keys off the table, and jumped in the Beast before I could second guess myself. I was headed to the morgue. I tried not to think about leaving James speechless and bewildered at the other end of our call. I didn't need any man telling me what to do, damn it!

Chapter Twenty Two

MORGUE MISCHIEF

Monday, December 5, 2022. 7:15 PM
38 hours and 15 minutes left

I felt nervous about driving after drinking—I was paranoid that way. I *never* drove after drinking anything and wished I hadn't been so insistent on doing so tonight.

To add to my paranoia, the vehicle behind me—definitely an SUV by the height of the headlights—was following much too closely for this snowy evening. With the snow falling and the night sky, I couldn't see the make of the car. The only thing I was sure of was that if I braked suddenly, that idiot was going to ram straight into my rear end. If someone hit my Beast, I would surely lose my mind after the day I'd had, especially since I had run out the door without my jacket and I was still wearing my slippers. I could not be stranded on the side of the road in 17 degree weather with no jacket or shoes. And what if it was an Escalade?

The SUV stayed with me until we entered the hospital parking lot and then entered the doctor's lot, which made it a forgivable offense to tailgate. He or she had lives to save. And I had made it to my destination unscathed as well.

The hospital parking lot was only dotted with cars, most people opting for the garage on this snowy night. I decided to use the parking garage as well so I wouldn't have to dig out my car with no jacket on when I was ready to head home. The level of stupidity—leaving home with no proper attire in the middle of a snowstorm—told me that I had no business being where I was. Nonetheless, I had no time to waste, so here I was.

The garage was packed so I had to park all the way on the bottom level. That's where I was headed anyhow, but it sure looked and felt ominous down there tonight. Not only had seeing Jeremy unsettled me, but the last time I was here, I was shot in the head. I put my hand to the bandage. It wasn't like Jeremy had shot me. He had nothing to do with any of this. *Right?* But what was he doing in town? I thought he had moved away after college. Shaking my head, I cleared that thought and got out of the Beast. Jake and I needed to talk right now and either he was very busy or had avoided the two calls I had placed to him earlier in the day.

Making my way down the same halls, to the same room I'd been shot in only days before, I suddenly had a flashback of Jake's greeting on that day. I had passed him as he exited the exam room to bring in a new victim. But wouldn't I have heard about the victim on my radio? Or seen the ambulance pulling in? I was too distraught on the night I discovered Angela's body to give it much thought, but now that I thought about it, it didn't make a lot of sense.

Entering the exam room, I found Jake there, where he always was like clockwork 10 am to 7 pm, Monday to Friday. He even ate his lunch in the room. As a matter of fact, the only time I had ever come by when he wasn't physically in the exam room was the day I was shot. But why was he working on a Saturday night? Shouldn't his assistant have been on duty?

"Hey Jake. How's it going?"

To say Jake jumped a foot wouldn't be an exaggeration. I think if the corpse between us had sat up and said "hi," he wouldn't have been more surprised.

"Dan! My God, where'd you come from?" A flush crept up his neck over his white lab coat, spilling onto his cheeks. Jake had a naturally ruddy complexion, so the addition of the flush made it look like his head was ready to pop off. Where'd I come from? Strange greeting.

"My mother's womb?" I tried to laugh. Jake's face changed from red to ashen so quickly, he looked like a lava lamp.

What a weird reaction. I'd shared this space with him many times before and I always showed up unannounced. "Jake? Everything okay? What's up?"

"Oh, uh, nothing. You just startled me. I wasn't expecting you."

I didn't buy it. This was not the Jake I had known since I was sixteen and doing volunteer work with the police, nor the Jake who had so graciously allowed me to learn from him during my summer internship. This was a completely different Jake, and he was making me feel very nervous. I laughed.

"If I didn't know any better, I'd say you were not very happy to see me, Jake."

I suspect my laugh was his undoing. The morgue was a generally somber place, and he did not personally know me well enough to know it was a nervous habit of mine. The laugh may have told him I knew something more than I knew.

"You have to understand, I didn't want to do it." He gulped.

"Didn't want to do what? Jake—did you shoot me?"

"No! Of course not! I would never hurt you!" To my shock and horror, he started crying. "I'm so sorry, Dan! He said I had to, or he would hurt my family!"

My eyes bulged. What. The. Heck. "Jake, please just calm down and tell me exactly what you are talking about."

"The implant . . . I had to get it out before anyone else knew. She was too old, and he knew it. She didn't belong in the trial."

Angela. He was absolutely talking about Angela now.

"Jake, *who* knew it? What are you talking about? Please slow down and explain what you are talking about!" I knew we weren't going to make progress as upset as he was.

Whoosh! Jake rocked back on his feet and hit the floor. I ran around the table. A red blossom began to spread on Jake's forehead, right between eyes that were staring through me. Automatically, I drew my weapon—except the only thing I drew was a chap stick. Damn! It was still hanging in my holster, by the front door, at my house. I heard echoing footsteps running down the corridor before the door closed. Dear God, what now?

I yanked out my phone, grateful that I had at least remembered to bring that much and dialed James.

"Hey Daniela. Look. I'm sorry if I offended you somehow—"

"Jake is dead." I said bluntly. "He was just shot in front of me."

"Where are you?" He was all business now.

"Morgue. Hospital." My mind was racing. I wasn't sure what I should do first. "I have alcohol in my system."

"Leave." James sounded certain.

"But I—"

"Leave." James repeated. "I'll send in a team."

I was desperate. I stopped thinking and just followed his directions. I ran down the hallway, praying at every turn that Jake's killer was not waiting for me. I shouldn't have come here. But had someone been trying to take me out again? And poor Jake got killed instead? He would not spend Christmas with his family this year or any year ever again and that was my fault. The tears that had been threatening all day began to fall and wouldn't stop.

When I reached the Beast, I jumped in and locked the doors. Then, spooked, I jumped back out immediately, throwing open all the doors on the SUV—even raising the hatch on the back—to make certain there was nobody hiding inside the car. All clear. I was frantic to get back in and close the doors again, locking them behind me once more. I was openly sobbing now and thankful that I didn't encounter anyone else, but I was also completely aware that every move I had just made was captured on camera in the parking garage.

I drove home very slowly, taking deep breaths, trying to regain my composure, and thinking the whole way. The last thing I needed to add to the list tonight was getting pulled over. How many times had I visited a crime scene and wondered "why"? Why had things gone so wrong? Why didn't the perp understand that the ten things they did after the first thing made it all a hundred times worse? Now I knew the answer to that question. When something happens that is out of your control, you lose the ability to react rationally.

Obviously, a cup of hot chocolate with a couple shots of Bailey's thrown in had not made me inebriated. But I also knew my lack of sleep and body weight factored in heavily and could have thrown me into the illegal zone. I read an article once that talked about the ratio of body fat, body weight, amount of sleep, adequate nutrition, and amount of alcohol and came to the scientific conclusion that I could drink approximately one teaspoon of alcohol without being "under the influence," and I'd had far more than a teaspoon tonight. Should I have stayed? Should I go back? Would my involvement have brought to light the fact that I was already lying about my relationship to the deceased? Would they ask how often I lied? How often I drank on the job? How often I forgot my firearm? Would I have become the next media victim?

This case really had my mind messed up. I could see why they said it wasn't safe when you were too close to the case. But on the other hand, who better to solve the case than someone whose heart and soul were involved.

I tried to focus on one piece at a time. The shooter knew I was at the morgue. Was I followed by that SUV that turned into the doctor's lot? Was it an Escalade? There was really no way to tell in the dark and snow.

And why kill poor Jake? Were they trying to shoot me again and accidentally shot Jake? Or had they intentionally killed Jake because he was about to tell me what had happened the first time? He had a family; I had no family. But as soon as I thought that I flashed on Mrs. Monn and how devastated she would be if she lost me too and, on my dad, last night when he was drunk. I felt something there I had never felt before. Maybe, just maybe, there were people who would care if I died.

The questions were swirling through my mind as my hysteria began to grow again. I kept taking deep gulps of air.

Calm down. Calm . . . down.

Realistically, the point-blank shot between the eyes said the shot was most likely meant for Jake.

What were his last words? "The implant. I had to get it out before anyone else knew."

So, Jake had been coerced into removing Angela's implant. But why? And *who* else knew about her diet? Was being too old such a grievous offense to the trial that it was worth killing for? My father—*Please God, do not let him be talking about my father!* — had vehemently denied being involved in the trial and the address for Lily Legacy was not at Neely Pharmaceuticals Headquarters. And what *was* that implant? Maybe James and I should visit the actual address and see whom we find in charge at the location.

Jake had said he was sorry. Was he apologizing for removing the implant? Or was he telling me that he had shot me? I wasn't sure. He had gotten so worked up so quickly. He seemed very frightened. I needed to tell James about the threat to Jake's family right away.

James . . . *Oh wow . . .*

One thing I knew for certain. I had only told one person I was going to go to the morgue.

***

My head was pounding as I pulled into my driveway, which should have been completely coated in six inches of snow like all the other houses on the block, but instead had recent tire tracks. *Who has been to my house?* Someone familiar enough to pull into my driveway? Don't most strangers park on the street? But maybe they didn't want to prevent the snowplow from coming through. Or maybe someone just turned around using my driveway for their K turn. These roads were narrow and with the snow accumulation, driveway turns made sense. I was overreacting because of my job and what was going on in my life right now. *That* was the logical explanation. It was probably just someone being considerate, and I was freaking out because I was still in freak out mode. I had to get into the house and get my bearings.

Opening the garage door, I held my breath, expecting to see a car or a person there, but it was just my garage with my bike hanging upside down waiting for spring to return and a pair of roller blades I hadn't had on my feet in at least five years.

Walking into my kitchen, I kicked off my wet moccasins and immediately noticed the box on the table. I had not left a box on my kitchen table. An icy chill went up my spine as I glanced all around the kitchen. My alarm. Had I forgotten to set my alarm in my hurry to get out the door? Dear God. That made four things I had forgotten: my coat, my firearm, my shoes, and my alarm. I was no longer qualified to be a detective. *Angela! I'm falling apart without you!* I silently cried.

I stopped. There was a chance an intruder had been in my house or still was in my house. I had to get to my gun. I suddenly appreciated that my home was not large. The distance between the kitchen and entry door was only about 20 feet; there were no hiding places in the kitchen. I picked up a large carving knife and made my way into the family room, my back flat against the wall. I was sure that if an intruder was still there, he could hear my heart pounding.

Finally reaching my holster, I was relieved to find the gun still in it. Weapon pulled and cocked, I thoroughly checked the room, strategically maneuvering to make certain nobody blindsided me.

No one.

Before I did anything else, I made certain to lock both doors and set my perimeter alarm. No more forgetting. My life was clearly at risk now.

I returned to the box on the kitchen table, cautiously pulling it open. *Oof.* I barely made it to the sink before the black dredges of cocoa and Bailey's came flying from the depths of my stomach.

Hanging my head, I splashed water on my face and took deep breaths, but it did no good. I was back in Trouble Triangle. I could see the sadistic look in Jeremy Richard's eyes. I could feel the hands on my arms and legs, holding me like I was an animal. I knew what he planned to do to me. I was reminded every time he brushed past me in the hallway, with whispered promises of more to come. I heaved again and again until I was only crying into the running water.

Who was in my house? How had they known I would be gone? Again, the only person I had told was James. How do you investigate the FBI agent assigned to assist you on the case you were working on?

I sat down at the table and pulled the items from the box one at a time. Size 12 slim girls' jeans. Light blue underwear. One white ankle sock with a navy Nike swish on the side. One Nike tennis shoe, size 5, white with a navy Nike swish on the side. My missing clothes. The "misplaced" evidence. Funny how it landed on my kitchen table at the same time both Jeremy and James had reappeared in my life—at the same time Angela's life ended. But not really funny at all.

Was James merely a very good actor? He seemed to have shown up at quite an opportune time after my shooting, and now, when this package showed up on my table, he was conveniently stuck in another state? If I were watching 48 Hours on TV, I'd be calling "bullshit" about now.

Then, once again, as if I summoned him just by thinking about him, my phone rang, and his number came across the screen.

"James." I said.

"Daniela. I just wanted to let you know that the scene has been secured."

And now I was indebted to James Hawthorne. How utterly convenient. Was this all part of the plan? So he could then blackmail me? What had I gotten myself into? My mind was reeling.

"James—" I stopped. Knowing I had to say something, I continued, "The security footage of the parking garage . . . I was on the bottom floor. I freaked out a little bit."

"There's nothing I can do about that, Dan. All I did was buy you some time to get the alcohol out of your system. But eventually, the evidence will lead them back to you, so you'd better be prepared to answer them."

I really didn't know what I would or could say to my captain about what had happened at the morgue. I felt all the pieces of my life unraveling beneath me. People I had worked hard to trust were not trustworthy. Jake hadn't been trustworthy. James might not be trustworthy. Poor Daniela, so desperate for someone to love her that she will believe anyone? The pain of that thought was so great it left me breathless.

"And Jake? What will his family think had happened to him?" I could not stop staring at the box on my table.

"We cannot sugarcoat what happened. The medical examiner was shot. Do you have any idea why someone would want to shoot him?"

It was the moment of truth. Did I trust him or not? I just couldn't be sure. I decided to give him the barebones version.

"We were just talking and all of a sudden, he fell over backwards."

This was a true statement. I had not lied to James. I just hadn't given him the whole story. For all I knew, James was crouched in my bedroom closet or in my basement or had been at the morgue the entire time. I had no proof that any of the cases in Maine even existed. I had no real proof that he had even driven to Maine or met with anyone there. That could all be a cover to give him an alibi. I just couldn't take the risk. Not with two people I cared about killed within days of each other.

"How about if we plan to talk tomorrow morning, first thing," he said.

I worked hard to keep my voice level. "How can we talk tomorrow? Aren't you snowbound in Maine?"

"I canceled my last appointment and secured a helo ride first thing in the morning from the field office in Portland. Leaves at 5 am. I should be there by 8 am."

"Be where? My house?" The very thought made me anxious, even though there was still a possibility that James was a good guy.

"No, at the Chelsea field office. I'll grab a car there and head to your place."

"Oh, do you really think that's a good idea? I'm sure I'll have a foot of snow by midnight." I countered.

"No problem. We've got an Escalade available at the Chelsea office for fly-ins. It'll get me where I need to be."

My stomach dropped at the mention of an Escalade. Could James have been following me all day long? There were a lot of nice SUVs in the Boston area.

"Dan? You still there? Everything okay?"

I kept expecting to hear his voice echo from the other room or waft up from the basement, but it was only coming through my cell phone. I took a deep breath.

"Yeah. I'm okay—just shook from earlier. Jake and I went way back, you know? He was good to me. Taught me a lot."

"You've been through a lot in the past few days. There would be no shame in handing the case over to another detective." He said it so earnestly, it was hard not to believe him.

The problem was, I no longer knew who to believe in. I felt so caught up in a web of deceit, and the only person who could help me clear my head was dead. She was the reason I was here in the first place. *Oh Ang!* I only had a mere 36 hours left to solve her murder. I was beginning to wonder if I could solve hers before someone would need to solve mine.

"We'll talk tomorrow, Daniela, okay? I'll be in town by around nine, okay? Try to get some sleep. Remember, you didn't sleep last night?"

Last night seemed a very long time ago, and I knew sleep would not come easy tonight either. I could still feel the presence of an intruder in my home. Even though the alarm was now set, I didn't feel safe. Had I set it before? What if someone had my code?

I thought of any possible way someone could get my code. James could have watched me enter it when we came in last night. That was a definite possibility. Other than that, my father had my code. He checked in on my house once weekly when Ang and I took trips, although it had certainly been a while since we'd done that. Mrs. Monn had my code. There were a few times she had graciously let in a repairman or a furniture delivery person for me. But as much as I scanned my brain, I couldn't think of anyone else who would know my code. Ang, of course. But that was a moot point now.

That thought allowed me to wallow in sorrow for the first time all day. Ever since I had opened my eyes this morning, I had been on the move, working every moment against the clock to solve the case. There was no time to think, to hurt, to grieve. And oh how I wanted to grieve. I wanted to roll up in a ball and allow sorrow to encompass my body, to become my body. There was a part of me that couldn't imagine a life without Angela in it. But I couldn't think about that part of life yet.

First, I had to take care of her in the last way I could. I started a list.

1. *Get detailed information on clinical trials from dad*

2. *Contact four local suicide victims with question: transgender? LGBTQ?*

3. *Get victim's computers and have FBI scan deleted content*

4. *Have FBI do deep dive on people who created Angela's fake ID from photo*

5. *Visit Lily Legacy location—find out who is in charge/Neely Pharma connection*

6. *Stop by my childhood home—who is staying there?*

7. *Get the box my clothes came in fingerprinted*

It was a lot to accomplish in one day, but my time was running out. As much as I hated to do it, I was going to have to handle some of the business over the phone and drop some into James's lap. I would give him items 2, 3, 4, and 7; I'd take 1, 5, and 6. I was beginning to suspect if I couldn't solve Angela's murder, I was next on the list.

Chapter Twenty Three

COMING UN-TUC-ED

Tuesday, December 6, 2022. 5:00 AM
28.5 hours left

Somehow, I had miraculously fallen asleep somewhere around 2 am amidst the crazy array of overstuffed pillows and cushions on my dependable old shabby chic Broyhill sofa that I'd pushed up against the door for added security. It looked old when it was new and now that it was no longer new, it really looked old. But I loved the way I sank into it at the end of a stressful day. Nothing in the home I'd been raised in had ever felt like its big, soft hug.

Moving it back into place, I almost knocked over the sofa table which held all of my most prized possessions: a simple walnut-frame photograph of my parents; an adorable pottery vase with coral, umber, and gold stripes that Angela had made in sophomore art class for me, filled weekly with fresh lilies; and a key ring that my father had given to me as a gift when he bought the house. The key ring was a miniature Brink's safe with the words "Home is your SAFE place" written on it. It sure didn't feel very safe right now. Nothing did.

Thinking of my dad reminded me that I still needed to get the details from my father about the clinical trial that James had told me about. Maybe if I knew more about it, it would shed some light on why I had become a target. I quickly flashed on the Markus Neely from a fortnight ago. My heart squeezed. No sense dreaming or wishing for things that couldn't come true. At least I had seen it— caught one glimpse of the man he could be. I would cherish it forever.

I dug my phone out, found it dead and plugged it in. Jeez, when was the last time I charged the poor thing? For that matter, when had I last bathed? I lifted my arm and sniffed my armpit. Not too bad. Eaten? So much work.

I was determined to do better after a night's rest. My time was rapidly deteriorating before the chief would pull the plug and Angela's death would be forever labeled a suicide. First things first. I made myself some scrambled eggs and then grabbed a croissant out of a baggie labeled Angel's Bakery. It was stale and had a small green patch on the tip that I flicked off with my fingernail. Ang had made that croissant. I was eating the darn thing if it killed me. I deserved it for not visiting my friend in the shop she'd worked so hard to create.

When I was done, I stacked my dishes and pan in the dishwasher where I knew they would sit for at least a month. Guaranteed I'd end up picking plates and cups out and hand washing them to use them or running the entire load for a couple of items. Someone should market a singles dishwasher that had a couple of spots for cups, a spot for a pan, a place for plates . . . I realized I was distracting myself with mundane, meaningless thought spirals.

Finally, after a quick shower, a fresh bandage, and some clean clothes, I picked up my phone and dialed my father's office. Voicemail. No surprise there.

"Hey Dad, It's Daniela again. Talking to your daughter two days in a row, must be a record for us. Anyhow, I was just checking in on you and also, I have one more question I really need to ask you. Can you please call me back as soon as possible? I would really appreciate it. Thank you, dad!" I tried to add a little more enthusiasm than usual. I *could* try harder.

I had just ended the call when my phone rang. Maybe he hung up on another call just to talk to me. Or maybe he didn't answer initially until he was certain he would want to talk to me. Maybe I was just trying too hard. But strangely, when I answered the line, my father acted as though we hadn't spoken the day before. Maybe it was his job to put the past behind him the minute it became the past. Maybe that's how it was so easy for him to forget he had a living and breathing daughter for the past 25 years. Daniela? Who is that?

"Dad?"

"Daniela. What a rare surprise. What can I help you with?"

He sounded genuinely eager to help which further confused me. I sighed aloud. Everything about him continued to be a mystery to me.

"Dad, when I was there, I forgot to get information from you about one other thing: another clinical trial that James Hawthorne told me about."

"Yes, I'm listening." He certainly wasn't going to give me anything I didn't specifically ask for.

"James said there was a trial that he and five other boys took part in growing up that began when their moms were pregnant. Does that sound familiar to you?"

"Yes, Daniela, that sounds familiar to me."

"Were you in charge of that clinical trial dad? Did you create it so you could have the sons you always wanted?" My voice broke on the last question.

My father was not affected by the borderline mad scientist question nor the break in my voice. "I was not in charge of the clinical trial Daniela. I headed up the team who created the supplementation and monitored its effects; however, that was the extent of my involvement with the project."

"I don't understand, Dad. How could you head up a team that created a supplement but not be involved in the project?" Although my father was not acting evasive at all, it felt like an evasive answer.

"Daniela, I am a top scientist in my field. I often work hand in hand with the Department of Defense on projects. My role in such projects is often very specific and small."

That did make sense, and it made me happy that the trial wasn't created by him as a method to have sons. That was just my own insecurity shining through. Angela was right.

"I know you cannot tell me any details or results of the trials Dad, but can you tell me what the participation criteria were?" Any information I could gain about these trials would be helpful; I could just feel it in my bones.

"Yes, I believe it would be appropriate for me to send that to you to further your investigation. Please treat it with care and confidence."

"Thank you, Dad. You can send it to my email address dantheman@ bpd.moc."

"Yes Daniela. I will do so immediately," he said. "You have always had such an unusual sense of humor."

There was something in his words—in his tone—that sounded almost amused. But I didn't think the great Markus Neely became amused, so perhaps I had imagined it. Suddenly, I remembered something else.

"Sorry dad, I know I said I only had one question, but could I throw one more in there for good measure. Must be the detective in me." I gave a half laugh which was completely wasted on him.

He remained silent, waiting.

"I was wondering why I need to give you notice before I visit the house. I mean, don't the caretakers recognize me after all these years? It just feels odd that I can't stop by my own home any time I want." I have never been a difficult child—certainly not one who questions adults or authority, but my conversation with James had been really weighing on me.

"Well, I guess you might as well know that someone stays there and appreciates the opportunity to clear out before you arrive. That person appreciates complete privacy, and I have agreed to respect that. So, we will continue as before."

I could tell that the conversation was done, although I was completely blown away by it. Some random person was living in my childhood home, so I was not allowed to visit it at will? *I'll be damned.* My next visit would be completely unannounced. I wanted to know who was staying at my home, quite possibly in my own bedroom. Not to mention the fact that ever since my father's drunken confession regarding a ledger, I was literally dying to search the house for it. I had never really lived "in" the house, only in my bedroom.

I ended our awkward conversation, hoping he would send the information over quickly, mulling his words over in my head. My father was a very private man. As far back as I had memories, we had never had a stranger in our home. Who would he allow to live there? As soon as Angela's death was solved, that would be my next serious investigation.

It seemed that once I began to feed my empty body, it thought it needed to stockpile food since I had been eating so erratically. Or maybe when you get up at 5, it's okay to eat again at 8. Then again, this could be what they call stress eating. Regardless, I grabbed a bag of Fritos, dumped them into a bowl, and poured some heated chili over them.

Frito Bowl. Breakfast of champions. It used to be a favorite of Ang's before she started the trial that controlled every bite that went into her mouth.

Then it hit me, bite midway to my mouth.

Your thalamus is the control center of your brain. TUC. Thalamus Under Control. He had said that to me. If your thalamus was being controlled, you could be convinced to do other unusual things, like the things Ang did her last weeks. It might not be related but what if . . .

Without thinking, I began to press send on James's number, only just catching myself at the last minute. Should I share it with James now that I was no longer sure if James was friend or foe? And now that I'd pretty much invited him into my home, things were going to be challenging, to say the least. The last thing I needed to do was continue to update him on my suspicions. What if he was somehow setting me up?

I put my phone down and finished eating my Frito bowl, running through all the possible scenarios in my mind. After all, who knew when I would find time to eat again, and James would be arriving soon.

When I finished, I grabbed my laptop and googled "thalamus." I was blown away by the wealth of information that was available online. According to the NIH, the mediodorsal nucleus of the thalamus affects things such as planning, cognitive control, working memory, and decision making because of its interconnectivity to the prefrontal cortex. It, plus several other informative articles went on to say that neuroplasticity stops at age 25, which makes it harder to develop new neural pathways at that point and afterward. Apparently, an excellent age for affecting the thalamus is 18. Each year after that, the body develops naturally to counter its malleability.

This in-depth description of the thalamus and its effect on the human body went a long way toward explaining why the clinical trial would only want 18 year olds involved in the study. They had the most malleable minds. It would also explain why Angela was the only one who left out a copy of her contract, a breadcrumb that might aid in the investigation—if in fact the other girls had been instructed to destroy those things to stall the investigation. The creeping feeling moving down my spine told me I was on to something. Something new. Something accurate. I needed that original contract.

I had to visit Lily Legacy.

Chapter Twenty Four

FRESH EYES

Tuesday, December 6, 2022. 8:00 AM
25 hours and 30 minutes left

I f I was going to survive to solve this case, I needed to step up my game. That much had become blazingly apparent. Leaned over my evidence board in the kitchen, I realized that whoever delivered that box also saw my "crazy board." I wasn't sure that mattered—whether the two were interlinked or just coincidence.

I checked my email and found the attachment from my father. I downloaded it. What I read made me feel more sick to my stomach than suspicious. What kind of parents would agree to these types of terms? Whoever sold this plan must've had one heck of a sales pitch. That could not have been my father. He did not have a charming bone in his body. He was just a scientist. Like me. Or rather, I guess I was like him. But we definitely were not charming. Still, that didn't mean he wasn't at fault: in charge of it. He was asking me to take the word of a stranger, because that's all he was to me. I had no idea what he was capable of.

The initial trial was called the VITAL Trial. I ran my finger down the screen over the list of applicant qualifications for the VITAL Trial and an icy chill settled over me as I read the criteria.

1. Father must hold a position that can either financially or influentially further future phases of the program

2. Healthy mother who has no family history of heart disease, cancer, diabetes, or inheritable genetic disorder

3. Only natural born male children

4. Single child family. It is imperative that the male child receives full attention for his abilities both intellectual and physical to ensure maximum success.

VITAL

Vitamin Integration Therapy Aiding Life

First injection begins 6 weeks after conception Injections monthly throughout term of pregnancy Injections monthly through age 2

Injections bi-weekly through age 4 Injections weekly through age 6 Daily oral tablets through age 18

Children will be tested before each injection beginning at age 2 for intelligence and ability.

Results will be put into monthly reports and returned to CIA liaison for monitoring/interpretation to ensure objectives are being achieved.

Upon graduation from supplemental integration therapy, children will be placed in key roles to further aid research.

If Phase 1 bears a success ratio of 93 to 96 % minimum, you may move to phase two.

James' role with the FBI would certainly be considered a 'key' role. I wondered where Jeremy worked. Something told me that James would know, and that fact made me very uncomfortable. I wondered where the other four had landed. James and I were going to have to have a heart to heart about this information. He was holding out on me.

The applicant qualifications for phase two were vastly different than Phase One. It was hard to make logical sense of the complete reversal of basic human requirements.

1. Candidate's base weight must be between 230 and 330 pounds.

2. Candidate must be between 18 and 20 years of age.

3. Candidate must be female at birth.

    4. Candidate must understand that details of side effects when participating in a pharmaceutical trial are strictly confidential.

TUC Trial

Thalamus Under Control

Implant placed at first visit

Effectiveness of implant monitored by regularly scheduled weigh ins

Upon reaching goal weight, trial participant will be required to continue wearing implant for up to two years.

Additional testing as to effectiveness of implant may take place after participant goals are reached.

The final phase of the trial simply stated 'Phase Three: fully integrated Soldiers On Command –phase name: SOL-COM. I wondered what the real trial for the TUC program entailed, if not for a diet. I wished I could have that information as well. And phase three just sounded like scary government stuff. Soldiers on command. I knew they had to do stuff like that to keep us safe over here in the States, but I didn't really like to think about it. I guess nobody really does. Perhaps the two programs were not even related, and this was all just a terrible coincidence. This could just be a serial killer on the loose from a place called Romeo to the Rescue or a sick guy named Sam who decided to kill the "freak" he was attracted to. My gut said it wasn't, but I knew I had to follow all leads.

I created one scenario after another until my eyes were burning like hot coals, and I didn't feel any closer to figuring out why Angela had been killed, why Jake had been killed, or why an attempt had been made on my life. None of it added up.

I decided that the only solution was to go back to good old fashioned police work. "Just do the homework, Neely." That's what O'Malley would have said to me.

I could see no alternative except to start with another visit to my father as well as Lily Legacy and hope that I didn't get killed in the process. Someone knew what the heck was going on here, and I was about to find out .

Chapter Twenty Five

FRIEND OR FOE

Tuesday, December 6, 2022. 9:00 AM

24 hours and 30 minutes left

As I opened the garage door, I could see that a black Escalade was battling with the snow drift caused by the early morning snowplows in front of the house. My heart jumped erratically.

James jumped out. "Dan!" he yelled. "Don't leave! I've been trying to park this damn beast of a car for ten minutes. How do people drive these things?"

Dread filled me. "Just pull into the driveway," I yelled. Was he trying to park out front now to throw me off from last night or was he really a guy who didn't park in other peoples' driveways? How could I possibly know?

James finally managed to pull away from the curb and pulled into the driveway. He really was terrible at driving the Escalade. There was something reassuring about that fact. I remembered how closely the Escalade that had tailed me had followed. That was someone experienced with the vehicle. I motioned him into the warmth of the Beast.

"Good morning," I said. "I'm grateful you could get here early."

"I told you I'd be here early. I'm a man of my word." He flashes me that smile, looking flawless as always. "One of the things I love about the Bureau are the bells and whistles we have available to us—especially when it comes to transportation."

Regardless of my doubts, I needed his resources and his help to solve Angela's murder. I only had 24 hours left. I thanked my lucky stars I took the time to finally eat, shower, and put on clean clothes, although I was certain I didn't hold a candle to his impeccable appearance.

"Were those bells and whistles able to get any information from the other victims' laptops yet?"

I refused to let him sidetrack me with his good looks. There was something about him that seemed to connect with my physicality that had never happened to me before. I found it distracting, disarming, and most of all, disturbing. It's sick to be attracted to someone who might be trying to kill you.

"Actually, yes. I dropped the laptops yesterday and got a report back this morning. There was basically nothing to suggest foul play. Complete dead end on the dark web angle with the Maine victims."

"Seriously?" I practically shouted the word in frustration. "Dead end?"

"I know you were hoping we would find something more, Daniela, but there was nothing else like the case. We were able to ascertain that each of the Maine victims *was* involved in the TUC clinical trial, so it looks like it is leading back to Neely Pharmaceuticals one way or another. Maybe the implant causes depression and suicidal ideation and they're trying to hide that result?"

He was speculating—guessing really—and we both knew it.

"Hmmm . . ." I muttered. I wasn't impressed by that theory in any way. It didn't explain why someone would try to kill me. It felt too contrived.

"I also wanted to tell you about the video footage we secured from High Life Dispensary across the street from Angela's apartment."

Now he had my full attention. "Did you see who went to her house?" I imagined what that slimeball Joaquin from Romeo to the Rescue looked like and what I would do to him when I got ahold of him. If we found out he was the one who killed her, I would hurt him bad before I arrested him. That much I was sure of.

"Yes. We were able to pull a facial rec on the guy who was trying to find Angela. Turns out, the people who live in that building don't have many visitors, so it wasn't too hard to weed through the extras with Mr. Smithers."

"You went to see Mr. Smithers again? Without me?" For some reason, that upset me, although it shouldn't have. We were working the case together. We were not attached at the hip.

He laughed. "Now how would I do that from Maine? There were only 6 people who entered the building during the past month who were not tenants. I sent the photos to Mr. Smithers on his cell phone. We had his number from the original call."

Of course. That made sense. Emotions made me an idiot. I was grateful they were not a regular part of my life.

"And?"

"And, as it turns out—you won't believe this—but the 'Sam' she met . . . You know, the one she was running with?" He looks at me to make sure I am following.

I nod at him to proceed.

"Sam Shoemaker. He works in IT for the Chelsea field office."

"What?" It made me sick to think a bigot was working for our government. "He works for the FBI?" I was incredulous.

"Before you get too worked up, let me tell you that I don't think he is a bad guy."

I rolled my eyes before I could stop myself. Of course he would say that about a fellow FBI agent.

"I talked to him. He told me that he met Angela, and they were really hitting it off. Then she just stopped showing up. She didn't seem the type to ghost him, so he wanted to make sure she was okay. That's all."

"That's all? Did he forget the part about calling her a freak?"

James looked down. "Look, I didn't think it would be appropriate to have that kind of discussion with him. I mean, how would I know something like that?" His face was red. But I could see his point. "Sam seems like a good guy."

Maybe he was and maybe he wasn't a bad guy. Sometimes people bash transgender people just to be cool or because they think that is what is expected. At the very least it makes him spineless, and I would never want Angela to be with someone that spineless. And now she doesn't get to be with anyone—spineless or otherwise.

I wanted to change the subject. "Let's go in so I can mark him off my board. I want to keep it updated."

He stopped briefly to stomp the snow off his boots.

I continued. "I was just getting ready to pay another visit to my father. And I have a list of things I need you to do today. I was up late prioritizing," I explained. "I'm running out of time."

"But . . ." James seemed genuinely puzzled. "I thought we were going to discuss what happened at the morgue last night."

Oh shoot. That was only last night? Now I didn't even know if I trusted him enough to discuss it with him.

"Oh, right. I'm sorry. I forgot that's why you came back early. My days and nights are getting all mixed up."

James looked concerned. "Really? Didn't you sleep last night?"

I wanted to tell him it was not his concern whether I slept. Instead, I asked, "Hey, did I happen to give you my alarm code the other day?"

"You forgot your alarm code? Daniela, I'm really concerned now."

I forced a laugh. "Of course I didn't forget my code. Just asking."

"But why are you asking?" I can see that he is not going to let this go.

"I just wondered if maybe I had given it to you in case you needed to get back into my house." I was not pulling this off as smoothly as I had imagined it in my mind.

"Of course not. Who gives out their alarm code? I wouldn't have let you." He looks disbelieving. "What's really going on?" he asked as we entered the kitchen.

I gave in and pointed to the box on the table. Even though I had promised myself I was not going to tell James about the box of clothes, now that he was here, I had to see his reaction. I felt like I would know.

James opened the flaps of the box, peering inside. Frowning, he pulled out a shoe, then a sock. He started pulling out the jeans when he suddenly dropped them like they were on fire. His eyes bulged. "Are these what I think they are?"

"Depends. Do tell." I said casually, watching him closely.

James had gone pale. "Are these your clothes from 'that' day? The day, you know, when Jeremy was going to . . ." He cleared his throat.

"You know James, I've always wondered if you believed Jeremy would've raped me. Do you think he would have?"

"So, these *are* the clothes? Where'd they come from?" James looked around the kitchen anxiously.

"Are you afraid someone is listening?" I also looked around. "You didn't answer my question, James. Do you think Jeremy would've raped me?"

"It wouldn't have been the first time." He lowered his eyes. "But it would have been the first time I witnessed it."

I gasped. I'm not sure what answer I expected, but that was not it. "You wouldn't have stopped him?"

"Jeremy was the strongest of all of us, even when we were little. Nobody could stop him from doing anything." he said simply. "We were all too scared of him."

"And do you still feel the same fear of him?" The answer to that question might tell me just how wrapped up in this James really was. Fear was the biggest motivator. Fear could make you do just about anything.

"I have special forces training now. I'd like to believe that is enough to go head to head with Jeremy Richards, but I guess I won't know the answer to that until I'm faced with it, will I?"

His honest answer did little to make me feel better. This guy was going to protect me? Hardly.

"I just happened to run into your friend yesterday in Angela's old neighborhood. What do you think are the odds of that randomly happening?" I said.

"I'd say slim to none. Jeremy doesn't live anywhere near there. He's proud of his expensive house in Bar Harbor and his Escalade."

"Black Escalade?" I ask, even though I already know what the answer will be.

"Yes. How'd you know?"

"The bigger question I have is how you know where he lives and what he drives when you say you haven't stayed in touch."

"I told you. Our parents became good friends during the trial. They have remained friends even though we haven't. Senator Richards—sorry, Mr. Richards, he was a senator when we were growing up—brags about his son all the time."

That made sense. Even though I had promised myself I wouldn't, I told him about being tailed by a black Escalade yesterday on the way to the station. But as I was speaking, he was shaking his head.

"No, I don't think Jeremy would tail you. It's not his style. Must be a coincidence like you said." Although these were the words coming out of his mouth, the expression on his face told a different story.

I cocked my head, my eyebrows forming the question I wanted to ask.

He put up his hand, silently asking me to follow along. "Look, I've got some documents in my car I need you to sign. Would you mind walking me out and I can head out from there?" he asked. "Sorry to cut you off, but I'm running late for an appointment."

I didn't understand what was going on. This cat and mouse game of "I do trust him; I don't trust him" was wearing on me. It was time to decide once and for all. But I didn't know how to make the decision without Angela here to help me. What would she have done? Angela always trusted James Hawthorne. I was the one who wouldn't forgive him.

I thought about that for a minute before I said, "Sure, no problem," and followed him out the door.

As soon as we walked out into the world that had been transformed into an enormous snow globe, James said, "I think your house and car are bugged."

Chapter Twenty Six

BUGGED

Tuesday, December 6, 2022. 9:30 AM
24 hours left

We slid our way down the driveway, finally climbing into the safety of James' SUV. It took a few minutes for us to warm up.

"What makes you think my house is bugged? Or my car?"

Two hours ago, James Hawthorne was on my list of suspects, and now I had to believe he was helping me. It *could* be true, but he could also be setting it up to look like he was helping me when, in fact, he could have bugged my house and that's how he knew. But I was down to 24 hours. It was time to take a leap of faith.

"Daniela, put together the pieces of what you told me." He said earnestly. "You said you were tailed by a black Escalade to the station. Since that point, it seems like someone has been one step ahead of you. The only way that happens is with a bug. How would someone know exactly when you were going to the morgue? When you'd leave, when you'd return to your home to find the box? There might even be a camera aimed at your keypad for your alarm," he continued.

I tried to hear his words with both my detective's gut and my heart, using all of my instincts. Angela always told me I had great instincts, but they got caught up inside my insecurity. I tried hard now to push my insecurity aside. I listened carefully, and every word that came out of his mouth made me trust him more. Although this evidence was all over the place and all I really wanted to do was work the case without worrying about someone killing me, I owed it to Ang.

"I'm going to need you to go back inside and pretend to call a repairman, Dan. If there is a bug in your house, whoever planted it needs to believe that you are not onto him or her. It is the only way to catch them."

I let this sink in for a minute. I could feel a dark cloud beginning to settle inside of me. I'd never felt such desperation and confusion. Is this what those girls felt like? Is this what Angela felt like?

"James, "I looked directly at him. "I am going to go back into my house, call you from my landline, and give you my alarm code. I am going to pretend that my heat has gone out and that you are a heat repairman. I am going to tell you that I am leaving until it is repaired because it is too cold to stay inside. Then you can send in your guys to work their magic in my home. My car will be parked at the rental agency on Worcester Street. You can send your men there to check it out. I will pick it up when you're done."

I said this all calmly, but I think he realized I'd reached my limit of what I could deal with and that this would not be a good time to question me.

"James, please write your phone number down. I will pick up a burner phone and as soon as I've got it, I will call you so we can talk about the remaining things that need to be checked out."

He scrambled in his glovebox, searching for a scrap of paper, tearing off the corner of the registration. He pulled out a beautiful pen from his inner jacket pocket that I knew had to be a gift at some point and quickly wrote his number. I wondered if the pen was a gift from an old girlfriend.

"Thank you. Now, I've got a phone call to a repairman to make."

We locked eyes briefly, and when I sensed he was going to reach out and touch me, I jumped hastily out of his car. I wanted to believe in him with every ounce of my soul. But life has taught me that men only pretend to care, and when you really need someone, they are not there. In such a brief period, James Hawthorne had become someone important to me. I didn't understand why, and I was not comfortable with those feelings at all.

I reentered my home, made the call as I told him I would, and then went to my room to pack an overnight bag, just in case. I knew exactly where I was going. At the last minute, I decided to put my clothes into a plastic Walmart bag and left my overnight bag sitting on the kitchen table. If James was part of the problem, I just outwitted him.

I stopped at CVS on my way, picking up a burner phone. I got detoured because of the snowplows and came very close to the running path by the Charles River. It made me think of Sam, and I again wondered about him as a potential suspect. Nobody was out running in this snow, not even those crazy die-hard runners whose faces looked like they were going to die any minute. But my gut instinct told me that Sam was just an anomaly, a bigot that Ang happened upon who made her sad for a day. I hated him for that, but it didn't make him a likely killer.

Putting my cell phone in the glove box of the Beast, I drove to the rental agency on Worcester Street. I had my pick—nobody was renting cars in the snow. Once I was safely inside a nice little Subaru that looked like it could cut through just about any amount of snow New England could throw its way, I activated the phone and called Mrs. Monn. Her number was etched into my memory for years.

"Hi Mrs. Monn! This is Dan. Would you mind if I come by again this afternoon?" I knew she wouldn't mind, but manners had been bred into me. "I'm having some problems with my house."

"Oh Dan, I would love that. I would really like some help planning Angela's . . . last wishes."

Dear God, how could I have forgotten that? I had been so obsessed with figuring out who killed her that I had forgotten there were important details that had to be considered related to her death.

"Your father contacted me, you know. He has generously offered to pay for everything. He's such a good man." She choked back a sob.

I felt like I'd been punched in the gut. My father had thought of Mrs. Monn when I had not. "Yes, well, I'll see you soon, okay? Do you need anything?"

"Just you, Dan."

Guilt flooded my body, making me feel weak. Would I never learn how to nurture people I loved? Was I incapable? Shaking my head, I refocused on the task at hand. I had a place to stay. Now I had to take care of the items on my list. I had less than 24 hours left to solve this case, and that wasn't going to happen if I sat around beating myself up over my personal failures.

First things first. I called James.

"Special Agent James Hawthorne. How can I help you?" James sounded so . . . FBI. A thrill shot through me.

"Hey." I said. Immediately, I wanted to pull the word back into my mouth. I don't think I've ever said "hey" in my life. I seemed to be diminishing in everything by the moment: emotional stability, skills, and now, intelligence. I cleared my throat and started again. "I wanted to provide you with a list of items that I need you—an FBI agent—to take care of today, please." Geez, back to my awkward self.

"Sure," he said. "I've been waiting for your call." I could hear the amusement in his voice.

I took a deep breath and dug in. "I'll need you to contact the four suicide cases in the Boston area and ask them the same questions you asked of the Maine victims yesterday. Also, please try to pick up their laptops and drop them by the Chelsea office for analysis. Additionally, I need you to do a deep dive into the people who made Angela's fake ID and see if they might be possible suspects and try to locate Joaquin. And last of all, can you drop off the box that the clothes came in and have it fingerprinted to see if any of the prints come up in the system?"

"Is that all?" he asked. "Consider them done."

"And please don't forget that I have less than 22 hours left until my captain pulls me off the case so everything needs to be rushed." I knew I was stating the obvious, but I still felt the need to say it.

And then, because he didn't ask, I felt obligated to let him know what I would be doing. "I'm going to stop by the actual address of Lily Legacy and try to speak with the person in charge to get a copy of Angela's contract. Hopefully, it can shed some light on some missing pieces."

I didn't mention that I was dropping by my childhood home, unannounced, since that seemed to have little to do with the case. But my detective's gut was telling me to go.

"What time do you want to hook up today?" he asked.

I felt a heat surge to my face like a schoolgirl. Hook up? I was glad that he was on the other end of a phone and couldn't see me. Geez, I needed to get over this physical whatever it was and quick. If Angela had felt like this before, I could fully understand why she hired the slimeball from Romeo to the Rescue. I wondered why it took a childhood enemy to bring this out in me. I think I'm defective.

"Let's play it by ear. I'll contact you." All I really wanted to do was end the call.

Lily Legacy was on the outskirts of Newton Upper Falls. A few companies occupied the space, and a great stairwell in highly polished old oak led up to the second floor. The office was just off the stairwell and to the left. The waiting area was circular around a great old brick fireplace that burned on every one of the four floors. You couldn't beat Boston when it came to original old English beauty. Of course, there was a price to pay for all that beauty—quite a price. I couldn't even imagine how much an office like that would cost in Newton Upper Falls. It was hard to understand how the trial could possibly be free.

A slightly plump blonde woman with hot pink oversized glasses greeted me warmly. She was not at all who I expected to greet me at a weight loss trial facility. But then again, I didn't know what else they did there. That may just be one small piece.

"Good morning. My name is Candace. How can I help you?" She smiled slightly. I caught a glimpse of overly whitened, perfectly aligned teeth.

"Hello Candace. My name is Daniela. A friend of mine came here for a weight loss trial?"

Candace's smile froze in place. "I'm sorry. You must be mistaken. We don't do weight loss trials here. This is a DoD facility. We only operate trials for the CIA and the FBI outside of the defense contractors." She showed me even more teeth in her next smile, but it did not reach her eyes.

Darn. I wished I had my phone so I could prove to her that I knew she was lying. Instead, I decided to lie too. "Oh—I must be mistaken. My friend gave me a copy of her contract and your name and address were at the top of the contract. The TUC trials?" I smiled widely. "She lost a hundred pounds on that trial—it was just amazing!" I gushed before she could say anything else. "The thing is---her doctor said he would see me because obviously I have hormonal issues too. Can't gain a pound no matter what I eat. So, I was just wondering if you could give me her doctor's name?"

I held my breath, waiting for her to ask me why my friend didn't give me the doctor's name. "Hang on," she said. I could tell that she felt I was nonthreatening. I think most people saw me that way because I am so small. "Okay now, what did you say her name was?"

"Angel Adams."

"It looks like Alejandro Zambrano oversaw her case."

Zambrano? *What a weird coincidence that he has the same last name as Margette.*

She flashed me her first real smile. "He doesn't have any initials behind his name, but you know how it is these days. Nobody's a doctor anymore. Everyone is an assistant of some sort."

"Isn't that the truth? Thank you for your kindness." I shook her hand, "Oh, one more question please? Does Dr. Neely work from this building?"

"I'm sorry miss. I don't know a Dr. Neely."

I nodded and left the building that Angela had visited for over a year. I had never once come with her. My feet felt leaden as I made their way back down the over polished oak stairs, turning the name of Angela's doctor over and over in my head. As soon as I got to the bottom, I stopped and googled "Is the surname Zambrano common in the United States?" My immediate response that there are 11,409 Zambranos in the United States did little to calm my mind. The coincidences were really starting to stack up in a strange way.

I stopped by Ang's bakery on the way back to my hometown. It was, for obvious reasons, Mrs. Monn's favorite. It was the least I could do for her. Thankfully, Sofie was on break. I wasn't sure I could continue to lie directly to her face. I didn't know what would happen to Angela's bakery now that she was gone, but the one thing I did know was that some of her original recipe peach cobbler would make her mother feel comforted.

That cobbler had gotten her listed in 'The Boston Foodie Guide' the past three years, a feat that had more than doubled her business. She called it Angel Cobbler. Experts called it a "heavenly experience" and labeled Angel Cakes an "essential stop in your visit to Boston." She had been so proud. I looked around the quaint little shop, buzzing with local business even on a snowy day like today. It wasn't surprising. Boston was a social city, and most places were walkable and easily accessible by public transportation. It takes more than 8 inches of snow to shut down the T.

Angela had handpicked the location. "It has to be in Jamaica Plain," she'd insisted, even though we had seen larger buildings for better prices elsewhere. But she'd done her homework, and she knew that Jamaica Plain was the most culturally diverse area in town and that was where she wanted to land her business. She had also hoped to move there one day, but Mattapan was as close as she could afford. Compared to the impoverished and crime ridden area where she had grown up and Mrs. Monn still lived, Mattapan was a step up.

I approached the turnoff to my childhood home in Blackstone. I was nearly past it when I suddenly swerved the wheel and made the turn. *I can do this.*

I drove slowly down the long, well-manicured drive. The trees had snowy boughs and crystalline icicles hanging from them. It was a magnificent sight. Almost as beautiful as fall, my favorite time of year to visit the house, with the mighty oak, maple, and chestnut trees lining the driveway like they were celebrating my arrival.

There were no cars in the drive, but I knew there could be some around back in the four car garage. I pulled up out front to a walk that was, as always, magically clear. Another of those things I took for granted and now wondered about since I had to shovel my own walks.

I put the key in the lock and pushed the door open, giving a shout out. "Anybody home?"

My voice echoed through the void. I did not hear any movement anywhere in the house, so I continued in, removing my shoes as I had been raised to do.

I stood and waited. It was a ritual I repeated every time I came. I waited for that "I'm home" feeling to wash over me. It didn't come. It never did.

The house looked the same as it always did. I was standing on a white marbled entryway that opened expansively into an enormous columned great room filled with white sofas and assorted side and end tables. The exotic rugs were the only splash of color in the room, and even those were muted shades of lavender, blue, and gray. At one side of the room was a floor to ceiling stone fireplace. But the only adornment was a massive seascape placed about 15 feet up the stone. At the rear of the room, a staircase curved out widely on both sides, as if inviting all who entered to the second floor. I always thought that was a weird place for stairs.

Behind the staircase lay the kitchen. I walked in that direction since the garage would be accessible beyond it—the easiest way to find out if anybody was currently occupying the home. The kitchen, modern and enormous, was immaculate save for one sheet of paper lying on the counter near the coffee pot, which, upon closer inspection appeared to have coffee in it. Walking over, I put my hand on the pot. *Cold.* Whoever had enjoyed this particular pot of coffee had not done so recently. I glanced down at the paper and froze. It was not a sheet of paper but rather a sheaf of papers. It was Angela's missing contract.

I whirled around quickly, expecting someone to be behind me. There was nobody in the room with me. I placed my hand on my gun, edging toward the garage door. I threw open the door and drew my weapon, fully expecting the intruder to attack. But I was pointing my gun at an empty garage. I reholstered my weapon, pulled a pair of rubber gloves out of my inner pocket and crossed back over to the contract. I photographed every page of the contract, and then took photographs of the contract as it sat on the counter. I desperately wanted to take it with me—to check for fingerprints or saliva. Almost every person turned the page of a contract the same: wet your fingers with spit, grab the lower right corner and turn. I scanned my brain for anything that would pick up the fingerprint or DNA on this contract. Then I had an idea.

First, I opened the dishwasher. Damn. No cups. Whoever drank the coffee must have washed their cup. But I knew I had tape in my room from my days of scientific experiments. So, I headed up the stairs toward my blue room. The house felt so eerie now that I knew someone else had been there—and not just any someone, but a someone who had the ability to steal evidence from the evidence locker at the precinct. I shook my head, trying to figure out who that could possibly be.

I entered my room. Everything looked exactly as it always had. If I had been born a boy, I would have been such a lucky boy. The room was quite beautiful. My heart swelled with grief over what could have been if only I'd been born the right sex. But then my dad's words from the other night came back to me.

"I left the hospital that day to meet the decorator. I didn't want my new baby girl to come home to a blue bedroom." Those don't sound like the words of a man who was sad about having a baby girl. Those sound like the words of a man who was excited about having a baby girl. What had happened? Why did he stop loving me?

I dropped briefly into the rocker—my nanny's rocker, until it became the only chair in the room and then it was my rocker. Rocking back and forth, I thought about his next words. "And then I found the ledger beneath the mattress. You weren't mine. I had to let your grandmother raise you." How could I not be his? Surely that was the alcohol talking because he had, in fact, raised me and I did not have any grandmothers.

But then the name from earlier sprang forward in my mind. Zambrano. The name of Angela's doctor. That was Margette's last name. Margette Zambrano. That's why the name struck a chord with me. I got out my phone and skimmed through the documents, finding the signature of Alejandro Zambrano on the last page. He was not a doctor. He was a Paramilitary Operations Officer for the CIA. What are the odds that the person in charge of Angela's experiment had the same last name as my nanny? I needed to look up the Zambranos in the immediate area to see how many there were.

I crossed to the crib and held my breath. Could the ledger possibly still be there 25 years later? I lifted the mattress end carefully. Nothing. Then I yanked the entire mattress out of the crib. Still, nothing. How stupid to think it would still be there. And what was I really looking for anyhow? I had no idea. A drunken man's imaginary ledger? Dear God. *Angela, I'm losing it. Really losing it. Come back! I need you. I cannot do this without you*! I closed my eyes, squeezing out the tears, silently begging her.

I took a few deep breaths, regrouped, grabbed the tape from the box labeled "science projects" still under the bed and left my room. On an impulse, I went down the hall to my father's room. I pushed open the door and froze stunned.

My father's enormous, perfectly manicured, masculine room looked like a disaster zone. Clearly the maid had not visited because of the snow. The bed was unmade. There were clothes—*women's* clothes—strewn about the room, draped over the chairs, headboard, and lying on the floor. There were crumpled towels, which I assumed to be wet (my nose involuntarily crinkled at the thought of mold and mildew growing there). I entered the room and crossed into the bathroom which looked equally disastrous if not worse. I made a quick decision then. Since I was still wearing my gloves, I grabbed the toothbrush, the hairbrush, the coffee cup (so she hadn't washed it after all—I doubt this woman had ever washed anything in her life) and rolled the three of them into a plastic shower cap sitting on the edge of the tub.

My heart began to pound furiously. I was afraid of getting caught. Now I had something to lose. I flew down the stairs, nearly forgetting to return to the kitchen to use the strips of tape for fingerprints. Although I might have enough DNA on the other items, fingerprints would come back much quicker. My hands were shaking badly. I was terrified in my own home. I listened acutely for any sounds. I didn't realize I'd been holding my breath until I was buckled into the rental and driving back down the lane. Then I realized the ignorance of my actions and burst out laughing, although it wasn't funny in any way. I didn't take the contract so nobody would know I was there, but I took her toothbrush, hairbrush, and coffee mug. She would surely miss those things. Geez. Sometimes I could be stupid. Also, someone was going to notice the mattress was ripped out of the crib. . .

I needed to get these items to James for quick analysis. Someone at the precinct had to have given this lady those papers. She couldn't have just walked in and taken them. Which means that I wasn't the only one who knew Angela was murdered. And I needed to talk to my father about who she was and tell him that she was involved in Angela's murder. I knew he would care about that at least—unless of course . . . but no—I couldn't believe he would hurt Angela. I just couldn't. But if I turned this new evidence over to my captain, it was all over for my dad.

I stopped at the end of the drive and dialed James. I didn't give him a chance to speak. "James. I need you to meet me at Mrs. Monn's house. I've got items that must be analyzed immediately. I think someone at the precinct might be involved in Angela's murder."

"Whoa!" he exclaimed. "What happened in the past three hours?"

"I can't explain now. This burner phone is a flip, and this rental doesn't have blue tooth so I can't drive and talk. I'm at my house—my dad's house. I need to leave before she gets back."

"Before whom gets back?"

"James!"

"Okay, yes. I'll head right over. Most of the roads are cleared now so it shouldn't be more than 45 minutes or so," he said.

"Thank you," I hung up. Every minute I sat in the driveway, my stomach was churning. All I wanted was to leave.

I began the short journey over to Mrs. Monn's house. Strangely, her unsafe neighborhood offered me great safety.

Chapter Twenty Seven

SAFETY IS HOME

Tuesday, December 6, 2022. 1:00 PM
20 hours 30 minutes left

I breathed a sigh of relief as I pulled in front of Mrs. Monn's house. Someone had shoveled the snow away from her curb. I smiled. The neighbors were caring for her. In a neighborhood where the police were called several times a week, I felt confident that no harm would come to her. She was well loved. She had earned the respect and trust of most simply by being who she was, never judging the drug dealer who looked like a thug or the ex-con who pawned stolen items. They received the same respect and offers of treats on a hot summer day that the old lady down the street did. "We're all just people trying to get by one way or another," was a favorite saying of hers. She was a beautiful human, and I was so fortunate to be part of her life. They even accepted me since I was someone she loved, and believe me, they hated cops.

Mrs. Monn was waiting for me and spread her arms wide as I came up the front steps onto her porch. After we'd embraced, I showed her what I had in my hand—the peach cobbler—and tears gathered in her eyes. "Oh Dan, you are such an Angel, my new Angel."

My throat thickened at her words. I didn't want to be her new angel. I wanted her old angel to be here. But she was a woman of faith, and she was prepared to move on, trusting in me to solve her girl's case. And she was also prepared to move on and love me—not in her place, but just as much.

As we dug into the magnificent cobbler, I wondered why I hadn't spent more time tasting and enjoying Angela's food. It would have made her so happy. I could have—should have—tried harder to make food more important to me since it was so important to her.

"Dan, I can see what you're thinking and it's okay." Mrs. Monn gently patted my hand. "Angela was never offended that you were not a foodie. She didn't understand it, mind you," she laughed, "but she knew food wasn't your thing. Saving people is your thing."

"It is?" I asked, shocked. I'd never thought of myself as someone who saved people. I just didn't want anyone to feel like me—like they had nobody to turn to, nobody who cared.

A knock at the door interrupted our conversation. "Oh shoot! I forgot to mention that my partner was stopping by to pick up a few items," I said, getting up to answer the door.

"Sit down, sit down. Surely, he has a minute for a piece of Angela's peach cobbler. I've never met anyone yet who didn't love it," she said proudly. She walked to the door and let James in. "You! What happened to Detective O'Malley?" she asked.

James looked like a deer in headlights. "I'm afraid I don't know Detective O'Malley. Don't you remember me Mrs. Monn? I went to school with Angela and Daniela. I graduated a couple of years ahead of them. James Hawthorne."

Her eyebrows shot upwards. "James Hawthorne of the 6-Pack? My goodness Dan. You've really come a long way sweetheart. I'm proud of you." Only I could see the mischievous twinkle in her eyes.

The awkwardness of the moment was cut by Mrs. Monn's tinkling laugh. "Oh, come on in now James. All are welcome here. We've all been blockheads at one time or another in our lives. Have a seat. We were just having some of Angela's peach cobbler," she said. And before he could protest, she added, "It's the best of Boston, you know. How could anyone say no to that?"

James took a seat and smiled warmly at Mrs. Monn. "You got me there." They were going to be just fine.

I finished my cobbler quickly. Three meals in half a day, a record for me.

"I'm going to run out to the car really quick and grab the evidence for you James."

As much as I was enjoying the time with them—with him—I desperately needed to know who was staying in my home.

When I returned, James and Mrs. Monn appeared to be fast friends. He was an easy man to like. I sensed something good in him that I hadn't wanted to believe was there. I hoped I wasn't imagining it because of my attraction to him.

Trying to be as polite as possible about getting him back out the door, I told him, "I left the evidence by the front door. There are a few things I need to tell you about it in confidence before you leave."

"Oh, of course,' he said, standing. "Thank you, Mrs. Monn. You are the most gracious hostess."

Mrs. Monn's cheeks were rosy. "Angela always liked you; you know? She always said you weren't like the rest of them. I trusted my girl's opinion then, and now that I've met you, I agree with her. You're good people. I feel it here," she said as she put her fist to her heart.

The whole thing really shook me. Why couldn't I be like her—like them. Why had I vacillated for days, wondering if he was trying to help me or kill me? What had made me so suspicious and untrusting? I hated the way I felt and wanted to be different. I wanted to trust James as easily as her. Was it only because he was male? Or was I holding a grudge from the past?

Mrs. Monn took the hint and began cleaning up our mess. I walked James to the door, briefing him on everything that had happened since we last spoke.

He looked up at me suddenly. "Angela's doctor shared the same last name as your nanny?" he asked in a disbelieving tone.

"Well, yes and no. Yes, they shared the same last name but as it turns out, he was not a doctor. He is some kind of an Operations Officer for the CIA—paramilitary I think."

As I spoke, I could see the look of disbelief in James eyes turn into something else. I couldn't decide exactly what it was. Excitement? Fear?

"James? What's going on?" I asked.

"Please just send me all the pages of the contract. I will drop these items by the Chelsea office and have Isaac process them. He and I go way back. I trust him."

I trust him? Were we now suspicious of the FBI too? Good God, how many agencies were involved in this coverup? And why? I knew asking would do no good. With the FBI, it was always "need to know."

"When will you have information about my house? My car? The box?" I wanted my life back. I wanted Angela back. I wanted to scream until all of the anguish in my chest was released.

"Dan, I promise, I will call you the minute I know anything. Keep doing what you are doing. I think you may have just blown the case open. This seems a safe place for you. She," he nodded toward the living room, "seems good for you right now."

"Yes, she is . . . but we are down to 20 hours. Please, please hurry. It will break her heart if she must bury her daughter as a suicide."

Mrs. Monn was busying herself in the kitchen. She asked if I could stay at her house for a day or two. I wondered how much she had heard.

"You'll sleep in Angela's old room of course. I've slept in there a couple of times, and it has brought me great comfort. You don't look well Dan. You *need* to sleep there tonight."

After the week I had experienced so far, I couldn't agree more, although I knew I had no time for sleep. I put my Walmart and CVS bags in the room, neither escaping Mrs. Monn's notice. "I plan to be able to return home tonight. These are 'just in case,' but thank you for the offer."

"Are you finding yourself in danger trying to solve this case, Dan?"

I couldn't lie to her. "Yes, Mrs. Monn. But don't worry, I won't let it deter me." I replied earnestly.

"I know you won't, dear. But remember, Angela would want you to be safe, too."

"I know. That's why I came here—for safety. I have so much to figure out and only a few hours left to do it. Somewhere in there, I promise to grab a couple of hours of sleep—safe sleep."

"We could make that happen," she replied decidedly. "Let's get you settled in and talk about happier times."

"Oh Mrs. Monn, I would love to, but I really need to talk to my father. I must ask him some questions and I really want to see the look on his face when I do. I was going to drive over to Neely Pharmaceuticals." This would be my third visit in two days and the fourth time I'd spoken with him. Normally, this multitude of interactions between us would have taken place over about a six month span.

"Well dear, you know that this time of the day, traffic is terrible with the work-weekers returning to their homes, and everyone gets especially worked up about the snow. How about if I just invite him over for some early dinner. You can't eat peach cobbler for lunch. Surely, anything you need to discuss, you can discuss here?"

Oh God, if only it was that simple. If my father was involved in Angela's death, Mrs. Monn was going to be crushed. To be honest, so was I. Even though we didn't have a typical father/daughter relationship, I still always respected him, and lately, I sensed that maybe there was something else there. I hadn't quite figured out what yet, but something.

However, I knew she was right about the traffic. I sent a prayer up to the heavens silently as I watched her dial his number. "Please mom, if you are up there and you can hear me, don't let dad be a killer."

Of course, the great Markus Neely could not make it to dinner. I would have been shocked had he shown up. His assistant said he was out of the country. I found that highly unlikely. You'd think that is something he would have mentioned that to me this morning. But it was hard to tell with him. As usual, I knew nothing about his life. I never had. For all I knew, he could have taken my call from a private airplane or from Switzerland. Worse yet, what if he was in country having an illicit rendezvous at the house. That possibility would make him the prime suspect.

Angela's contract had been sitting openly on the counter and he had denied knowledge of the trial. I hoped that was not the case.

I made a decision that spending a little time with Mrs. Monn was as important as finding Angela's killer. Angela would want me to be there for her. I could sacrifice a few hours for her. I would beg Cap for an extension on my hands and knees if I had to. The day I was attacked in high school, Mrs. Monn left work with no hesitation, even though she was low income. For all I know, she couldn't pay her rent that month, but still, she came. Unlike Margette, who didn't work—I was her only job—who arrived two hours later. Mrs. Monn and Angela defended me to the police officer, and when Margette offered money to Mrs. Monn, even though I knew she needed it, she refused.

"Here, sit Dan. Let's talk." She patted the sofa next to her. "I've been reading through Angela's recipe journals and want to share some of them with you. They ease the pain in my heart, and I know they will help you too."

"That is so kind of you." I replied. I wondered how long we would avoid the unpleasant topic of Angela's funeral arrangements. Why didn't we think of things like that while we were alive? How horrible that the people left behind had to make decisions about what to do with your dead body.

"There is one page that I think will make you happy. It is from the day Angela created her friendship bread recipe."

Angela's friendship bread had been a major hit at her bakery. Orders were placed up to six months in advance for friends, sisters, mothers. Once she had even received an order for a parish minister to share with his staff of elders.

"I hope that someday you have the time to read all of her entries, but for today, I want you to read just this one."

I took the book from her and settled in to read the entry.

"I'm going to make a care package for you—some dinners to microwave when you're home—while you read sweetheart."

Angela's Recipe Book

October 21, 2013

I have so much to tell you about Daniela! But first things first, I have to write down the new recipe I just created—with 'us' in mind. It is especially awesome because I could bake two smaller loaves and let Daniela take one loaf home too. I love the concept. I LOVE HAVING A BEST FRIEND!!!! When I sell it in my bakery someday, I will sell it as two small loaves and they will be labeled 'for you,' and 'for your friend,' but they will be tied together, side by side with a huge ribbon (preferably pink!). I think people will love buying it to share with their best friend or someone they love. I need to figure out a way to ship it to different states for loved ones who live far away. I'm going to have such an amazing bakery! I have incredible ideas every single day. I was born to bake!

For the record, it is a cinnamon-based bread because cinnamon is not only good for your physical health, but also helps you with emotional challenges in your life, pushing away bad feelings and thoughts. Win/win. I wonder if people would like it if I put little note cards on the bread that said that? IDEA to remember!!!

Cinnamon Friendship Bread

Ingredients:

½ tsp baking soda

2 tsp baking powder

3 tsp ground cinnamon 2 tsp Almond extract

¼ cup extra virgin olive oil 2 large organic eggs

1 cup of buttermilk

1 cup of light brown sugar

2 cups of almond flour

Mix all ingredients in large bowl, preferably with a wire whisk, until well combined.

Pour into two (or three, don't overfill pans) well buttered mini loaf pans

Cook at 350 degrees for 40 to 50 minutes (when a toothpick comes out clean) Upon removal from oven, roll butter over top of hot loaf and allow to sink in.

Cover with foil after cooling.

SHARE WITH YOUR FRIEND or SOMEONE YOU LOVE!!!

Now, onto my news about my new friend. It wasn't my imagination. We really have become best friends. It was worth every minute of the 15 years I had to wait. I think we bring out the best in each other, although for some reason, she can't see much goodness in herself. That makes me sad, but I am determined to help her find her groove—her one thing that fills her up inside. Maybe she can't find that until she feels loved. (Or maybe she just needs to eat healthier first! She is so skinny and barely cares about food—that is unbelievable!)

I can see so many things I have always taken for granted are actually really big things. But she said the same thing to me after the first time she left my house. Funny. She said she never really noticed before how things just 'happened' at her house. Like the gardeners showed up to groom the landscaping, which was insane and definitely a full time job. Or how food just showed up at their house. She never once wondered how or when it got there. <u>She has never been to the grocery store in her life</u>! Have you ever heard of something that crazy? She kind of lives in this weird little bubble world where she gets up, eats, does everything she is told to do like school and gymnastics, studies [a LOT because she loves to learn] and goes to bed. I have definitely rocked her world with my mad cooking skills. Oh, and there are fresh lilies delivered every single week just because her mom's name was Lily (Lillian). How creepy is that? We don't hang out at her house very often because it feels so awkward there. Here's a perfect example. Her bedroom is decorated for a boy. And she is a girl. I know you know that but she's not like me. She was born a girl and always wants to be a girl. It's not just a blue room either; it is seriously a baby boy room that still has a crib in it. Lions and tigers and bears, oh my! Of course, she doesn't sleep in the crib—she sleeps in the bed her nanny used to sleep in, but still . . . it is just so awkward that her room looks like that! Why? She said she never asked. But why would she even need to ask?

My mom has always been so sensitive to my gender preference. She has never made me feel awkward or uncomfortable. She has never made me feel guilty that we have to live in a small house in this neighborhood so she can afford the treatments. My dad would freak out if he knew what his support money paid for! (That actually makes me happy—pretty sure that is called poetic justice.) Mom just encourages me and says things like, "Aren't we lucky to live in Boston where you have access to the treatments you need." My mom is a champion like that. From the time I was little—she was one of the first to buy Lili Elbe's book when it was released in the US—Man into Woman. That book gave me so much hope for my future. It always feels good to know you're not alone—that there are other people like you, who fought to live their life the way they knew they should. And she didn't stop there. She kept searching for ways to help me. When we found out that Boston Children's Hospital was starting a gender management service, my mom went there in person to meet them and make sure I wasn't just a 'number' to them. That they saw me for the valuable person I was. And she succeeded. They are so nice to me there when I go for check ins and shots.

I felt guilty, standing in Daniela's little boy bedroom, knowing my mom works extra shifts and would use her very last dollar for my puberty blockers and estrogen. How can parents be so different? Why don't all parents love their children?

I will love my children the way my mom loves me. I will cherish them. And eventually, my mom and I will make Daniela feel loved—I know we will—and we'll help her see her value as a person. She's so smart and so deadpan blunt that it can be pretty funny sometimes. But the best is when something bad happens and she laughs . . . the look on people's faces? Like she is a monster. Itty bitty Daniela is a monster. She doesn't have a mean bone in her body. She's just afraid—pretty much of everything and everyone.

But speaking of monsters, Jeremy Richards got away scot free. No kidding. He did not get into trouble at all for what he did to Daniela. It's interesting how evidence can go missing when you have a powerful daddy. She is still really scared of him. She believes he will come after her again. It's been 6 weeks since the assault, and he's still leaving scary notes in her locker almost every day. My mom thinks she might need some therapy. She is still very jumpy and afraid. But Daniela said therapy is not on the table. It's not like they can't afford it. Maybe she's right and nobody does care about her. I don't know why her nanny couldn't take her. That lady has no other job except to take care of Daniela. She's a strange one. If I didn't know Daniela's mom was dead, I would've thought Margette could be her mom. She just kind of looks like her but I guess she is pretty old. She sure doesn't treat her like a daughter though. She treats her like she is someone she just met. I don't understand that at all. How could you not love someone you've watched their whole life? Someone as sweet as Daniela?

Daniela thinks her dad doesn't love her but maybe he just needs to work all of the time to pay for all of those expensive things. I met him once and he seemed kind of nice—sad, really worn out and tired, but nice. He said he liked my ribbon cupcakes, so I know he has good taste. I always send home extras for her dad and Margette, but Margette has never mentioned it once—not even to say "thank you." Like I said, she's a strange one.

But Daniela doesn't need to rely on her anymore. She's got me and mom. Every day I can feel her loving and trusting us more. We won't ever let her down. Right now, we've just got to get her through this school year. I think once the seniors—Jeremy and his buddies—leave town for college, she might be better.

P.S. I think she'll love the bread!

When Mrs. Monn came in to check on me, I was re-reading the entry. Angela had always told me that she instantly knew we were meant to be friends forever, but this entry was so heartfelt. She really loved me. I looked up at Mrs. Monn through the glimmer of my tears.

"I know, Dan. She loved you immediately." She patted my shoulder. "I can't lie. Even though I always supported her decisions 100%, there was a small part of me that always wondered if I hadn't, would the two of you have met and married? Were you meant to be?"

I was shocked at this postmortem confession from a woman who had never done anything but openly support her son's decision to become a female from the time he was five years old. "But deep inside, I always knew that she knew herself so who was I to question?"

Yes, if anyone knew herself, it was Angela. I wonder how that happened. I wished it could happen to me. I wished I could feel comfortable in my own skin.

"We'll get through this together," I assured her.

True to her word, Mrs. Monn described the wonderful dinners that she packed up for me. I was eager to eat for a change. I had forgotten what an amazing cook Mrs. Monn was. Angela could make her bakery goods, but when it came to a home cooked meal, Mrs. Monn was the real deal. I felt so sad for a man so shallow and stupid that he would leave two wonderful people like them just because Ang wanted to be a girl. It made me almost wish him misery in his second marriage. He just didn't deserve happiness after throwing away such great people. But I never was as good a person as Ang, who wished him no harm. "I'm happy. I hope he is too." She'd always said. She was so good.

As much as I hated to, finally, I excused myself, telling her I had very important phone calls to make. Going into Angela's old bedroom, I dialed the first number on my list and got voicemail.

"Hey Chief, this is Detective Neely. I'm calling to see if I can get any extension at all on my case. I've collected numerous additional facts that point to homicide, and I'm working with FBI special agent James Hawthorne around the clock trying to not only solve this murder but also tie it into four identical suicide situations in Maine." I hoped that the mention of the FBI and the additional cases would buy me the extra time I might need. My gut told me I was close. I continued. "I discovered that my vehicle, my house and my phone were bugged so I am not staying at home, and you can reach me at this number temporarily: 857-555-1212."

My chief had been very clear about time allotted to me and I thought it highly unlikely he would grant an extension, but I had to at least try—just in case.

My next call was to James. He picked up before the first ring had finished.

"Dan, we've struck gold! Although a lot of what I've learned is going to be hard for you," he spoke.

My stomach dropped. My dad had left the country. I could pretty much guess what he was going to tell me.

"Did my dad kill my best friend?"

How could he? He knew she was all I had—the only person who had ever loved me. How could he take away that one little thing that brought me happiness?

"What? No!" He sputtered. "Definitely not! Sorry—didn't realize your mind would go there."

I sat up straighter, drawing back. Definitely not? Where else could my mind go? What other possible news could be hard for me?

"Okay, first things first," he said. "I spent all afternoon speaking to the families of the Boston victims, cross analyzing the data from the Boston victims to the Maine victims, and they are basically identical except for Angela. They all took part in the clinical trial that utilized an implant with quarterly check-ins at the local office of, you guessed it, Lily Legacy. The whole virgin thing was pretty much random and how do you really know anyhow? I mean, don't all girls tell their parents they are virgins? Other than the two discovered through autopsy by Jake, we don't really know. So, that's two definite virgins out of 8, *and* LaTonya's Romeo was an actual guy named Romeo—not in any way affiliated with Romeo to the Rescue. Three of the four parents are willing to drop off their computers for analysis, but quite honestly, I don't see that goinganywhere. But that is the only the bad, bad news. I've got plenty of good, bad news too."

I took a deep breath. So far, it sounded as if we didn't have a leg to stand on—like we'd done nothing but spin our wheels for four days. But

I knew that police work often looked like that before a case split wide open, so I hoped his good, bad news was a whole lot better.

"I'll start with the bugs. Only your vehicle and house were compromised, not your phone. Your car had a tracking device, which we removed. Someone planted it behind your front right wheel well."

I was relieved. I missed the Beast. I needed it now more than ever. I remembered being tailed by the black Escalade as far as the station and tried to visualize where I had parked there.

"I'm pretty sure the bug would have been planted on my car at the station," I told him. "We could probably pull surveillance cameras to see who planted it."

"Great idea. I'll get right on that," he said.

"And my house?" I asked.

"So, I was right," he said. "Your home was bugged in several places. But there were no cameras, so either you forgot to leave the alarm on or the someone who placed the box has a sophisticated device that disarms them. They exist."

Of course they do. And who exactly would have such a device? The FBI? The CIA?

"The next thing I have to tell you, you're not going to want to hear," he said. He sounded apologetic. Since he had already told me my dad was not a murderer, I couldn't really understand his hesitation. The only other person in my life I trusted was Mrs. Monn, and I knew she would never hurt me.

"The fingerprints on the box—the only sets of fingerprints on the box, and there were quite a few of them—belonged to Detective Thomas O'Malley."

My body doubled over involuntarily, a sharp gasp escaping my lips as the air seemed to rush out of me, leaving me breathless and struggling to regain my composure. O'Malley did this to me? How had I forgotten about him? He was my partner. I trusted him with my life every day on the job. I trusted him with my alarm code because we had stopped by many times during an investigation. He didn't need a camera or a sophisticated device. He had the code.

"Dan?" James' concern was evident. "I wish I could say that was the worst of the news but there is more coming."

"More coming that is worse than my partner betraying me? Dear God, James, why don't you just shoot me and get it over with?" The bitterness in my voice oozed through every word.

"Dan, don't forget what your goal is here. To find Angela's killer. I believe we are going to do that."

He said this with such conviction that it snapped me out of my self-pity. But I wasn't going to let it go. As soon as we hung up, I was going to call O'Malley and let him know that I knew. No more nice guy.

"What else?" I asked, bracing myself.

"Well, I did a little digging, and it turns out that one Margette Zambrano had a son named Alejandro Zambrano. I doubted that was a coincidence when you mentioned it. Boston has a very small Ecuadorian population."

What? Margette said her family lived in Ecuador and that she never got to see her "one perfect son." If she lived and worked locally, why couldn't she see him? Didn't she know?

"That doesn't really fit with the things Margette said to me," I told him.

"Well, it gets better than that. Alejandro was your mother's first assistant, so there is no doubt she would have met Margette through Alejandro."

Nausea twisted like a snake through my churning stomach. Every moment I was putting together a worse picture in my mind. I was afraid to find out what was next.

"Is there any way you can dig into Alejandro's background? See if maybe my mother hired Margette to help him pay back student loans or help him through the academy or something?"

I liked that idea—that my mother had been their savior. Surely someone was a good person in all this mess. Maybe it was my mom.

"I already did the digging Dan. This part is strange. I don't know what it means or how it fits—or even if it has anything at all to do with anything. It might just be information and nothing more."

He hesitated.

"Just say it."

I hated the dejected tone in my voice, but so far, I was unable to put together any clear picture of why anyone would want to hurt Angela and why. Surely Margette's son wouldn't have hurt her because he was jealous that his mother lived with me? Was it my fault Angela was dead? Was he still trying to kill me?

"Alejandro is married to the man who delivered you."

I didn't see that one coming. And he was right. I didn't know if that had anything to do with anything but if life had taught me one thing it was that coincidences rarely happened.

"Hmmm," I said. "How incredibly odd and convenient." Was this even more reason for Alejandro to hate me? Was this guy Alejandro responsible for both Angela's death and trying to kill me? And Jake? *He knew she was too old.* That would make sense if Margette had told him that she was my friend—my age. Is that how he knew?

"I'm almost afraid to ask if there is anything more, James."

Even I could hear the defeated tone in my voice. I felt like a pumpkin that had been hollowed out for Halloween. The grimace on my face probably resembled one too.

"Well . . . The fingerprint on the contract came up with a top secret clearance match. I haven't been able to get that result released yet, and of course, none of the DNA is back yet. I know those are critical pieces of evidence and that you went through a lot of stress to get them. I'll pull every string I can to push them through."

"Thank you, James. Right now, I can't make heads nor tails out of any of it, but please, if you come up with anything, please let me know immediately." My voice had become husky by the end of my speech and cracked as I finished, "I'm thankful for your help. I guess Angela was right about you all along."

I said my goodbyes to Mrs. Monn, reiterating how much I loved her and how grateful I was for her love and support, just in case things didn't work out good for me during the remainder of the investigation. I suggested she think about taking over Angela's bakery.

"Angela would be so happy to have you there, and her staff knows her recipes," I encouraged

"I was thinking the same thing," she said. "It will keep me close to my girl."

To my girl. What a wonderful mother. I wish every transsexual child in the world could be born to a mother like Mrs. Monn.

"Thank you for everything. See you at Christmas?" We both knew we would see each other sooner than that and for a much sadder occasion, but we each chose to ignore it. We each had jobs to do before then—important jobs—to take care of Angela.

"Wouldn't miss it for the world." She kissed my cheek.

Chapter Twenty Eight

BACKED INTO A WALL

Tuesday, December 6, 2022. 5:30 PM
16 hours left

O'Malley. I knew the sound of his voice was going to hurt me. I'd trusted him and had been burned—again.

"Dan, what's going on? I hear your corpse buddy is dead. How you doing?" O'Malley sounded concerned.

"Yes, my friend Jake is dead," I said. "His family will never see him again. And I've been working day and night, trying to crack Angela's case." I barely trusted myself to talk to him, but I pushed on.

"I thought we agreed it was a hate crime?" He says this like we had solved the case days ago and I was a complete idiot for pursuing it further. I wondered how many times he had spoken to me like that, and I hadn't noticed—didn't want to notice—because he was the only one of the guys willing to even give me the time of day.

"No. We didn't agree. That was your living room deduction of probable cause, not mine. That angle is dead in the water."

I could barely suppress my anger, and it was becoming obvious.

"What's got your panties in a wad today?" he asked, nonchalant as always.

I didn't know how he could have a conversation with me so easily, feeling no guilt, knowing what he had done with a box of evidence 10 years ago and knowing what he had done again yesterday.

"My friend James, who works for the FBI, fingerprinted a box that was left on my kitchen table for me." I paused to let the words sink in, wondering if he would confess or continue to lie.

He took a deep breath and sighed. "I'm sorry, okay? I just thought maybe if it showed up, you would look over your shoulder a little bit. I saw that guy the other day—that Richards guy—you know the perp on the original case? He's back in town. I didn't want nothing happening to you."

Oh, he was not getting off that easily, making himself look like a hero. "How did you know where the box was?" I practically yelled at him.

"Look, back in the day, when I was a new detective, I did what I was told, you know? You do what you're told and keep your nose clean, and you move up in the department. I didn't ask no questions. I was told to file a box under the accused's name instead of the victim, so I did. The order came down from the top—DoD—not internally. Nobody ever thought to look there . . . hiding in plain sight, you know, so they could say no law was broken. Just misfiled."

I felt sick knowing that the man I'd respected and been partnered with for the past 18 months had also been the man who prevented my case from being heard as a teenager. He was the reason I'd had to live in fear for so long. I remained silent, letting him squirm.

"Then, it ain't too long afterward, a lady comes forward and tells them that there is another piece of evidence, and she tells them where to find it. Now this lady must have stayed with the evidence all the way to the lab, because this one did not get lost."

"Wait," I said. "A lady? What did she look like?" James told me he had reported the other shoe.

"That's just it. I don't know. Never saw her myself. Seems nobody did. That's why I say she musta taken it in herself. The report just says it was a lady."

I felt sick with the realization that James has lied to me too. Of course. As soon as I decide to trust him, I find out he is a liar too.

"Why give it all to me now, O'Malley? Ten years later?"

"I already told you. To protect you. And also, because back then, it was just a box and you was just 'a case.' Now you're my partner—someone I care about, and the guys at the precinct told me someone tried to kill you. I put that together with Richards being back in town and . . . Well, it don't take no brain surgeon to figure this one out, does it?"

His rhetorical question sent a chill down my spine. O'Malley thought Jeremy Richards had tried to kill me. But why would he? Making the leap from assault to murder was a huge one, and not one that often happened without a progression. Was there a progression I didn't know about? Did James know about it?

"Thanks O'Malley." I appreciated his strangely misguided effort but knew I could never trust him again, and what good is a partner you can't trust? "And you planted the bugs too? On my car and in my house? For my safety?"

"Sorry kid, I didn't plant no bugs. I just had the box delivered to me and then I dropped it off at your house. Your alarm was off, you know—with your firearm right inside the door. You gotta be more careful than that."

So I had forgotten to set the alarm. "Thanks again, O'Malley."

I would ask the Cap for a new partner as soon as this case was wrapped up. I had to think of a viable reason for it first.

"Yeah, whatever. Take care of yourself."

He hung up, already uncomfortable with the help he had provided. I wondered what the cost would be to him professionally.

His call changed everything and nothing. But I was done beating around the bush. I called James' number before I could change my mind.

"Special Agent James Hawthorne." He sounded so brisk and abrupt, nothing like the way he normally talked to me.

His tone startled me. "Is everything okay?"

"Oh, sorry Dan. I was expecting someone else," he said. "What's up?"

"I just had a discussion with the 'box delivery person,' and I have a question to ask you. According to police records, a 'lady' reported the other shoe and took the police chief to the location to find it." It all rushed out, an accusation rather than a question.

"Yes," James admitted. "My father doctored the report. There is no name of the lady because the lady was me. We wanted to keep my name out of it. We were afraid of retaliation from the trial. I don't know if you know this, but the oversight was run by the DoD. I'm sorry I was so spineless back then."

His immediate admission released my shoulders like someone had let all the air out of a balloon. I was glad I hit this head on instead of allowing my mind and insecurities to run away with me. I did not like how often I was hearing the words Department of Defense come up in relation to both the trial that the 6-Pack had participated in and potentially the trial that Angela had participated in.

"James, I didn't mean to be so accusatory. I just don't know who is on my side. I always had Angela to ground me, and I haven't figured out life without her yet," I said sadly, praying now that my chief would grant the extension since I had only 15 hours remaining.

"If you'll let me, you can count on me Daniela. I won't let you down again. I promise."

I could almost hear Ang saying to me, "Go ahead and take a chance Dan. It's worth it! You might get something you always wanted."

I took a deep breath and jumped in the deep end of the ocean with both feet. "Okay . . . So, what do you know about Jeremy Richards? Is O'Malley way off base here or has he been escalating in Maine?" I asked.

"I haven't heard anything about him escalating. I know he dropped out of MIT after one semester. He kind of fell apart after his mom died. Rumor has it that he blames the trial for everything that happened after he graduated, and after learning about the twin sister situation from you, he might be right." He sounded apologetic when he said this.

"It's okay. My dad said the trial was my mom's project, although I'm still not sure if that was the half carafe of bourbon speaking or him since she didn't even work for Neely." I gave a small laugh.

James was quiet on the other end of the phone. I wondered what I'd said that shut him down.

Eventually, he said, "I think we have no choice but to draw the killer out. And since it seems like the killer finds you to be of particular interest,

I don't think we have any choice but to draw him or her out through you," he said.

Him or her? Well, that was a new twist. I shivered involuntarily. Were we now throwing Jessica into the mix? My mind raced. What possible reason would she have to hurt Angela or me?

Although James had not said it, I felt my dad was the elephant in the room, so to speak. Who better to draw out a killer who might be their own dad? I knew when I became a detective that I would have to do difficult things like go undercover, but I never in a million years dreamed that I would be in a situation like this where the killer might be my own father. It made me shake. But at the same time, I knew it was the only logical solution. From the time all of this started at the morgue, I was the common denominator, and I had promised Mrs. Monn to solve Angela's murder.

"I agree James." I said, trying to sound confident, even though I didn't feel it. "I'm leaving the Monn house now. How about if you formulate a plan while I pick up the Beast and drive to the Chelsea office?"

"Sounds good," James said. "And Daniela?" "Yes?"

"When all of this is over, could we try to be friends?" He sounded so hopeful.

"We could try James, but you'll be back in Portland, and I'll be here so we probably won't cross paths all that often, you know?" I was just trying to be realistic.

"Actually, I just got a transfer to the Chelsea field office, and I could really use a friend in the area—one that didn't ingest steroids for the first 18 years of their life."

That made me laugh—a real laugh, not a nervous or sarcastic one. "Count me, Dan Neely, as your official first friend in the greater Boston Area."

"Well, then I'd better make sure you don't get hurt on this sting," he said wryly.

"Please do." I whispered and I closed the flip phone.

Chapter Twenty Nine

THE PLAN

Tuesday, December 6, 2022. 8:00 PM
13 hours and 30 minutes left

When James greeted me at the field office, his voice was raspy. I could tell that he hadn't had much sleep in the past few days either.

"What did you come up with?" I asked.

"I feel that everything comes from the clinical trial in one way or another."

"You mean Neely Pharmaceuticals." I state bluntly.

"Maybe. Maybe not. Don't forget, when you went by Lily Legacy, they said there was no Dr.Neely working there, and when I called the Maine location, I received the same response. Also, didn't you tell me your father denied involvement with that company? And said the TUC trials had been your mother's project?"

"Yes. But first, my mother has been dead for 25 years, and second, there is also the small detail that he chose this moment in time to leave the country." I didn't want to believe my father was a serial killer of young women and that he had also tried to kill me, his own daughter either. "That doesn't really sound like something an innocent man would do, does it?"

"Daniela, I don't want you to convict him or decide anything. I'm just collecting the facts of the case, and there are some major facts involved in this case of which you are currently unaware. I would like to put a wire on you for that 'when and if' you run into the killer and put a tracking device on your SUV."

"Well, what are the facts of which I am unaware?" I felt annoyed that he worded it like that instead of just explaining it to me. "Am I now on a 'need to know' too?"

"Some of the facts of the case are top secret—DoD—and yes, 'need to know.' I'm sorry but the powers that be have determined that you do not need to know." His face flushes all the way down his collar as he said this, letting me know he isn't happy about saying it to me.

He explained the rest of the details he has come up with, including a safe word, which all make perfect sense, but I dread it, nonetheless.

"I'll do it---for Angela---because my Cap left a message denying me an extension so I'm almost out of time. But I'll be honest with you, it makes me feel more like a victim than a detective." I said.

"Okay. Let's get you set up then," he said, ignoring my 'victim' comment. "What safe word would you like to choose?"

"Let's keep it simple and easy for me to remember. Lily."

He winced. I wondered if he thought it was painful for me to mention my mother. I'd gotten past that long ago.

They put a microscopic camera and wire in a cute little necklace that I could wear without worrying. It looked just like a Kendra Scott original. "Just remember to take it off before you shower. We don't need to see your private things," the agent told me.

"What private things can you see with this?" I asked James. He laughed. "Just try to go about your life and business as naturally as possible. We will be following you, and if you run into a problem, the cavalry will be there in a flash."

It all sounded too good to be true. If it was really that easy, informants and undercover cops wouldn't die all the time. Nonetheless, the plan was officially in motion. I drove home, feeling edgy and needing to talk to someone. I decided to give O'Malley another quick call on the way. I didn't tell him I was wired. I just told him the evidence was pointing back to my father's company in the deaths of 9 young women.

"Look kid, you got no choice. You gotta go where the evidence takes you." He says sympathetically. "Nobody wants to believe their daddy did it."

Impulsively, I couldn't wait until he was back at work. I decided I *would* forgive him. In the end, he cared more about me than the job. I didn't realize how "fatherly" he had become with me. Maybe that's why the chief had put him with me. Well, that and my bedside manner.

I parked out front since my driveway still wasn't cleared. That never even crossed my mind while I was gone. Now I knew why James was struggling to park. The snowplows had piled the snow so high on the sides when they cleared the streets. I sashayed up the front walk and unlocked the front door, immediately noticing the alarm was not on. I commented aloud to myself, hoping the wire was working loud and clear. "How odd, I guess the heater repairman forgot to turn the alarm back on."

I left the door very slightly ajar; not enough that anyone would notice, but enough so it could quickly be opened if need be. Then I removed my holster and hung it on the coat tree but slipped my gun into the back waistband of my pants. I felt I had no choice but to follow my regular routine as much as possible or it would be a dead giveaway if indeed there was an intruder.

Nothing looked out of place, so I relaxed. They really must have forgotten to reset the alarm. *Geez---idiots!* I walked into the kitchen with my care package from Mrs. Monn. The cold weather had worked nicely as a life hack for a cooler. I was grateful for the homecooked meal because as usual, the cupboards were bare except for some Triscuits.

I struggled to open the lid, the airtight seal stubbornly refusing to give. Without warning, the hairs on the back of my neck rising to attention alerted me to a presence in the room before I heard the voice.

"Need a hand with that?"

Jeremy. His voice was calm. Unhurried.

Despite my inner turmoil, I did not flinch. I knew this day had been coming for a very long time. Now that it was finally here, the terror that had gripped me so many times on a dark street and when I searched my back seat fanatically before each drive seemed to have finally exhausted itself. Or maybe I just cared a little less about my own life now that Angela was no longer in it. Regardless, what was left in its place was something icy and determined. I made him wait for a response. I wouldn't give him what he expected from me this time.

I wrapped a paper towel around the pot pie carefully placed it in the microwave oven, including the fork that I used to break the seal. I set the timer for 6 minutes, then turned to face him.

"Jeremy." Even as I stared into his bottomless, glittering eyes, I couldn't imagine him killing all those women. But then neither could I imagine my father doing it. Maybe I was just a terrible judge of character.

"Where have you been? I've been waiting here since the heat came back on." He smiled, a rather beautiful smile, I had to admit, on a rather evil man. It would be so helpful if evil people looked evil instead of just looking like normal, everyday people.

"And you are here because . . .?" My voice did not sound like me. It was scratchy and barely audible. I hoped it could be heard on the wire. Now that he was here, in the flesh, it was like my throat refused to work.

"You and me—we've got unfinished business—and this time your *boy*friend isn't here to interfere." His smile widened.

Even as terrified as I was, hearing him call Ang a boy filled me with an unholy fury.

"You always thought you were so smart," he continued. "First you got me arrested and almost kicked out of the whole project. But I'm a patient guy and I knew my time would come. I've been waiting and watching you for a long time."

Although his words sent a chill down my spine, I could not let him know how he had controlled my life over the past 10 years.

"I guess I should be flattered," I said. Somehow, the anger had returned my voice to its natural tenor. "I heard you moved away. I thought you might have a new love interest by now."

His low chuckle held no humor. "There is no love in revenge. I always get even."

A loud clanging sound came from the microwave.

He continued. "I knew it was Monstrosity the minute I set eyes on her. We'd already established our four for the trial—she was my own special bonus participant, just for fun. You have to admit, I owed her big time." He'd been saving up his words for a long time and now he wanted to hurt me with them.

He grabbed me suddenly, whirling me around, pressing my back to his chest, rubbing his nose through my hair, inhaling deeply.

I wondered why Jeremy was involved in selecting people for phase 2 of the trial and in this area.

James had said he lived in Bar Harbor. Did he actually work for my father's company? For Lily Legacy? That was a chilling thought. His nose brushed the gauze on my head, and I flinched.

"Yeah—sorry about that." He kissed my wound and I cringed. "I swear, I didn't plan to hurt you. I was just trying to get you out of there so old Jakey wouldn't get in any trouble. Poor guy— thought he was going to have a heart attack over removing a little implant. Wouldn't even take the money we offered him. Such a boy scout." He chuckled softly.

"Why did you have to kill him?" I rasped. I couldn't hold my tongue any longer. It hurt me to think of what Jake had gone through, and for what?

"You see, that's where you're mistaken," he said smugly. "I'm not a killer. I'm just a guy who likes to have a little fun." I felt the warmth of his hands slide underneath the front of my shirt, moving upwards toward areas no man had touched. Panic began to blossom in my chest.

"So, you're saying you didn't kill Jake?" I was trying to buy time, willing my plan to work as I watched for the sparking I prayed should soon begin.

"I told you I didn't." He was suddenly annoyed. "Why would I kill Jake?" His response made me wonder if he'd liked Jake.

"You know, I almost caught up to you before she opened that damn door." He was putting the conversation back on track. "If she hadn't opened it, you would've been mine and I guarantee you would've never forgotten me." His erection was apparent now against my back, his breath hot on my neck.

I strained away as hard as I could, worried he would feel my gun in the back of my pants waist. For the first time in my life, I was thankful for being short—thankful he was over a foot taller than me, forcing him to hollow out his torso to keep his face next to mine.

The clanging and popping increased in the microwave. We both glanced over involuntarily.

"I have never forgotten you, Jeremy." I choked out the words, trying to draw his eyes away from the microwave.

"But always that moose of a man or woman or whatever it was, watching over you, I knew I didn't have a chance."

Hatred burned in my gut, hearing him call Angela such ugly words.

"We would have had such a good time, me and you," he cooed softly in my ear. He was slowly rotating his hips in a figure 8 against my back as if we had all the time in the world. "Thanks to good old Monstrosity, we're gonna have it now. I've been waiting soooo long . . ."

He was lost in his own world now, filled with pleasure and grandiosity. He was oblivious to the increased noise coming from the microwave.

"When she called in the damn shoe . . . she almost ruined my entire career. But in the end, I got her, didn't I? I got that little freak good. Oh, I had a little fun with her first—making her check her mail naked. I laughed my ass off over that brilliant idea. I wish I could've seen the look on her neighbor's faces when they saw a dick hanging between her legs."

Jeremy's crude comment told me he did not know about Angela's gender change surgery.

Good. Ang got one over on him and he didn't even know it. The body she showed the neighbors was actually a very nice looking fully female body with just some extra skin from when she was heavier—but all woman, nonetheless. *Go Ang!*

The microwave door burst open; sparks shot out. Jeremy jumped back in surprise. This was my moment---the one I had been fantasizing for 10 years. Even though his words and actions made me feel weak with fear, what Jeremy didn't know was that the 'freak' he was talking about taught me to love myself and to use what God gave me to deal with this sometimes cruel world. I breathed deeply, feeling Angela's faith in me shoot through my veins as I threw my right elbow back with all the strength my fury could muster and stamped on his foot at the same time. As he began to recoil, I bent and flipped him over my head. I drew my gun.

"You asshole, you're not as smart as you think you are. Angela was a woman, not a man. You didn't make a fool out of her. You are only making a fool out of yourself." I knew I shouldn't feed into his game, but I couldn't stand to listen to him disparage her for one more minute. "How could you kill all of those innocent young women?"

He laughed in my face and droned on, even lying on the floor with a gun trained on him, impressed with himself as always.

"I told you I'm not a killer. If you knew who was really behind all of this . . ." He laughed again. "Angela was my special one. Just one little suggestion into the command center and she always did as she was told. She even ordered me a holiday pie—my favorite: caramel apple. It was so easy to convince her to buy the pills. She thought all of it was her idea. But nobody—"

I screamed and started to kick him, but he grabbed my leg and took me down hard, my gun firing as it skittered into the living room. He was up instantly and quicker than me, but my years of gymnastics were my advantage. I jumped high and did a dive roll coming up within inches of my gun just as Jeremy rammed me into the door, slamming my only means of escape solidly shut.

I quickly rolled out from under him and leapt onto the sofa, grabbing the vase, and swinging all in one motion. I watched the vase explode against the side of his head, but it didn't slow him down at all. He was like the freaking terminator. *What the hell was in those drugs?*

He looped his arm around my waist and slammed me down hard to the floor, his body on top of mine. I began to scream. I might not win this fight, but I would make it miserable for him. I would scream my guts out through the entire thing.

"You Neelys think you are invincible, don't you," he growled as he grinded against me. "You've taken everything from me my whole life:

my mother, my sister, and now my son. We'll see how mommy likes it when someone hurts her little girl."

His eyes shone with madness. His words were no longer making sense.

Suddenly, the front door hit the wall as it was flung open behind us. The widening of Jeremy's eyes seemed to be simultaneous with the rapid *pew pew* before he crumpled on top of me. Frantically, I shoved him aside, rolling from beneath him. Using my feet and hands, I crab crawled backwards into the corner rapidly, never taking my eyes off Jeremy, expecting him to pounce again.

I raised my eyes to his killer, cowering beneath her icy gaze.

"Daniela, I believe it is time we met."

I gasped, recognition knocking the air from my lungs. Tall, blonde—I instantly recognized her from the photograph in my father's bedroom. I did the only thing I could do. I laughed. "Lily," tumbled from my lips.

The woman's features twisted in confusion.

Chapter Thirty

THE UN-DAD

Tuesday, December 6, 2022. 10:00 PM
12 hours 30 minutes left

The shock of seeing my mother—alive—superseded the horror I felt only moments earlier when I thought Jeremy was going to finish what he started 10 years ago. James, who rushed in the door as soon as I had finally uttered the safe word, though it was accidental, didn't seem as shocked as me as he reached out his hand to help me get up. Nor did the other two men who casually strode through the open doorway behind him, as if they hadn't just entered a crime scene. One man was small with dark eyes and hair, and the other was my father. Clearly, he was not out of the country.

"You knew," I accused James in a hushed tone. Had the four of them been working together this whole time?

"No. I wasn't with them. I was in the van, waiting to hear from you. Although I was beginning to strongly suspect. I couldn't find a death certificate for her," he said.

"I don't understand. What does this mean?" My body trembled. He held onto my hand.

Looking down, I saw Jeremy's blood spatter on my clothes. He was dead. My mother had shot him. *My mother had saved me. She was alive. Had been alive? My whole life?* After not seeing me for over 25 years, she somehow knew that Jeremy was going to attack me and showed up to save the day?

Bewilderment and confusion engulfed me. I had to be unconscious. Or dead. This was not real life. In real life, my mother would have thrown her arms around me and sobbed, telling me how much she had missed me. She wouldn't say, "It's time we met."

I closed my eyes and shook my head wildly. *What is happening? Am I hallucinating*? But when I opened my eyes, all of the same people were in the room, all peering at me with different expressions on their faces. My father looked ashamed. The short, dark man looked uncomfortable— like he wanted to be anywhere but here. My mother—my MOTHER—looked irritated, not at all like she had just shot a man to death and was staring at his blood all over the daughter she hadn't seen in 25 years. And James . . . James's eyebrows were drawn so tightly together over his forehead they nearly met in the middle. I felt warmth and realized he had taken hold of my other hand. He was holding both of them firmly now.

I didn't realize tears were running down my cheeks until a drop hit my hand. I was the most unwanted human on the earth. At least before, I could believe that it wasn't my mother's choice not to be with me, but she was the same as everyone else. She just didn't want me.

"We'll get through this Daniela. You've still got me." It was as though James could read my mind. He pulled me close, his mouth near my ear: whispering now. "I started to suspect after your visit to your home. Especially when the fingerprints came back needing a top secret clearance," he said, nodding toward the lady---my mother.

I glanced toward her and realized she was speaking to me.

"So, just to clarify, you understand that uncovering the trials would be a national security breach, right?" Lillian was looking pointedly at both James and me.

A national security breach? This is what she had to say to me? And what the heck was she talking about? We didn't do anything wrong. She's the one who walked in guns a blazing. I still wasn't sure Jeremy deserved two shots through the back of his head. Couldn't she have shot his leg or something? He was unarmed.

Eyes wide, I took in every detail of her. She was beautiful by traditional standards. She had glossy, thick blonde hair that was pulled into an elegant knot at the nape of her neck. Certainly, I looked nothing like her. She wore a deep red suit that perfectly complimented her coloring, the legs of the pants trim to the ankle where her black pumps didn't even faintly resemble the practical Clarks I favored. I didn't even like the way my mother spoke. She was dismissive, arrogant, and cold. Could I truly have been born from this woman? And did she really think she could just show up and act like nothing happened? I spent 25 years grieving her death. I lived with no mother. I had nobody to love me for 15 years. She wasn't going to get away without answering some questions.

"Why did you leave me?" My voice broke as I said it. I hated how pathetic I sounded. "And how did you know to come back now?"

She waved her arm around the room. "Time is of the essence, and this is not the place for this discussion. If you feel we must discuss this further, we can move this meeting to our house."

This *meeting*? There was a dead body in my living room. Who would call that a meeting? What a stupid comment. How could we *not* discuss this further? As I followed her gaze and saw Jeremy's dead body, I felt both relief and sadness. I would no longer live in fear, but Jeremy's last words had told me he had a son. A son---who would grow up without a father. I knew firsthand what it was like to grow up without a parent—without any parents really.

And *our* home? She'd never lived there with us. But maybe she was the one who was living there now. Wow. Has my dead mother been living in my house for the past 10 years while I lived in a house purchased with her life insurance money? My dad committed insurance fraud? Oh my God! Why? He must have known. My thoughts were beginning to spiral out of control again. I laughed.

Lillian recoiled as if I'd slapped her. "I hardly find this a laughing matter," she said. She didn't know me or understand me at all. But the laugh did throw her into action.

"My team will get Jeremy out of your home. You'll never know he was here. We'll discuss him later."

I hated the way she dictated orders to everyone, and we all just followed them like little minions.

Why would people take orders from her? What "team" was she talking about? Who was the short guy anyways?

"What about my neighbors?" I asked. "They must have heard my gun go off. Someone would have called the police." This was a nice neighborhood. People took care of each other here. Nobody would just look away.

"It's nothing I can't handle," she said confidently. "But you—you need to go." She flicked her hand toward me as if I were any annoying fly. "And you—go wait in my car," she said, jerking her head toward dad.

"I'm going to ride over with Daniela. I think she might have a question or two specifically for me." She narrowed her eyes in disapproval. I could see that she was accustomed to being obeyed. Who the hell was she?

"And you?" With a flick of her head, she dismissed James altogether. "I'm sure you can see we've got a handle on this."

He didn't bother answering her.

I eagerly left my home; James kept a hand on my back to steady me. My dad was ready to answer questions? God yes, I had questions! *Were you involved in Angela's death? Why did you hire Jeremy? Did you know my mother was alive the whole time*? I wasn't sure he understood the full magnitude of the questions I did have, or he may have run from me. Nonetheless, I wanted to hug him for the simple act of rebuking this person but knew we didn't do hugs. I just gave him a grateful smile. He pressed his lips into a thin line that didn't much resemble a smile.

James gave my hand one last quick squeeze before closing the car door. "I'll meet you there. Do not start the meeting without me—got it?"

He looked so deeply into my eyes, I felt myself melting into him. There was something so incredibly comforting about James Hawthorne. I suppose most men wouldn't appreciate being called comforting, but that is the first word that came to mind. When he looked at me like that, I could feel the warmth spread all the way through my body. It was a new and scary feeling to me, not one I'd ever felt with a man before. I wondered if this was trust. Maybe Angela sent him to me.

It was gratifying to slip into the comfort of the Beast. My old friend wrapped its leather heated seat beneath my bottom, and I was instantly soothed. Before I switched the radio off, Taylor Swift was singing the words to Anti Hero. How many times had I belted that song out, believing that in most cases, I really was the problem. Turns out, it may not be me after all.

I switched the radio off and told my dad, "Fire away. I need to hear it all, no matter how bad it is. Please. For the first time in my life, just tell me the truth." If he had been responsible for Angela's death, even indirectly, I needed to know right now before we faced *her* again.

"The first thing I want to tell you, Daniela, is how sorry I am for being such a coward." His voice was thick with unshed tears.

Oh wow, we were really going to do this. My dad was going to have emotions, and he was not drunk. Holy cow. I braced myself.

"I told myself it was best for you to be raised by your grandmother—a blood relative—and never even checked to make sure she was being good to you. You seemed to be thriving. You excelled in school. You excelled in gymnastics. But when you said that about the boys attacking you . . ."

"My grandmother? What are you saying? Margette was my *grandmother*?" My arms felt so weak, I nearly let go of the steering wheel. Zambrano/Zambrano. James had said it. But I still refused to believe it. Surely a grandmother couldn't treat her own flesh and blood with such indifference. "Were you adopted?" I was grasping at straws.

"No, Daniela, I wasn't adopted. My parents passed the way I told you," he said. "Margette is Alejandro's mother. He has been your mother's assistant for a very long time."

"I tried to stay out of her way. I had no real legal claim to you. I thought she would love you. Her only son's child . . ." His voice trailed away.

"But, how did you know?" He couldn't possibly have noticed the resemblance on the face of a newborn baby.

He hung his head and sighed deeply. "When your mother was pregnant with you, I began to hope for the first time that we were going to have our child at long last. I didn't know that Lillian had aborted our other children because they were girls. I wanted to change the nursery and surprise her, redecorate it for a little girl. "

Just hearing these words made my heart hurt. How many days had I lain in that room wondering why I was raised in a little boys' room? Too many to count.

"So, I arranged for the decorator to meet me at the house while Lillian was in the hospital. When she removed the mattress from the baby blue crib, there was a ledger sitting right in the middle of the dust ruffle. Of course, she gave it to me."

He stopped and I could see that it was extremely hard for him to tell this part of the story. "I immediately got the feeling that something wasn't right. I didn't think it was a normal thing to find a ledger hidden underneath a crib mattress, so I excused the decorator for the day and began to read it. I found in it detailed facts such as conception, parentage, dates of shots, etc."

He went on to tell me that he had discovered that Alejandro was my father through IVF, that Margette (whom Lillian had recently brought into the home to prepare as a nanny), was Alejandro's mother, and that I was a part of her experiment. He was crushed.

I had just turned into the tree-lined drive that would take me to the front door of the home I grew up in. Each time I turned up the lane, it felt less like home.

"I was a part of the experiment?" I asked, truly shocked. "But I never took any shots or supplements."

Even as I said this, I also knew that I was always physically superior—small, but superior—to my peers, and academically I was always years ahead as well. I thought it was because I was a nose to the grindstone kind of girl but turns out, I was just another Frankenstein.

"Your mother abandoned your participation in the experiment when she could not chart sufficient growth. All the male participants were born at a minimum of ten pounds. You were born at six pounds. She believed that was too small to be a significant part of the experiment, so she made the decision to remove herself."

Remove herself. I'd failed her twice before I was even born. Female. Petite.

So, Margette had been a victim of my mother's schemes too. I recalled the time Jenny and her friends had put the wad of gum in my hair on the bus. I had begged Margette not to cut my long, thick hair. It was the only part of me that even faintly resembled my mother. Back then, it was so important to me to have even one part of me that was like her. But Margette had taken me in for a bob and we kept it that way afterward. She said it was easier than the incessant braiding for my gymnastic meets. That's when Jenny started calling me Dan the Man. When I cried to Margette, she told me the words I carried with me for the rest of my life. "Everyone's life would have been much easier if you had been born a boy, Daniela." Now I understood the full meaning of her words.

Although Margette always made certain I was well cared for, she never gave me anything extra, like love or attention. She must have been too filled with resentment. She had been required to give up her life in Ecuador. And she had blamed me for all of it—my mother's control, her own son's selfishness. It wasn't my fault that he was for sale.

"The day she left you at the hospital, she told me not to worry; your grandmother would raise you. I took that as a 'hands off' although now I realize it was just another one of her self-rationalizations for what she'd chosen to do." He was shaking his head, as if he couldn't believe he had been so foolish. "I went on a weeklong bender---the only week I've ever missed work. I finally had my daughter and had been told 'hands off.'"

We had arrived at the house. As much as I wanted to talk this to death with him, I had something I had to know before we went in. "Dad, we can talk about this more later---and there will be a later for us, I promise---but before we go in, I have to know what your part is in the clinical trial that took Angela's life." I turned to face him and then, uncharacteristically, put my hand on his arm. "Please, Dad. I loved her very much. I love Mrs. Monn very much too. I can't let her believe her daughter killed herself. She doesn't deserve that."

Even though the interior of the Beast was dimly lit by the lights of the dashboard, we were able to make eye contact with each other.

"When those boys attacked me," I continued softly, "they were the only two people who were there for me, and they have been there for me every day since." If I had to use guilt, then I would use guilt. I would use any tactic I had to use to discover Angela's killer.

"Daniela, with God as my witness, I did not know that the TUC trial was being experimented upon young girls in this way. When the implant was originally designed, the trials were to be consensually run on 18- to 20-year-old enlistees on a volunteer basis only. And I was never informed that the trials had even begun. As a matter of fact, when the first phase had so many mental health complications, modifications were made to the drugs and phase 1 was restarted with the new drugs and has not reached completion. Phase 2, the TUC trials, was not scheduled to begin until the results of the new variation were completed. As far as I know, they are only about halfway through the new variation of phase 1."

I nodded slowly. "So, Jeremy Richards wasn't the only one of the six who had problems during the first trial?"

"I cannot comment on who had what, Daniela, you know that. These are DoD trials, and I only oversee the results. But what I can tell you is that six was just the local number. When the trials are run, external factors must be added into the picture as well, so they are spread out nationally."

Oh. My. God. How many Jeremy Richards had been created across the nation? Was his mental instability created by the drugs and injections or by losing his mother to alcoholism or by eventually losing her to suicide? And wasn't the experiment ultimately responsible for all three?

"If not you, who was in charge? Please. I have to know." I was begging him now. I had to give my Captain a name or Angela would forever be called a suicide.

"I thought you would have figured that out by now, Daniela. Your mother, of course. She's a CIA operative. Lily Legacy is a company wholly operated by her. I knew it the moment I saw the name," he said. "More than anything else, your mother wants to make history."

Out of the corner of my eye, James walked past the Beast and gave me a thumbs up. I assumed that meant we were good to go in—that he had my back.

My shoulders slumped in defeat. I couldn't very well accuse the CIA of killing Angela, could I?

Maybe it was Jeremy, despite his protests? But he seemed like a guy who would brag about something like that if he'd done it. Maybe . . . I shook my head, clearing the thought.

"We'd better get inside. Wouldn't want to keep Lillian waiting." I said drolly. I caught the shadow of a smile on my father's lips. It felt like we were starting to "get" each other.

Chapter Thirty One

LILY LEGACY

Wednesday, December 7, 2022. 12:30 AM

9 hours left

A fire was already blazing in the grand fireplace when we walked in. The short, dark-haired man seemed to know exactly where everything was: wood, kindling, matches. I wondered if this was from his many visits to his mother or to see my mother—his . . . boss? co-worker? benefactor? I wasn't exactly sure what she was to him at this point, but I had to know what I was to him.

I walked directed over to him, extending my hand. "My name is Dan Neely. And you are?"

He hesitated briefly, considering how to respond. "I am Alejandro Zambrano."

"You are Margette's son?" I asked, knowing both the answer and the implication.

He nodded.

"She told me about you once. She said she had one perfect son." The conversation had taken place 'that day,' on the way home from the Monn's house. It was the only time she had ever mentioned having a family to me. "She told me her family lived in Ecuador."

"They do—all except for me. I am not accepted there."

I raised my eyebrows.

"I am married to a man. It is forbidden in Ecuador."

"And you are my father?"

"Genetically only." He emphasized the second word, as if to make certain there was no mistake about it.

"Obviously," I said, sarcasm dripping from the word.

I stared at him, dissecting his features. I didn't look like him other than the similarity in coloring, but I did look like Margette. How many people had said that when I was young? Even Angela had written that in her recipe book. I thought they were just trying to make me feel better— like I fit in, like I had a mom. But I could see now that I did look like her. I knew I would never think of this man as my father. He would never be anything other than a sperm donor to me. My father was my father. Knowing what he knew, he still provided for me my entire life. He even helped my friend anytime I asked. And in his own way, he watched over me—perhaps more than I had ever given him credit for. The people who were related to me—my mother, sperm donor and grandmother? They were the ones who didn't care. It had never been a gender thing for my dad. He didn't reject me because I was a girl. Gender had nothing to do with it. He was like Mrs. Monn, and I never even knew it. But somehow, Angela did. God, how was I going to get through life without her kindhearted and wise guidance?

"Why didn't your mother accept me as her grandchild?" I asked Alejandro. "She raised me from the moment I was born."

"She is devout Catholic. She believes invitro is immoral and you are an abomination. Children are begotten not made." He said this all matter of fact, as if he hadn't just proclaimed me spawn of Satan.

"Are you kidding me? My nanny—my grandmother—who raised me believed I was an abomination?" The implications made me feel sick. No wonder she was so "hands off" with me. She was probably waiting for my head to start spinning.

"Enough! "Lillian had arrived. "Your parentage and upbringing have nothing to do with anything here. No more."

Seriously?

She continued. "You must understand. This project is my life's work. I never intended to have children, but the possibilities were so exciting, I couldn't resist trying to become part of the trial myself."

"What?" I tried to force myself to refocus on what she was saying. Even though it was difficult to continue to listen to her diatribe, I knew my answers lie in there somewhere, and to reach them, I would have to indulge her endless narcissism.

She flashed an annoyed look. "Ale`. Make some coffee. Daniela seems to be falling asleep over here," she ordered.

"I go by Dan," I said, smartly.

"Yes, of course. What a shame you aren't." She continued, "I tried four times to have a boy with your father, but each time, we created a girl, so the pregnancy had to be terminated."

I saw my father flinch when she said this so casually. She had killed four of his natural daughters without his knowledge. I'd spent my lifetime thinking men couldn't be trusted but she was blowing that theory clean out of the water. I suppose there are good and bad within both sexes. I'd just been so caught up in my own head, I couldn't see it.

"By then, we had to fill the sixth spot in the trial. We just had to eliminate one more girl."

"But you didn't eliminate me." I said with uncertainty, wondering if my mother had tried to abort me but it had failed. The thought made me shiver involuntarily. James slipped his arm around my shoulder. I glanced over at him, surprised. Is that what we were now? An "arm around the shoulder" couple of people? Did friends do things like that? I'd always let Angela know I wasn't very comfortable with physical contact, so she'd respected my wishes. Was I comfortable with James doing that?

James gave me a single nod, as if to say, "We're good." Playing it safe with my emotions hadn't kept me safe at all. It had left me feeling vulnerable and afraid all the time. I sensed a change taking place inside me. I was shedding my old insecurities and becoming something more—a stronger version of myself. A me who I could trust and a me who trusts other people.

"No, before you," she said irritably. "The Richards Twin. We offered the parents a spot for their boy—he would be the smartest, the most athletic; everything a parent could ever want for their son—plus make history. All they had to do was give their daughter up for adoption. It was too late to abort her."

James squeezed my shoulder as she continued.

"That mother was a stumbling block; she didn't want to give up her daughter, but the father understood the value of what we were offering. He wanted his place in the history books." She sighed dramatically. "Don't we all?"

Every word that came out of her mouth disgusted me. As if she was talking about selling a cow, not giving away your newborn child. But, I reminded myself, this was a woman who walked away from her newborn child—me—and never looked back. She had no conscience whatsoever. Which suddenly made me wonder anew why she had come back today, of all days, and more importantly, why she had shot Jeremy. It certainly wasn't to protect me. My head started to spin with partially formed questions. My mother---if I dared call her that---would only have come back if it served her. I continued to listen while my mind raced with the possibilities.

"Of course, we provided the money and supplied them with a wonderful couple, but to make sure that crazy mother didn't go behind our backs, we had to put in a contingency clause. If she ever contacted the girl, the child would lose everything, and she could do nothing about it." She clapped her hands together and brushed them off, as if to indicate presto, problem solved.

"And I just happen to know that when the girl, Jessica is her name by the way, contacted the family, she lost everything. You fail to mention that." I couldn't resist letting her know I was aware of how cruel she could be.

I stared her directly in the eyes, wanting her to know I was not intimidated by her in any way.

She was wrong about me. I was stronger than she knew. I was stronger than I had known. Her beauty, her money, her intelligence—none of it held a candle to the kind of people I'd been exposed to like Angela, Mrs. Monn, and . . . my father.

"Oh please, don't be a drama queen, Daniela. It's unattractive." She gave a dismissive wave of her hand and looked away from me as if I was nothing. "She got it back, didn't she?" She gave a brittle laugh.

Yes, Jessica had gotten it back, at the cost of her mother's life—Jeremy's mother's life. I wondered how Mr. Richard's felt about his son's place in the history books now.

"Anyhow, after those six boys were born and we immediately began to chart such remarkable results both intellectually and physically, well, I'm afraid my own desire to succeed got the better of me and I just had to try one more time. The results were so exciting!" The sparkle in her eyes reflected her excitement but then she looked at James. "But you—you've turned out to be quite the disappointment, sitting on the wrong side of it all."

"Sorry to disappoint, mam. I like which side I'm sitting on just fine," James said, giving me another comforting squeeze.

My stomach began to churn over the words I knew were coming next.

"So, statistically speaking—and we *are* working in statistics here—if you've produced four female embryos with the same person, you are going to produce a fifth. Therefore, I made the decision that Alejandro would assist me in my final attempt in hopes of creating that one special boy." She gave Ale` a quick, fake smile.

"Unfortunately, IVF wasn't as foolproof back then as it has become. There was only about a 60% accuracy rate on the gender selection. You," she nodded toward me, "were part of the unfortunate 40% that turned out wrong. But I still upheld my part of the bargain," she said, clearly waiting for us to ask what it was so she could let us all know how wonderful she was. So I asked, just to get it over with.

"And what was your part of the bargain?"

I tried hard to keep my tone light so she wouldn't notice the sarcasm that had seeped in, but she had become so engaged in her own story, she didn't even notice.

"Why, I simply made a phone call and a "reasonable" donation to the powers that be and voila`! Boston became the first city in the United States to allow same sex marriage." She beamed her best "aren't I amazing" smile. Ale's future husband performed the invitro. It was all so perfect. Until it wasn't, of course."

As I listened to her drone on, a one man show, so to speak. I remember my father's drunken proclamation that she was a monster. I realized he was right. This woman was indeed a monster. At the very least, she was a psychopath. I'd spent my entire 25 years pining over her, wishing I knew her, dreaming I was just like her. Now, I thanked God I was not. Somehow, even though I had spent little time with him, I had managed to pick up quite a few of my father's traits. I smiled.

"I found myself carrying another girl, so I thought, 'Why not?' and started giving myself the injections. Women can be physically superior, too, and are almost always intellectually superior." She was still telling her story, as if any of us wanted to hear it.

I don't know how my father, and I realized I would always call him this, could just sit there and listen to her. Maybe he spent years doing it already. I wondered how long before she left, he realized that she was a monster.

"But the shots proved to be too much for your little body Daniela. I guess I should've chosen a bigger, stronger specimen of a man, but it never occurred to me you would come out with dominant genes from the father. I thought you would look like me."

"Well, she might not have a big body like you, but she is strong as shit and one of the smartest people I've ever met." These words seemed to come out of nowhere. Everyone turned to look at James. They'd all forgotten he was there.

"I'm sure." Lillian said, with her tight fake smile.

I would never think of this beast as my mother. Suddenly, I felt overwhelmed by the smell of lilies in the room. I knew I would never be able to see or smell another lily as long as I lived without thinking of her—the real her—and hating them both. I wanted to get up and throw them on the floor and stomp on them, crush them beneath my feet.

"No, don't brush him off. What he's saying is true." My father said. "You don't even know her. We do. Daniela graduated high school when she was sixteen because she took online courses and summer school and the whole time, she was also volunteering at the police department. She is the youngest detective on the force. And she did that with no help from anyone apparently. It appears Margette was not the person I believed her to be—certainly not grandmother material."

"Well of course she did. The boosters during pregnancy gave her superior intelligence. I thought you understood that much." Lillian looked upward—the mature equivalent of eye rolling, I guess. "And don't be too hard on Margette. Not everybody enjoys children you know. They can be very taxing."

My eyes filled with tears. I didn't even know my dad knew these things about me. After the incident with Jeremy and the 6-Pack, I had become completely obsessed with police work. Although I started by volunteering for filing and running errands, the guys liked me and eventually relaxed and discussed cases in front of me. I learned a lot from them. And I believe my mother made it clear how she felt about children.

Lillian quickly interrupted. "Are we done with the questions now? I don't have long before I need to leave. Phase 2 was a complete success, and we must get to work on Phase 3 immediately."

Lillian's words reminded me why we had come to the house in the first place.

"No," I stated emphatically. "We are not done." I sat up straight, making James' arm drop in the process. I glanced at him apologetically. He gave me a "go get her" look.

"I have two more things I need to know. First of all, why did you fake your death?"

"Daniela," she began.

"Dan," I insisted.

"Yes, of course, Dan. It is not a crime to leave your family. I made the decision to say I had died in childbirth. I felt it would be best for you. I always traveled extensively, internationally in my position with the CIA and had no desire to be a mother," she said. "Had you ever bothered to look, you would have seen there was no death certificate. You are a detective, correct?"

I refused to be bullied by her. Why would I suspect that my parents had lied about my mother dying? Of course I'd never looked. I pushed on. "The second thing I need to know is how and why you showed up at my house today at the exact moment Jeremy was attacking me. You certainly weren't here 10 years ago, when I was a scared kid who really needed your help." My words were full of accusation.

She hesitated, but only for a moment. "I received intel that Jeremy was becoming a liability so we placed surveillance in places we thought might be problem areas."

"So you were the one who bugged my house?" I asked.

Lillian nods with that upward glance again as if to say, "obviously."

Instead of clarifying things for me, her response had further muddied the waters, so I decided to go for a more direct route.

"Did Jeremy kill those girls?" I asked.

"Of course not," she exclaimed. "He wasn't a murderer. Just an unstable man."

"Did you kill them? Did you know one of them was my best friend?" *My only friend* I thought.

"Daniela, honey, nobody killed them. That is the beauty of it all. We made a little suggestion through their implants and then they killed themselves. We had to *know,* don't you understand? If a person who has reached the happiest point in their life could be made to do something completely contrary to that, our weapon . . . our implant had perfect acuity—"

Honey? Beauty? Perfect acuity? I couldn't hold my tongue any longer. We were talking about human lives here.

"Perfect acuity for what?"

She pursed her lips, clearly annoyed at my interruption. I doubt that few people interrupted Lillian Neely.

"Since you have no imagination," she began, "I'll give you an example." Then she fully rolled her eyes. I was really frustrating her.

Despite the edginess of the situation, it made me laugh. I'd fought that habit so hard in my life thinking it made me look young and foolish, and here was the great Lillian Neely, rolling her eyes at her less-than-nothing daughter.

She physically recoiled. "You really must do something about that hideous habit, Daniela. It makes you appear a monster."

I refused to drop my stare. *I guess it takes one to know one.*

She continued, "Many people who enlist in the armed services today are what we call 'family oriented.' While that sounds like a good thing here in the US, on the battlefield, that is nothing but a guarantee that lives will be lost—American lives. If we order a soldier to bomb a village where we know a lead terrorist is hiding, and he hesitates, even for a few minutes, because he sees women and children there—the family thing—the terrorist escapes. But this implant will eliminate the hesitation. The response will be instantaneous. We'll get the bad guy every time and save American lives."

"I think the one thing you are forgetting is that American lives are not the only lives that matter," James said. "That hesitation you speak of eliminating is humanity."

She narrowed her eyes. "Make no mistake about it—this is not a request. You'll do as you're told, both of you, or you'll be dealt with. It's really that simple."

She picked at the skin on her right index finger as if bored by this whole "meeting" and was ready to head out the door.

"I've made the decision that we will say Jeremy killed your friend. It is my understanding that you don't want her death to go on record as a suicide. We will say he then came after you—because we have to explain his death now, don't we—but *we will construct the story* and you will stick with the story we construct. It will all be some kind of hate crime. Even regular people commit those. Got it?"

Yes, unfortunately they do. And there was plenty of hate in Jeremy. "What about Jake. Who killed him? And why? Jake was harmless."

"There are things that must be done for the overall good of this country. If a few lives have to be sacrificed, so be it. It is better than the alternative. You have no understanding of this project. It is the greatest thing I've ever done. If phase 3 is as successful as the first two, I will save thousands and thousands of American lives."

"So Jake's life—an American life—is an acceptable sacrifice because you say so?" I hated that she believed she had the right to choose which American lives should be saved and which should be sacrificed in the name of her great project. "Jake had a family that loved him. He mattered to a lot of people."

And if I had been girl embryos number one through four, even I wouldn't be here.

She looked at me and seemed to decide that I was never going to understand the necessity of what she did. She stood up and offered her hand to me. "It was nice to finally meet you."

I started to reach up to take my mother's hand, but it was caught by James' hand instead. "This isn't over," he said. "You killed at least 9 innocent young women. Young women who had bright futures ahead of them. You don't get to just walk away."

"Oh really?" she said haughtily. A lifetime of money and CIA privileges had taught her that she could do anything she wanted to do and walking away was one of them. "Watch me."

She smirked at us as she donned her full-length cream cashmere coat and walked toward the front door. I hoped she was dying again and would stay dead this time.

When Lillian pulled open the enormous, solid maple door, a flood of flashing lights reflected on the marble floor. There were people gathered outside—a lot of people. She whirled around, eyes wide.

"What have you done?" The smugness in her voice had been replaced with something that sounded a little more like panic.

My glance shot to James. "What's going on?" I asked, alarmed.

He tapped his chest and pointed to me. My wire had captured a full confession from Angela's killer.

This neighborhood wasn't like Angela's neighborhood. If the police were here, everyone wanted to know why. A lot of curious people witnessed Lillian Neely's walk of shame.

Chapter Thirty Two

ANGELA'S REDEMPTION

Wednesday, December 7, 2022. 5:00 AM
4 hours 30 minutes left

I staggered into the precinct, the soles of my shoes squeaking loudly. Wet rubber and polish are noisy—and when you haven't slept in a while, the sound sends chills up your back like nails on a chalkboard.

I had stopped by my house long enough to change out of my bloody clothes and shower. I would burn those clothes. I knew I'd never be able to forget that Jeremy's blood had been on them. I'd burn them along with the clothes in the box still on my kitchen island. Two cups of coffee and one semi moldy croissant later, I was back in the office, ready to get back to work filling out my report—ready to name Angela's killer before my 48 hours were up, and also ready to put a lot of sad parents' minds to rest.

I looked around. Everything looked different than it did four days ago. These were my people—my family. Why hadn't I felt it before? These were people who would have my back and go to bat for me. With their help and the help of the FBI, I had solved my friend's murder and 8 other murders. I was giving peace to nine families for Christmas. I couldn't bring their daughters back, but I could take away their guilt.

Angela was right. I was meant to do this job. I helped people. And I had one more thing I planned to do before I would lay her to rest.

I glanced at the clock. 5:55 AM. Why not? Seems like it helped last time. I closed my eyes and made a wish. Then I picked up my phone.

Epilogue

The world will be a sadder place without Angela in it. The day is gray, misty, and just bone cold. It is one of those New England days when all you wanted to do was snuggle up with a thick, fluffy blanket and some hot cocoa in front of the fireplace with a sweet guy like James Hawthorne. I wish Angela had lived to see this day, the day when I finally grew into who she knew I could become all along. She wouldn't have been surprised. She had such belief in people. She told me once that sometimes good people are bad and sometimes bad people are good, but we should always be ready to meet people where they are.

I also don't think she would be at all surprised that her father is sitting a row in front of me in the family section with his wife and two children, mourning the loss of a daughter he never knew. Or that her mother has graciously invited them all over to her home afterward to look through pictures and share stories of the beautiful person who graced her life for 25 years. Or that James Hawthorne sits to my left and my father sits to my right—two men who I realize I care deeply about. I guess it is never too late to change and we can only do so if we have loving people to teach and support us.

Thank you, Angela.

The End